No. 378
$22.85

THE COMPLETE LIBRARY OF METAL WORKING, BLACKSMITHING, & SOLDERING

METAL WORKING

MODERN BLACKSMITHING & HORSESHOEING

SOLDERING AND WELDING

Published in 1976 by
Drake Publishers Inc.
801 Second Ave.
New York, N.Y. 10017

Copyright 1971 by Oscar Almeida
All Rights Reserved.

ISBN: 0-8473-1172-4

Printed in The United States of America
Book Club Edition

Metalworking

by Oscar Almeida

DRAKE PUBLISHERS INC.

NEW YORK   LONDON

Contents

I
Design

Everything designed to be made in metal should have a purpose. The designer must understand this purpose and know the materials and processes used in the carrying out of his design. He must design within his knowledge and experience.

Even purely decorative work must perform its function, i.e., to be decorative. Apart from decorative work, providing your design functions, the simpler it is the better. There is a tendency among students to make designs much too involved. This tendency can be rectified, once having made your design, by asking yourself can I simplify it? This often leads to a more efficient design.

Efficient things must be made from the materials best suited for the purpose. For instance: stainless steel for kitchen utensils and cutlery; mild steel for tools which have to be case hardened; aluminium where lightness is required; gilding metal, nickel silver and brass for decorative work, and so on. This choice of materials must take into account cost, methods of joining the metals, ease of fabrication, strength, weight, etc.

The dreadful moment comes in designing when you sit down with a large piece of blank paper in front of you. Perhaps one of the best ways to start is by making a number of small sketches of the thing you are designing, then developing your best design. This calls for practice. The ability to draw is not heaven-sent: it comes only by hard work.

However, hard work on its own is not enough. You must keep abreast of the latest developments because we live in a changing living world in which many forces influence the shape and the kind of things we use. If you are wise you keep up to date, if you are a genius you are ahead of your time.

Time permitting, it is often advisable, once having completed your design on paper, to make a model of the thing you have designed. This is known as a "mock-up". By doing this you learn a lot about the design which it is not possible to learn from the drawing. "Mock-ups" can be made from any suitable material that comes to hand and they are not necessarily made the same size as the finished work, although this is advisable wherever possible.

When your design is finished you wonder, quite naturally, whether it is good or bad. Listen to the opinion of people who know, but ultimately the best test is time. By this we mean that a good design survives all the changes of fashion and taste. This is a rare quality.

2
Metals

Before considering particular metals and alloys there are terms applied to all metals which should be understood.

Brittleness. The tendency of a metal to break with little deformation and under low stress. Cast iron is brittle.

Compression. The opposite of tension. It is the ability to stand pressure. Metals such as cast iron which are strong in compression are known as "good load carriers".

Conductivity. The ability to allow the passage of electricity or heat. Silver and copper are very good conductors of heat and electricity.

Creep. This is the slow yielding of metals under a load. This yielding may take months or years as in furnace and steam boiler parts. Creep takes place more often at high temperatures, but soft metals such as lead, tin and zinc suffer from creep at room temperatures. The lead sheets on church roofs thicken towards the eaves.

Ductility. The property which enables a metal to withstand mechanical deformation without cracking particularly when being stretched as in wire drawing.

Fatigue Failure. Metals which have withstood all the normal tests under heavy stress have been known to fracture when a much lighter intermittent stress is applied millions of times. Over one hundred years ago Sir William Fairbairn found that a wrought iron girder would stand a single load of up to 12 tonnes, but if a load of little more than 3 tonnes was applied 3,000,000 times the girder would break.*

Impact Resistance. This is the ability of metal to withstand a severe impact without failure. A machine developed by Edwin G. Izod is much used in Britain for testing this kind of resistance. On this machine, a notched metal test piece is broken by a heavy swinging pendulum and the amount of energy required to break it is measured.

Malleability. The property enabling a metal to be hammered or rolled into thin sheets or similar forms. Gold is the most malleable metal as it can be hammered to 0·0000063 mm thick. In this form it is translucent and is known as gold leaf which is used for applying to surfaces for decoration such as in sign writing.

Shear Strength. The ability of a metal to withstand the action of two parallel forces acting in opposite directions as in a guillotine.

Specific Gravity. The ratio of the weight of a substance to the weight of the same volume of water.

Tensile Strength. The maximum pulling stress which a metal can withstand before breaking. A test piece of a known cross sectional area is stretched until it breaks and the power needed is recorded. Tensile strength is stated in Newtons per square millimetre (N/mm²). The tensile strength of a piece of metal is known as its tenacity.

Toughness. This denotes a condition intermediate between brittleness and softness. Or it can be said to be a combination of strength and ductility.

Stress. The term is used to denote the intensity of load applied to a material in relation to the area of its cross section.

* From *Metals in the Service of Man* by W. Alexander and A. Street.

IRON AND STEEL

More than any other metal steel has made our present technological age possible. From the finest hypodermic needle used by the dentist to the heaviest industrial machinery, steel is predominant. Steel is an alloy of iron and carbon. In fact steel is composed mainly of iron with, in some cases, only as little as 0·1% carbon. There are many kinds of steel consisting of iron alloyed with carbon together with other metals such as chromium, nickel, molybdenum, silicon, manganese, vanadium and cobalt. Iron, however, remains the basis of all steels.

The modern steelmaking processes can be grouped as follows:

1. The converter processes.
2. The open-hearth process.
3. The electric furnace processes.

In considering these processes we must also take into account some of the early achievements which led to the development of the present industry and we start with ironmaking.

THE PRODUCTION OF IRON

At the beginning of the seventeenth century Dud Dudley made the first improvement in iron smelting. By using coal as a fuel he was able to produce about 3 tons of pig iron in one week. However, the first big improvement was brought about by Abraham Darby in 1709 when he used coke for smelting. This was the beginning of the iron and steel industry as we know it now. In those early days the iron was smelted from ores found locally, but now much of it is imported.

The best ores for iron making in order of quality are magnetite, haematite and limonite. About half the ore used in Britain is obtained in this country. The rest is imported from Canada, the United States, U.S.S.R., Brazil, Sweden and Venezuela. Some ores lie within 100 feet of the surface and can be mined by open-cast working, but haematite often requires deep mine working.

Magnetite ores contain the mineral magnetite. It is grey-black in colour, magnetic and is the richest ore, containing up to 65% iron as mined. Haematite is reddish brown and contains between 20% and 60% iron. Limonite ores contain between 20% and 55% iron.

Iron ores are known as "acid" or "basic" which are terms derived from the type of furnace lining used. The slag made in each process is consequent on the kind of ores used.

Basic or high phosphorous ores, with up to about 2·5% phosphorus, are the kind usually found in Britain. These are often mixed with imported ores of the haematite group to improve them. Acid, or haematite (low phosphorous), ores contain up to about 0·04% phosphorus and have a relatively high silicon content. In Britain the greater tonnage of iron is basic.

Here are some typical analyses of irons made from British ores.

	Basic	Haematite (Acid)
Carbon	3·5	3·75
Silicon	0·85	2·0
Sulphur	0·08	0·04
Phosphorus	1·6	0·045
Manganese	1·0	0·5

Before the ores are used in the blast furnace they are treated to remove some impurities. They are then mixed with coke breeze (fine coke dust) and limestone and roasted to produce sinter, or made into high iron content pellets and charged into the furnace with the coke and limestone. The coke used in the blast furnace is produced in coke ovens which are adjacent to the blast furnace. Limestone is used as a flux and is usually quarried near the blast furnace site.

SMELTING IN THE BLAST FURNACE

A large furnace is about 30 metres high and over 10 metres in diameter at its widest part (fig. 1). The fire brick lining can be almost 1 metre thick and the outside plates are 38 mm thick.

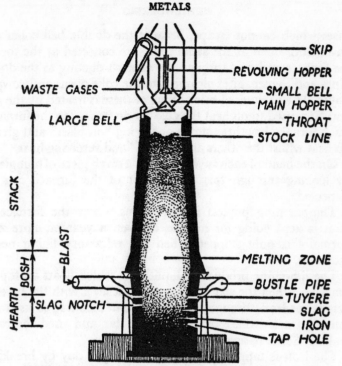

SKIP
REVOLVING HOPPER
WASTE GASES
SMALL BELL
MAIN HOPPER
LARGE BELL
THROAT
STOCK LINE
STACK
BLAST
MELTING ZONE
BOSH
BUSTLE PIPE
TUYERE
HEARTH
SLAG NOTCH
SLAG
IRON
TAP HOLE

FIG.1. DIAGRAM OF BLAST FURNACE

The prepared ore, coke and limestone, known as "the charge", are put into the blast furnace by means of the skip.

The coke, in addition to producing heat and the reducing agent (reducing iron oxide to iron), combines with the iron to make a lower melting point alloy.

A preheated air blast passes through the large bustle pipe, which encircles the base of the furnace, and is blown into the charge through the tuyères (pronounced "tweers"). The oxygen of the air blown in at the bottom causes the coke to burn fiercely. This generates heat and large columns of reducing gas. As the coke burns away the charge descends in the furnace against the stream of gas rushing upwards. The gas and heat act on the ore and together with the limestone bring about the extraction of the iron and its separation from the earthy matter. The hot gases which cannot escape, because the double bell cones are never both open at the same time, are collected at the top of the furnace and pass through the exhaust ducting to the down pipes and thence, after cleaning, to the coke ovens and cowper stoves. The chequered brick lining of these is heated by the gas and later used to preheat the cold air on its way to the furnace. Each furnace has three stoves one being "on blast" and giving up heat whilst the others are "on gas" and receiving heat.

On the bend of each tuyère there is a small piece of blue glass; by looking through this the interior of the furnace can be inspected.

The smelting process is continuous. Once the furnace is lit it is kept going for months or even a year or more and normally is only stopped when the refractory lining needs attention.

The limestone produces a liquid slag which floats on top of the iron. When the slag has risen almost level with the tuyeres it is tapped off through the slag notch. This slag is used for railway track ballast or coated with tar and used for road making. Some basic slag is used for fertiliser.

The iron is tapped four or five times per day by breaking through the clay plug of the tapping hole thus allowing the molten metal to gush out. The impure iron-carbon alloy is either cast into metal moulds or it is cast into moulds of sand which originally looked like pigs feeding from a sow. For that reason the iron at this stage was called pig iron. (This term now applies to all the iron as it comes from the blast furnace.) Often however the pig iron is run into large refractory lined ladles which take the iron in the molten state to the steel making plant.

Recently the efficiency of blast furnaces has been improved by the injection of oil, fine coal, oxygen or steam into the blast.

Cast Iron

Cast iron is usually made from pig iron in a foundry where it is remelted and refined in a small furnace, not unlike a blast furnace, but which is only about 6 metres tall. A general characteristic of cast iron is that it is brittle and cannot be forged into shape. However there are various kinds of cast iron.

Grey Cast Iron. This is the commonest form of cast iron. When fractured it has a grey appearance. The properties of this iron are regulated to suit various requirements. The higher grades are used for machine beds and other machine parts, and the lower grades for grates, drainpipes, guttering, etc.

White Cast Iron. Is very hard and brittle and is difficult to machine. It has a white appearance when fractured. It is used for machine parts, such as those found in cement works, which have to stand great pressure and often rough usage.

Malleable Castings. These are produced by packing white cast iron components in an oxidising material and heating to red heat for several days and allowing to cool slowly. This causes some of the carbon to be removed by oxidation.

Malleable castings are tougher than ordinary iron castings. They can be machined and are used for machine parts which have to withstand shock.

WROUGHT IRON

Wrought iron is probably the oldest and, at its best, the purest form of iron. It was produced long before the Christian era and in its purest form contains only a very small amount of carbon and fibrous slag.

Primitive furnaces are still in existence in Africa which reduce iron ore to iron using charcoal as a fuel and goatskin bellows for the air blast. Most of the carbon is removed by oxidation thus raising the melting point of the iron which remains in the pasty stage. The almost pure iron which is obtained is hammered into the desired shape. Before the eighteenth century iron was made in this way in Sussex and the Forest of Dean in furnaces known as bloomeries. Wood charcoal was used as fuel.

In 1794 the puddling furnace, which provided a much cheaper way of producing iron, was introduced by Henry Cort. The small amount of wrought iron produced today is made in furnaces similar to the one used by Henry Cort, (fig. 2). It is a reverberatory type furnace and unlike the blast furnace the metal is not mixed with the fuel. The furnace is charged with pig iron and flux. The fuel is burned in a grate at one end of the furnace and only the hot fumes are in contact with the charge. The heat is reflected from the roof on to the charge to melt it.

Soon after the metal melts the carbon monoxide gas burns on the surface and it appears to boil. It is stirred or puddled by men with long heavy iron bars. The almost pure iron rises to the top and because of its higher melting point remains pasty and separates from the slag. The puddler manipulates the iron and unavoidably some of the slag, into blooms on the end of the iron bar. These weigh about 36 kilogram. After removal from the furnace the blooms are rolled then wired together in a faggot and brought to welding heat and re-rolled so that they are united. This disperses the slag throughout the metal and gives it its characteristic fibrous structure.

Wrought iron resists corrosion well and for this reason it is used in boiler making. It has also a good resistance to fatigue and sudden shock and is thus used for chains, hooks and haulage gear. Only a limited quantity of wrought iron is made today having been largely superseded by mild steel.

MILD STEEL

In 1856 Sir Henry Bessemer introduced the Bessemer Converter which could make steel quickly and cheaply. The converter is shown in figure 3. The outside casing is made of steel and the whole furnace can be tipped on trunnions through which the air pipe, which is connected to the air holes at the bottom passes.

The refractory lining is either "acid", made from silica bricks, or "basic", made from crushed dolomite rammed with tar.

The original converters had only acid linings, until in 1878 Sidney Thomas and Percy Gilchrist introduced the basic lining thus making it possible to use high phosphorous ores.

A known amount of molten pig iron which may contain 3%–4% carbon is poured into the converter together with some

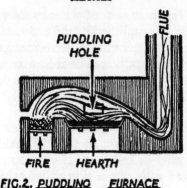

FIG.2. PUDDLING FURNACE

FIG.3.

CHARGING   BLOWING   POURING

THE BESSEMER CONVERTER

limestone. The air blast is then turned on at low pressure. As the converter is turned on its trunnions to the upright position, the air pressure is increased. This prevents the steel from going into the holes.

The air blowing through the steel burns out the carbon and the other impurities. This is known as "the blow". It causes a spectacular show of sparks which lasts about 20 minutes. When the flame drops it means there is no carbon left, but the blast is kept on to burn out the phosphorus and the flame becomes a dense brown smoke. This stage is known as the "afterblow" and lasts for two or three minutes. The carbon has been eliminated from the metal but it contains oxides and gases which have been formed during the blow and which must be removed. The inclusion of the necessary carbon and the de-oxidation are accomplished by the addition, at the end of the blow, of a calculated quantity of ferro-manganese, an alloy of iron, manganese and carbon. The converter is rotated and the steel poured into ladles and then cast into ingots. Mild steel contains less than 0·25% carbon.

The Cementation Process

This is the oldest known method of making steel. It was probably first used in India about 1400 B.C. Bars of wrought iron were packed with charcoal in sealed crucibles and kept at red heat for several days. In this process the carbon in the charcoal combines with the iron to form cementite at the surface of the bars; for this reason it is called the cementation process. The bars were then bundled together and reheated to welding heat and forged together into a single bar to obtain a more even distribution of carbon. The bar could then be cut into short lengths and welded together again. This was repeated as often as desired. The steel thus obtained was known as shear steel. Small quantities of shear steel are still made. This process was quite good for small articles such as knives and shears, but it was not possible by this method to obtain an even distribution of carbon for large work. The cementation process is similar to the present-day case hardening process (see Chapter 7).

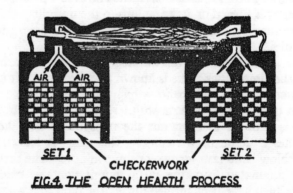

FIG.4. THE OPEN HEARTH PROCESS

The Crucible Process

Benjamin Huntsman who was a clock maker realised that to make good clock springs he needed steel in which the carbon was evenly distributed. In 1740 he developed a method of introducing the carbon to the iron when it was molten. This was done in small quantities in a crucible (because this steel was poured into moulds it was known as cast steel). It is actually an alloying process and is similar in principle to the modern induction process.

Open-Hearth Process

This was developed in 1867 by Charles W. Siemens in co-operation with Pierre Martin, by whom it was first patented.

Today more steel is produced by this method in Britain than by any other.

Figure 4 shows the open-hearth furnace. This is a reverberatory furnace in which the heat from the burning fuel, after passing over the charge, heats the chequered brickwork of one set of preheating chambers. When this set of chambers is hot the passage of gas and air is reversed so that it now passes through the hot bricks and becomes itself preheated and, after passing over the charge, heats the other set. The direction of the flow of gases is reversed periodically. This is known as the regenerative principle, and by this means a sufficiently high temperature is obtained to treat large quantities of metal and to keep it molten throughout the process.

The furnace is charged with pig iron and steel scrap. When this is melted, iron or millscale is added mainly to remove carbon by oxidation. During this process samples are taken from the furnace and analyses are made of the metal and slag. When the refining is complete either the tapping notch is broken or the furnace is tilted, depending on the type, and the steel is tapped into a ladle. The steel is then teemed from the ladle into ingot moulds. The furnace is tapped about every 12 hours. Some furnaces charged with hot metal are ready for tapping after 8 hours.

By using either a basic or acid lining, according to the type of charge, this furnace produces low and medium carbon steels. The average capacity of these furnaces is 250 tonnes and they are fired by gas or fuel oil.

ELECTRIC FURNACES

These are either electric arc (fig. 5), in which the heat is generated by an arc between graphite electrodes and the metal, or induction furnaces.

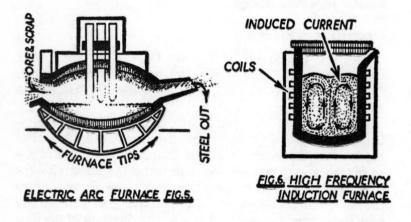

ELECTRIC ARC FURNACE FIG.5.

FIG.6. HIGH FREQUENCY INDUCTION FURNACE

The high frequency induction furnace (fig. 6) is a hollow vessel with a refractory lining round which is wound a water cooled coil of copper wire. The charge consists of carefully selected scrap to which the necessary alloys are added. When the coil is energised with an electric current an induced current in the charge causes it to heat up and melt. There is very little slag in this process.

Both processes are used for making high grade alloy-steels including stainless steel. For these high grade steels the temperature must be carefully controlled and impurities kept to a minimum.

Since the cost of electricity has not risen as rapidly as the cost of other fuels electric arc furnaces, with a capacity up to 100 tonnes, are being used on a large scale. One steelworks in Britain is now making 1·35 million tonnes of ingots in one year with six high powered arc furnaces which in the past it took 21 openhearth furnaces to make.

Modern Converter Processes

Since Bessemer introduced his converter in 1856 and thereby started the "Steel Age", improvements have been made notably by the introduction of oxygen to the process. By injecting oxygen and air, or steam, or carbon dioxide, a greater proportion of scrap can be added to the charge: up to 15% as against a maximum of 5%.

The most recent converter processes are known as the L.D. process, the Kaldo and the rotor.

The L.D. process is named after the initial letters of the Austrian towns Linz and Donawitz where it was first developed. In this process oxygen is blown on to the top of the molten pig iron in the converter, which is vertical (fig. 7). This process is mainly used on pig iron with a low phosphorous content.

The Kaldo process is so named from Professor Kalling its inventor and Domnarvet, the Swedish steel works where it was

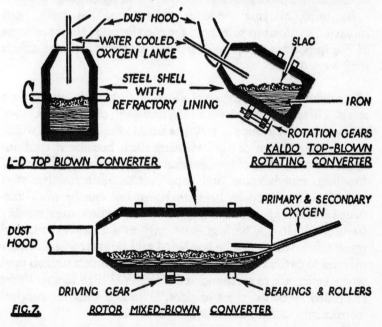

FIG.7. ROTOR MIXED-BLOWN CONVERTER

developed. It is a basic process. The converter, which is inclined at an angle of 20° to the horizontal, slowly revolves about its axis whilst a jet of oxygen is directed on to the surface of the molten metal through a lance (fig. 7). This process takes about 90 minutes and irons with up to 2% phosphorus are used. The rotation of the converter allows the heat to be evenly transmitted to the charge and the quality of the metal obtained can be more closely controlled than by other converter methods. A fairly high percentage of scrap can be used in this process and a wide range of steels obtained.

The rotor process was developed in Germany. It uses a horizontal converter with two nozzles. One jet of oxygen blows into the molten metal as the vessel slowly revolves, and the other jet blows on to the surface of the metal (fig. 7).

Alloy Steel and Alloying Elements

Plain carbon steels have certain limitations such as lack of strength, hardness and high ductility, also non-retention of hardness at temperatures developed in metal cutting.

By using alloying elements special qualities have been imparted to steels to suit them for specific uses. Here are some of the important alloys and alloying elements and the effects they have on steel.

Chromium. This is the chief alloying element in all stainless steels. These contain between 12% and 30% chromium. One of the best known groups of stainless steel is the austenitic, which is generally known as 18/8 stainless steel, because it contains approximately 18% chromium and 8% nickel with additions of titanium, molybdenum and copper. Austenitic stainless steel cannot be hardened by heat treatment but can be work hardened. There are two other groups of stainless steel namely ferritic, which can be hardened only to a small extent, and martensitic, which can be hardened and tempered in a similar manner to carbon steels. A wide variety of stainless steels is used where resistance to corrosion and strength at high temperatures is needed, such as in jet engines. It is also used for surgical instruments, cutlery and kitchen utensils.

Cobalt. It is highly magnetic and is used in cutting tools to increase their hot hardness and in heat resisting nickel base alloys.

High Speed Steel. In 1868 Robert Mushet discovered that certain tungsten alloy steels could "self harden". Later, in 1900, he produced high speed steel which contained between 14% and 18% tungsten. This steel keeps its hardness at high temperatures; for this reason it is used in cutting-tool steels and for hot dies used for hot working of metals.

Manganese. It is usually added to steel in the form of ferromanganese, an alloy of iron, manganese and carbon. Above 10% added to steel makes it very difficult to machine. Small additions to steel improve the elasticity.

Molybdenum. It has a very high melting point—2,625°C which is exceeded only by four other metals: tungsten, rhenium, tantalum and osmium. It is used in heat resisting steels and where 18% tungsten is used in high speed steel it can be replaced by 9% molybdenum—it is said to have twice the "power" of tungsten.

Nickel. Alloys of iron and between 36% and 50% nickel are used for length standards, pendulum rods and measuring tapes, because they expand and contract very little at room temperatures. It is used in nickel chrome steel which has approximately 4·4% nickel, 1·2% chromium, 0·5% manganese, 0·3% carbon and 0·2% molybdenum and a tensile strength of up to 100 tons per square inch.

Silicon. It is a non-metal. When used in conjunction with manganese it makes excellent steel for car springs and bridges. Silicon improves the elasticity of steel. When up to 4% is added to steel it greatly increases its magnetic permeability.

Tungsten. It has the highest melting point of any metal—3380°C. It is used in steels which need to keep their hardness at high temperature such as high speed steel.

Vanadium. This is used as a de-oxidising agent in steel manufacture. It also gives steel grain refinement. 0·5% vanadium added to chromium steel makes it easier to forge and stamp and more resistant to shock.

Two metals which are neither iron nor steel but which are so much used in engineering that they must be mentioned are: cemented carbides and stellite.

Cemented Carbides. These are very hard and brittle. They are used as tips on cutting tools which are brazed on to carbon steel shanks. Cemented carbides consist of particles of tungsten carbide in a matrix of metal with a lower melting point; this matrix metal is usually cobalt. Cemented carbides are classified as:

1. Tungsten carbides which are used for machining highly abrasive metals such as irons and bronzes.

2. Titanium tungsten carbides which although less hard than tungsten carbides are used to machine steels because they resist the tendency for "chips" to become welded to the tip.

Stellite. This is an alloy of cobalt, chromium and tungsten. It is produced in an electric furnace and cast into shape; it cannot be forged into shape. Since it will retain its hardness and cutting edge even at red heat, it is used for rapid machining of hard metals. Stellite contains about 50% cobalt, up to 33% tungsten and 3% carbon. As it contains no iron it is not a steel and is non-magnetic.

METALS AND THEIR PROPERTIES

Non-Ferrous Metals

Aluminium. It is extracted from bauxite, an ore rich in aluminium oxide, which derives its name from Les Baux near Arles in France, where it was first worked commercially. Although aluminium is the most plentiful metal in the earth's crust (of which it forms 8%) it does not occur in its metallic

WORKSHOP DISTINGUISHING TESTS FOR FERROUS METALS

Test	Mild Steel	Carbon Steel 0·4% C to 1·5% C	Cast Iron	High Speed Steel	Wrought Iron
Grind on emery wheel	Bright yellow sparks with a few star-like sparks	Streams of bursting star-like sparks	Non-bursting dull red sparks close to wheel	Dull red sparks, some cling to the wheel	Bright non-bursting sparks
Sound—drop on anvil	Medium pitch metallic sound	Ringing high pitch sound	No ring dull note	Ringing sound not as high as carbon steel	Almost no ring. A little higher than cast iron
Make red hot and hammer	Works readily	Not as malleable as mild steel	Breaks up under the hammer	Does not work readily	Works readily
Make red hot and cool slowly	No effect	May become softer	No effect	May become brittle (depends on kind of steel)	No effect
Make red hot and quench	No effect	Becomes hard and brittle	May crack otherwise little change	Becomes hard and brittle	No effect
File	Files easily	Difficult	Filings dark, skin hard	Difficult	Files easily
Nick thin bar and hammer in vice	Bends then breaks. Grey crystalline fracture	Bends little then breaks. Fine silver crystalline fracture	Breaks easily. Light grey crystalline fracture	Bends little then breaks. Fine blue grey crystalline fracture	Bends well. Coarse grey fibrous fracture
Turn in lathe	Turns well. Swarf long and curly	Less easy than mild steel. Swarf breaks into short chips	Under hard skin, turns well. Chips crumble	Less easy than mild steel. Swarf long	Turns easily but finish is poor. Swarf long and curly

state, and only within the last hundred years has its production been developed.

Napoleon III of France had spoons and forks made from aluminium. The King of Siam, when he visited the French court, was delighted to receive a watch charm made from this rare metal, which was considered more precious than gold. At that time aluminium could only be manufactured by costly and laborious methods from bauxite and other salts of aluminium.

Bauxite ore is usually found near the surface and is mined in large quantities by open-cast working in Jamaica, U.S.S.R. France, Surinam, U.S.A., Guinea, Guyana, Greece, India and Australia.

Before smelting, the ore is refined by the concentration process devised by Karl Josef Bayer in 1890. In this process the almost pure aluminium oxide is dissolved in hot caustic soda while the impurities in bauxite are insoluble and are left behind. After drying the pure aluminium oxide is then converted into aluminium by electrolysis.

The electrolytic process requires a powerful electric current: for this reason aluminium reduction plants are often situated near fast flowing rivers where cheap hydro-electric power is developed. The electrolytic method was developed by Charles Hall in America and Paul Heroult in France. Although they worked independently they both arrived at the same solution to their problem.

They found that a mixture of 10% to 15% alumina in a mineral known as cryolite would become molten at 1,000°C when an electric current was passed through it. When the mixture was kept molten by the heat from the electric current the aluminium oxide split into aluminium and oxygen.

Cryolite is mined in Ivigtut in south-western Greenland. In recent years cryolite has been made synthetically.

Figure 8 shows an aluminium furnace.

Aluminium is an important engineering material. It is light and will not easily corrode in the atmosphere. This resistance to corrosion is due to the oxide film that rapidly forms on the surface so that the aluminium becomes insulated from further attack. Commercially pure aluminium is relatively soft but this lack of strength is overcome by alloying.

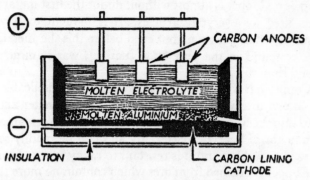

FIG.8. EXTRACTING ALUMINIUM BY ELECTROLYSIS

Aluminium Alloys. Many alloys have been developed but they are used in two forms—wrought and cast. The wrought forms are those that have been forged, rolled, extruded, pressed or drawn. The cast form is made by gravity or pressure casting the molten metal in steel moulds or alternatively the metal can be poured into sand moulds which can only be used once.

Most of these alloys are classified by the British Standards Institution. They are referred to by code letters and numbers. A popular casting alloy used in the motor industry contains 7% copper, 3% zinc and 3% silicon. Another much used alloy contains 3% copper, 5% silicon and about 0·5% manganese.

Wrought components are made from an alloy containing small quantities of manganese or magnesium or magnesium and silicon, or for high strength they may contain copper or zinc.

Some alloys, containing approximately 4·25% copper and 0·5% magnesium, after heating and quenching in water will become harder and stronger after a few days. This is known as age hardening. Age hardened aluminium alloy is used in large quantities in the aircraft industry but because these alloys are not good corrosion resisters they are covered on each side with a thin layer of pure aluminium. This is known as cladding.

Cladding is performed by rolling a thin sheet of pure aluminium in each side of the alloy sheet. The total thickness of the pure aluminium front and back is about 10% of the thickness of the sheet.

Copper. Copper is almost without doubt the first metal to have been used for everyday articles. It is thought to have been first smelted in 3500 B.C., but even before this the metal, which can be found in the pure state (native), was hammered into useful shapes.

Copper has a reddish-gold appearance; it is malleable; it can be drawn into wire as fine as 0·0254 mm diameter and rolled into thin sheets, forged, pressed, beaten or spun. It is an excellent conductor of heat and electricity and can be readily soldered, brazed or welded and it is resistant to many forms of corrosion.

Copper is crushed from ores which contain no more than 4% copper. These are ground to a fine powder and the copper bearing grains are separated by the flotation method. The flotation process is worthy of note, not only because it is widely used, but because it is unusual in that the dense metal compounds are caused to float in a bath of frothed-up liquid, while the unwanted minerals are wetted and sink to the bottom. A reverberatory furnace is then used to remove more of the impurities. This leaves a mixture of copper and iron sulphide known as the matte. This is heated in a converter, which is similar to the Bessemer converter, to remove the iron and sulphur and then it is finally refined either by fire refining or by electrolytic refining.

Fire refining is a process whereby the impure copper is melted and some impurities burnt by oxidation. After the slag has been removed, hardwood poles are forced into the molten metal to remove the oxygen by combustion. This is known as poling; the copper is then poured into moulds.

Electrolytic refining produces high purity copper. In this process large pieces of impure copper (anodes) are suspended in dilute sulphuric acid. These are interleaved with thin cathodes of pure copper. By electrolytic action copper from the anodes is deposited on to the cathodes and the impurities go to the bottom of the bath.

Brass. This is the best known copper alloy consisting of copper and up to 40% zinc. Apart from zinc some brasses may contain small quantities of aluminium, lead, manganese, silicon and tin.

Cartridge Brass or Best Brass, from which cartridges and shells are made, contains 70% copper and 30% zinc (usually referred to as 70/30 brass) and is the most ductile of the cold working brasses.

Admiralty Brass is similar to cartridge brass except that it contains up to 1% tin which increases its corrosion resistance.

Gilding Metal contains copper and between 20% and 5% zinc. It derives its name from its golden colour. It is used for decorative work on buildings and for jewellery and beaten metalwork.

Muntz Metal or Yellow Metal contains 40% zinc. It is used for casting and for hot working operations such as rolling and extrusion and as a brazing alloy for steels.

Bronze. Properly speaking it is an alloy of copper and tin, but it has come to include alloys such as silicon bronze and aluminium bronze which contain no tin and others such as manganese bronze which contain only a small amount. Bronze was used for weapons as long ago as 2000 B.C. In parts of the world where tin and copper ores exist together it was probably first smelted by accident. Later copper and tin ores were smelted together in varying proportions to produce bronze for particular purposes. Bronze is harder than copper, it casts well, has good corrosion resisting qualities and good wearing qualities.

Phosphor Bronze contains 3·75% to 12% tin and between 0·1% to 0·5% phosphorus. This is a good bearing material but as the phosphorous content increases so the ductility decreases.

Lead Bronze containing about 30% lead has been used with great success on aero engines. The lead in the bearings acts as a metallic lubricant when the oil film breaks down. Small amounts of lead (about 1%) are added to bronze to improve its machinability.

Aluminium Bronze, containing 5% to 10% aluminium, is produced in strip, wire, rod and tube forms. This alloy is used as a substitute for steel where strength and non-magnetic properties are required. It is also used for ships' fittings and components which need to be corrosive resistant.

Gunmetal was used, in early times, for casting cannon. It is a bronze which contains a small amount of zinc and is excellent for casting. Admiralty gun metal contains 88% copper, 10% tin and 2% zinc and is widely used for marine purposes. A gun metal which contains 85% copper and 5% each of tin, zinc and lead (85–5–5–5) is a much used casting material in foundries.

Tin. It is smelted from cassiterite which is a tin oxide known also as tinstone. It is mined in Malaya, Indonesia and Bolivia. The tin ore is washed out from the tin deposits, most of which are alluvial. The ore is then crushed and roasted in a reverberatory furnace to remove the sulphur and arsenic present. Then it is washed and mixed with slaked lime and anthracite and smelted in a reverberatory furnace. The crude tin is then poured into moulds. Later this is purified in another reverberatory furnace in which most of the impurities are skimmed off as slag.

Tin is a shiny white metal which is very soft and weak and has a low melting point (232°C) and has excellent corrosion resisting properties. The "cry of tin" is the name given to the sound a piece of tin makes when it is bent backwards and forwards.

The most common use of tin is in tinplate, which consists of steel sheets coated on each side with a thin layer of tin from which containers are made to store food, paints, lubricants and many other commodities.

Almost 50% of the tin produced goes into the making of tinplate. The mild steel sheets before being coated with tin are hot rolled to 1·8 mm thick, then cleaned by pickling in dilute sulphuric acid, then cold rolled to about 0·26 mm thick. After annealing it is rolled again which gives the sheet the correct surface finish and degree of hardness. The prepared sheet is then tinned either by electro-deposition or by hot dipping. The former process accounts for about three-quarters of the world production.

The electric process is carried out in large automatic plants which can make tinplate at an average rate of 300 metres per minute; the tin being in long strips which are coiled. In the hot dipping process the sheet steel is cut into small pieces which are passed through a bath of molten tin equipped with rollers which remove the excess tin on the surface. The thickness of the tin coating by this process is approximately 0·002 mm and by the electric process approximately 0·001 mm.

Tin Lead Solders (see Chapter 4 on joining metals).

White Metal Alloys. These are alloys chiefly of tin, lead, copper and antimony. The best known white metal is Babbits metal which consists of 88% tin, 4% copper and 8% antimony. This is used for bearings. Apart from bearing metal the term white metal includes pewter, printers' alloys and solders.

Type Metal is an alloy used for printing type and consists of 50% to 85% lead, up to 25% tin and between 10% and 30% antimony. This has the unusual property of expanding on cooling, thus it forces itself into every corner of the type mould giving an excellent casting.

Pewter is a white metal and consists, today, of approximately 94% tin, 4% to 5% antimony and 1 to 2% copper. This alloy is also known as Britannia metal. It can be cast, rolled or spun and is suitable for food vessels. Ancient pewter was composed of lead and tin and was used for utensils and coins. Between the fourteenth and eighteenth centuries it was widely used for plates and other vessels. In this country the pewterers had their own guild and "touch mark", which was a hallmark and ensured a certain standard of workmanship and quality of material.

Zinc. This is a blue-grey metal which is obtained from zinc blend (a sulphide) mined chiefly in North America and Australia. The metal does not occur in its native state but is obtained either by electrolysis or distillation. Zinc was first made in Sumatra and China and was not commercially produced in England until 1740.

In the electrolytic process concentrates of zinc are dissolved in sulphuric acid and after purification deposited electrolytically on aluminium sheets from which it is later stripped and cast into slabs. This method produces an almost pure metal. The distillation or thermal process is one in which a briquetted mixture of roasted ores and bituminous coal is heated in a vertical retort made from silicon carbide bricks, in which reduction can proceed continuously. The zinc forms as a vapour and is caught as a liquid metal in condensers.

A large proportion of zinc produced is used for making brass. Another important use is for coating iron—galvanising—which gives excellent protection against rust. It is also used in the form of zinc-base alloys for die casting.

Lead. It is a heavy bluish-grey metal (specific gravity 11·3) which is easily fusible and lacks strength. It is obtained chiefly from the lead ore, galena. After the ores are crushed they are separated from the impurities by the flotation process and after roasting they are reduced in a blast furnace.

Lead was used in antiquity; the Romans made extensive use of it for lining baths and making water pipes, the seams of which they fused together by pouring hot lead along the prepared joint. This was known as "lead burning". "Plumbum" was the name they used for lead and our present-day workers in lead are known as plumbers. Lead has a low melting point (327°C) and casts easily from the molten state. It is used for roof covering and water pipes and for fonts and rainwater heads. It resists acid well and is used for containers for these corrosive liquids. A more recent use is for shielding against radiation in atomic energy establishments. It is estimated that at present 15,000 tonnes of lead per year are used for this purpose in Britain.

Nickel. This is a silvery white metal which takes a good polish and is resistant to corrosion and is magnetic. It can be cast, forged, welded, brazed and hard soldered; and it is strong both at low and high temperatures. Its melting point is 1,454°C, nearly as high as iron. Eighty-five per cent of the world's output of nickel is obtained from ores mined in Sudbury, Ontario.

The ores usually contain copper and iron and sometimes precious metals. The name "nickel" is German and is derived from "Kupfer-Nickell" which might be translated as "devil's copper". It was so called by miners in the Hartz Mountains when they produced a nickel-copper alloy when struggling to obtain copper. The original process for separating nickel from its ores was developed in 1751. This process consisted of melting metallic sulphides with nitre cake which, when cooled, formed two separate layers, the top one containing copper and the bottom nickel. Since then nickel production has been greatly improved.

Nickel is used chiefly as an alloy in ferrous and non-ferrous metals and as a pure metal in plating.

Nickel Silver. In China, two thousand years before nickel was isolated, an alloy called "paktong" was made by melting a mixture of copper-nickel ore and zinc ore. A number of alloys of this type were made in Europe in the early part of this century and were known as German silver.

Nickel silver with 5% to 35% nickel, 50% to 60% copper and 15% to 35% zinc is used, because of its colour and resistance to corrosion, for tableware which is silver plated and known as E.P.N.S. (Electro Plated Nickel Silver). It is widely used for contact springs in telephone exchanges.

Gold. This is the precious metal of antiquity. Its malleability has been mentioned, but it is also the most ductile metal: one grain Troy can be drawn into wire 2·4 kilometres long. The pure metal is too soft for general use so it is hardened by alloying. The term "carat" used in connection with gold means a 24th part: e.g., 18 carat gold has 18 parts by weight pure gold and 6 parts alloying elements. The alloying elements are often 3 parts copper and 1 part silver.

Silver. It is the best conductor of heat and electricity; it is malleable and ductile and its pleasant white colour makes it a pleasure to handle. Sterling or standard silver has contained, since 1696, 92·5% pure silver. Silver can be cast or wrought and it is available in sheet, strip and tube form. Apart from its use in silversmithing it is used in large quantities for making silver solders.

Platinum. This is white in colour and is malleable and ductile. It is superior to gold in its resistance to corrosion. Because of its colour and strength it is used for making the fine settings in jewellery for precious stones, particularly diamonds.

3

Fitting

MEASURING, MARKING-OUT AND TESTING

Accuracy is the word that comes to mind when we mention engineering. On bench work this accuracy is ensured by careful measuring, marking-out and testing.

The Rule. The most common measuring tool is the steel rule. These are available in lengths from 100 mm to 2 metres. They are divided into mm and cm.

Scribers. The scriber (fig. 1) is the marking-out tool most used with the steel rule. It is made of hardened and tempered carbon steel. It should be ground to a point in such a way that the lines of the grindstone are in line with the axis as shown, otherwise the tip will break off more easily.

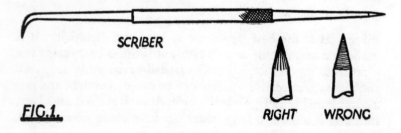

SCRIBER

RIGHT   WRONG

FIG.1.

To ensure that scribed lines show clearly it is usual to clean the metal and then colour it with copper sulphate or some proprietary marking-out fluid. Castings can be rubbed with white chalk or given a coat of whitewash.

Dot Punch. Some engineers like to dot punch the lines after marking-out so that the scribed lines are not "lost" when further work is being done on the workpiece. Dot punching is done with a sharp centre punch (fig. 2). The dot punch mark should be heavy enough to be seen, but not so large that it disfigures the work.

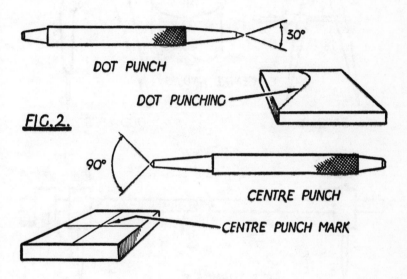

FIG. 2.

Centre Punch. Before a hole is drilled the exact centre must be centre punched (fig. 2).

Dividers. Spring dividers, trammels, odd-leg calipers (also known as jenny calipers or hermaphrodite calipers) are used for marking-out (fig. 3).

Calipers. Calipers are used to facilitate measuring, both for outside work such as checking the diameter of a rod, or for internal work, e.g. checking the diameter of a bored hole. These are shown in figure 4. Both spring type and firm joint calipers

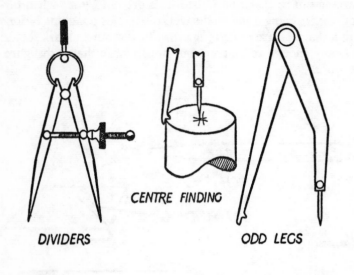

CENTRE FINDING

DIVIDERS   ODD LEGS

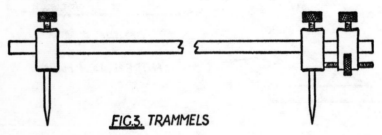

FIG.3. TRAMMELS

are available for internal and external use. Spring calipers are
used in schools more than the firm joint kind because they are
easier for a beginner.

Firm joint calipers are sometimes known as "tap" calipers
because many engineers tap them to open and close them
(fig. 4). By tapping a very fine degree of accuracy is obtainable.

Try Squares or Engineers' Square. Testing or "trying" a
right angle is done with a try square. These are precision tools
and should never be dropped or otherwise misused. They are

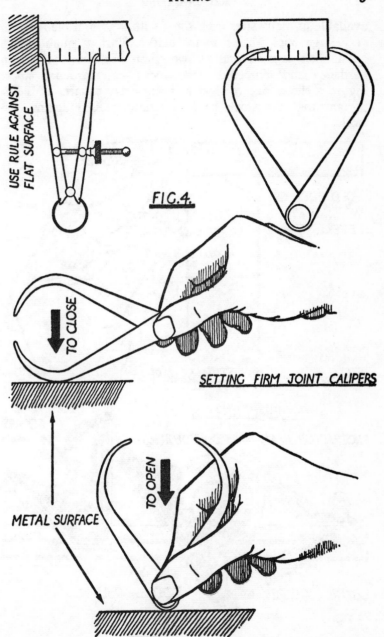

USE RULE AGAINST FLAT SURFACE

FIG. 4.

TO CLOSE

SETTING FIRM JOINT CALIPERS

METAL SURFACE

TO OPEN

available in many sizes from those with a 50 mm blade up to very large ones with 1 metre blades. Various qualities are obtainable: a good one for workshop use has a 125 mm hardened and tempered blade and a case-hardened stock. Figure 5 shows one method of using a try square. It is important that the stock be kept firmly pressed against the work.

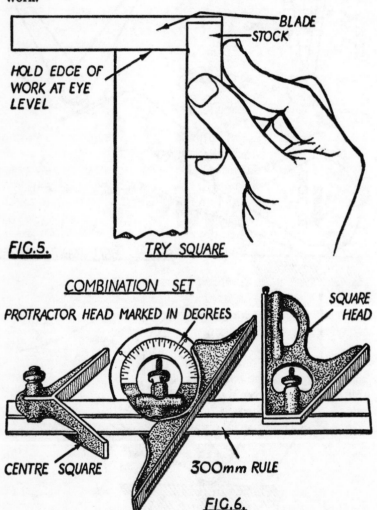

BLADE
STOCK
HOLD EDGE OF WORK AT EYE LEVEL

FIG.5. TRY SQUARE

COMBINATION SET

PROTRACTOR HEAD MARKED IN DEGREES

SQUARE HEAD

CENTRE SQUARE

300mm RULE

FIG.6.

Combination Set. A combination set is shown in figure 6. It comprises a rule which is usually 300 mm long, a centre head or centre square which can be used to find the centre of circular work, a square head with which angles of 90° and 45° can be set out, and a protractor head for obtaining angles which can be read direct from the scale.

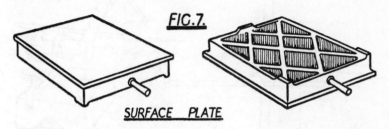

FIG. 7.

SURFACE PLATE

Surface Plate (fig. 7). Surface plates provide an accurate flat surface from which to mark out work. They are made of fine grained cast iron with a thick top and heavy ribbing underneath to resist distortion. They stand on three legs for stability. The surface is planed and on the best plates it is hand scraped. A wooden cover into which a piece of thin felt is stuck should be used for protection when the plate is not in use. The felt inside the cover should be soaked in oil to prevent rust on the plate.

Surface Gauge or Scribing Block. The surface gauge is used on the surface plate for marking-out lines parallel to the surface of the plate (fig. 8). The height of the point is set against a rule which is stood vertically on the plate or against the rule of the combination set held upright in the square head. The fine adjusting screw allows the point to be raised or lowered fractional amounts. The base of the scribing block is vee-shaped so that it can rest on round sections. Often there are two small pins which can be pushed to protrude below the bottom surface. These are used in special circumstances such as in figure 8a.

Vee-Blocks. Vee-blocks are useful for holding round work for marking-out on the surface plate, as shown in figure 9.

Vee-blocks are made in pairs and each block of the pair is stamped with the same number. They should always be used as

SCRIBING BLOCK

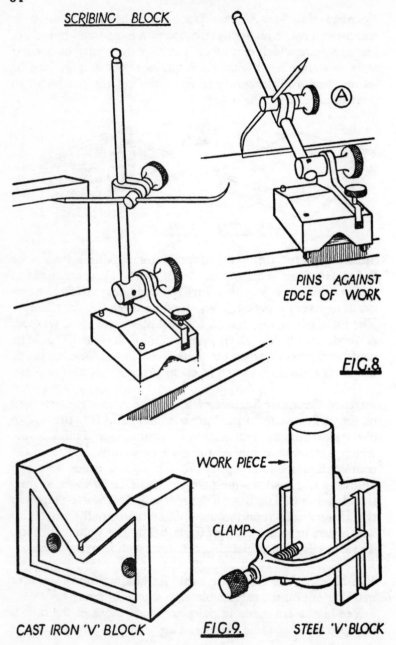

Ⓐ

PINS AGAINST
EDGE OF WORK

FIG.8

CAST IRON 'V' BLOCK

WORK PIECE →

CLAMP →

FIG.9.

STEEL 'V'BLOCK

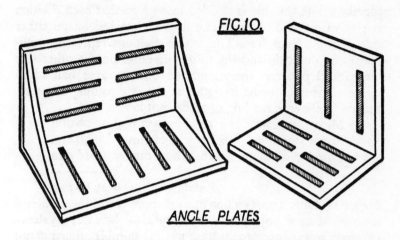

FIG.IO.

ANGLE PLATES

a pair unless only one block is required. The larger blocks are usually made of cast iron, but the smaller, more accurate, vee-blocks are made of mild .steel, case hardened and accurately ground. These are made with grooves along the side for clamps which secure the work as shown in figure 9.

Angle Plates. Angle plates are made from fine grained cast iron. They are available in a large variety of sizes and qualities. Small ones are about 75 mm long and the largest ones take two men to lift them. They are made either machined all over or with webbed ends (fig. 10). Large irregular shaped work pieces can be clamped against them for marking-out. The ends of the angle plates are machined so they can be stood on end if required.

Micrometer Caliper. This is an almost indispensable precision measuring instrument in the Metalwork Room. They are available in sizes ranging from 0-25 mm 25-50, 50-75 and so on. Figure 11 shows a 0-25 mm micrometer.

In principle they are simple. One end of the spindle is threaded and this screws into the sleeve. The thread has a pitch of 0·5 mm which means that each revolution of the spindle opens or closes the gap between the anvil and the spindle space 0·5 mm. The spindle and the thimble move together. The thimble is divided into 50 so that each division is 1/50 of 0·5 = 0·01 mm. The sleeve is marked off on either side of the datum line. The major divisions represent millimetres on one side and the minor divisions on the other side are placed between the numbered ones to give half millimetres. The micrometer in figure 11 shows a reading of 7 mm. Figure 12 shows a reading of 10.66 mm i.e.

Major divisions   = 10 × 1·00 mm = 10·00 mm
Minor divisions   = 1 × 0·50 mm = 0·50 mm
Thimble divisions = 16 × 0·01 mm = 0·16 mm
                                     ————
            Reading   = 10·66 mm

Figure 11 shows a part section of a micrometer. (1) the hardened faces of the anvil and spindle (2) spindle (3) lock nut (4) sleeve (5) main nut (6) screw adjusting nut (7) thimble adjusting nut (8) ratchet (9) the thimble (10) frame (11) cut away on frame (to allow measurements to be taken in restricted spaces).

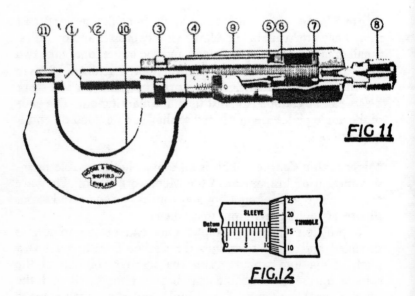

FIG 11

FIG.12

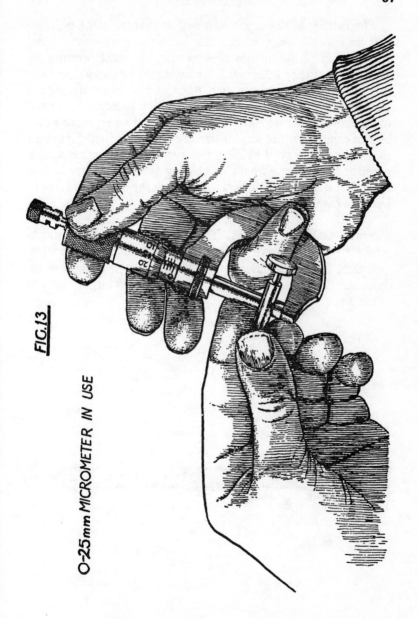

FIG.13

0-25mm MICROMETER IN USE

The ratchet at the top is provided so that the same pressure will be applied whoever uses the instrument. However, most engineers know when they are exerting the right pressure by "feel" so that they seldom use the ratchet. The locknut sets the instrument at a given reading, but this can cause damage if used by beginners because so often they try to force it over the work being measured. The locknut is useful when large numbers of components of similar size are being checked. Figure 12 shows the best way of holding the micrometer. It takes a little practice to learn the knack of holding the micrometer in one hand, but it is invaluable because it leaves the other hand free to hold the component to be measured.

Vernier Caliper Gauges. These are precision instruments used for taking internal and external measurements to within 0·02 mm. Figure 14 shows a vernier caliper. For normal workshop use they are 150 mm long, although much larger ones are available.

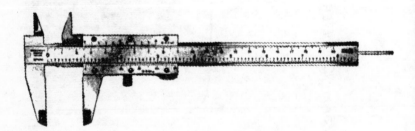

VERNIER SCALE

| 0 | 1 | 2 | 3 | 4 | 5 | 6 | 7 | 8 | 9 | 0 | 0·02 mm. |

| 5 | 6 | 7 | 8 | 9 | 10 | 11 |

MAIN SCALE

a.	53 MILLIMETRES	53·00
b.	8 TENTHS	0·80
c.	2 HUNDREDTHS	0·04
		53·84 mm.

FIG 15

How to read the Vernier Caliper. Figure 15. Metric reading —0·02 mm. The Main Scale is graduated in millimetres and the Vernier Scale is divided into 50 divisions over a distance of 49 mm, each division equalling 49/50ths of a millimetre (0·98 mm). The difference between a division on the Main Scale and the Vernier Scale is 1/50th mm (0·02 mm).

Main Scale:
a Each large number = 10·00 mm
b Each division = 1·00 mm
  Vernier Scale
c Each number = 0·10 mm
d Each division = 0·02 mm

(a) 5 × 10·00 mm = 50·00 mm
(b) 3 × 1·00 mm = 3·00 mm
(c) 8 × 0·10 mm = 0·80 mm
(d) 2 × 0·02 mm = 0·04 mm

Caliper reading = 53·84 mm

To read the vernier it is helpful to use a magnifying glass to check the coincidence of the line on the fixed scale with the one on the sliding scale.

Screw Pitch Recognition Gauge. This is used for checking the pitch of a thread. It is also useful for checking the radius at the crest and the root of the threads when screwcutting on the lathe. The pitch of the thread is clearly marked on each blade and they are available with blades ranging from 0·25 mm pitch to 7·0 mm pitch. Figure 16 shows one of these gauges.

Radius or Fillet Gauge. Radius gauges are used to check radii on internal and external work. These are bought in sets and are available in decimal, fractional or metric radii. Figure 17 shows a radius gauge which has 20 blades.

Feeler Gauge. These are in sets as shown in figure 18. The thickness of the blades ranges from 0·03 mm to 1·0 mm. They are used for checking narrow gaps.

Thread Angle Gauge. These are used for checking the angle when grinding a tool for screw cutting and for setting the tool in correct relationship to the axis of the work on the lathe (fig. 19).

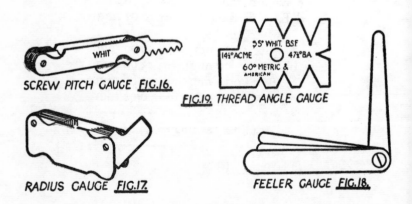

SCREW PITCH GAUGE FIG.16.

FIG.19. THREAD ANGLE GAUGE

RADIUS GAUGE FIG.17.

FEELER GAUGE FIG.18.

BENCH WORK

The bench vice is the important holding device at which most of the bench work is done. Usually each pupil in the metalwork room has a vice place.

Engineers parallel jaw vices (fig. 20) are usually made of cast iron with inset steel jaws. These may or may not have a quick release mechanism. This is for quick opening and closing of the vice and it is operated by a lever which lifts and lowers a half nut which engages on a buttress thread. Heavy hammering or bending should be done on the leg vice (Chapter 6, fig. 3) not on the bench vice. The roughened surface of the jaws is sometimes covered with vice clamps to protect the work. These are made of some soft metal such as copper, aluminium or lead.

Hand Vices (fig. 21). These are useful for holding thin pieces of metal when using the drilling machine. Hand vices are made of drop forged steel. The jaws are roughened to improve the grip, but for this reason it is advisable to use two pieces of thin cardboard as temporary vice clamps to prevent damage when holding non-ferrous sheet metal.

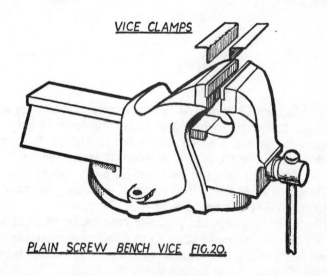

VICE CLAMPS

PLAIN SCREW BENCH VICE FIG.20.

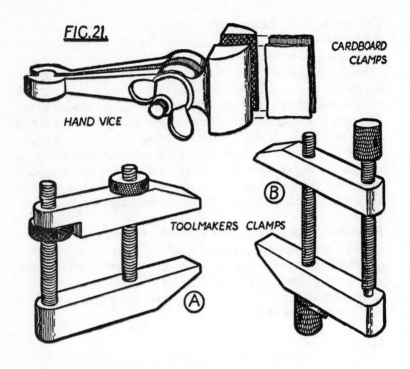

FIG. 21.

HAND VICE

CARDBOARD CLAMPS

TOOLMAKERS CLAMPS

(A)

(B)

Tool Makers Clamps. As the name suggest, these are much used by toolmakers who often make their own. Many toolmakers prefer the kind shown in figure 21A to those at B. because they have one jaw uninterrupted by the head of a screw. This plain jaw can be rested on a flat surface such as a drilling machine table. When gripping work the jaws should be adjusted so that they are parallel.

Toolmakers clamps are made of case hardened mild steel. It is a mistake to make these from small square section stock because the strength is required in one direction which is better obtained using oblong section stock.

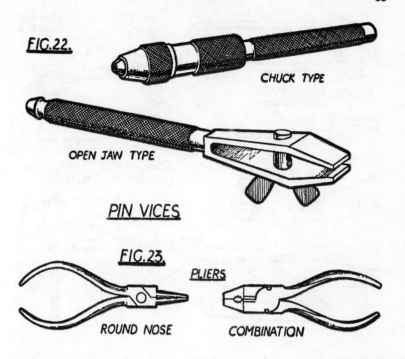

FIG.22.

CHUCK TYPE

OPEN JAW TYPE

PIN VICES

FIG.23.

PLIERS

ROUND NOSE   COMBINATION

Pin Vices (fig. 22). They are used for holding small work. The handle is hollow to allow long lengths of metal to be held. Pin vices will hold work up to 2 mm diameter.

Pliers (fig. 23). Some of these can be used as holding devices, although many pliers, such as side cutting and round-nosed, have other uses.

Hack Saws (fig. 24). The illustration shows a tubular frame hack saw, but there are other types available. In principle they are all similar. There is always provision for adjusting the frame to suit the length of blade, and for turning it axially through 90° as shown. The blade is always held in tension.

The adjustment for length on the saw shown is provided by the tubular frame which slides through the top of the handle and is locked in place by a knurled set screw.

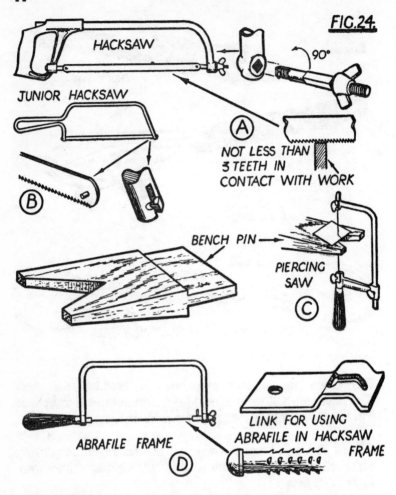

FIG.24.

HACKSAW

90°

JUNIOR HACKSAW

A
NOT LESS THAN
3 TEETH IN
CONTACT WITH WORK

B

BENCH PIN

PIERCING
SAW

C

ABRAFILE FRAME

LINK FOR USING
ABRAFILE IN HACKSAW
FRAME

D

The blades are usually 254 mm or 304 mm long, 12 mm deep and 0·6 mm thick. The pitch of the teeth varies between 0·8 mm pitch to 1·5 mm pitch. Note the length of a hacksaw blade is measured from the outside edges of the holes. These are made of either high speed steel, which is more expensive but will last longer and cut harder metals, or of low tungsten steel. Low tungsten steel blades are made either as "flexible", which have teeth hardened but the back soft and are very tough, or "all hard" type blades, which are hard throughout. These are preferred by skilled men because they are more rigid.

When choosing a blade it is important to select one which will have a minimum of 3 teeth always in contact with the work (fig. 24A) otherwise "chatter" will result and teeth will start to break off. When inserting a blade in the hacksaw frame, the teeth must always point forward, i.e. away from the operator. Remember to use the full length of the blade when hacksawing and to take about one second for each cut, i.e. don't try to cut too quickly because this often causes the blade to twist or brake and results in bad work.

Junior Hacksaws. These are useful for smaller work (fig. 24B). The blade, which is 150 mm long, is held in tension by the spring of the frame itself. The blades have a small pin inserted at each end by which they are held in the frame.

Piercing Saws (fig. 24C). These are for very fine work such as that done by jewellers and silversmiths, but they are sometimes useful in the school workshop for piercing out motifs in sheet metal.

For piercing the saw should be used in the upright position and the work held by hand on a bench pin which is made of wood as shown. The teeth of the blade should point downwards, i.e. towards the handle.

"Abrafile" Tension File. This is really a file but it is used as a saw. The blade which is like a thin round file is held taut in the frame (fig. 24D).

Tension files are available in lengths from 150 mm to 275 mm approximately 2 mm diameter. Special links are made for using these blades in a hacksaw frame.

Power Hacksaws (fig. 25). These are used in workshops where a lot of sawing is necessary. The machine might be a small bench model with a jaw capacity of 50 mm by 50 mm, or a heavy duty type with a capacity of 250 × 250 mm. Special large blades are made for these machines.

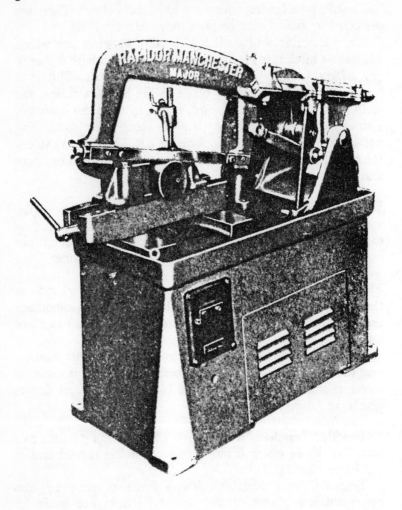

Chisels. These are usually called cold chisels because they are used for cutting cold work. The flat chisel is the most used.

Cold chisels can be made from hardened and tempered carbon steel or bought made from "non-temper chrome alloy steel". These are extremely tough and yet can be sharpened with a file. Flat carbon steel chisels should be ground as in figure 26. The lines left by the grinding wheel should be as shown, i.e. they should be in line with the axis thus helping to prevent the extreme edge from breaking off. The cutting edge is ground in a slight arc so that when cutting the main thrust is taken in the centre. The top of the chisel which is soft will become "mushroomed" with continued use unless ground off from time to time. If this mushroom is not ground off it can be dangerous because a glancing blow from the hammer might cause a piece to fly off.

Flat chisels are useful for shearing thin stock as shown in figure 26A, or for cutting out sheet metal on a chipping block as shown at B.

Half round chisels are often used for cutting oil grooves and "cleaning up" corners as shown at C.

Cross cut or cape chisels are used where a narrow groove is required such as a key-way (D).

The diamond chisel can be used for cutting into sharp internal corners. A typical example is shown at E.

Hammers. The engineer's ball pein hammer is the type most used in the metalwork room. The heads are made from hardened and tempered carbon steel. Popular weights in the workshop are 0·2 kgm, 0·3 kgm and 0·4 kgm. The handle is of hickory or ash. The hammer head is made fast on the handle by wood wedge which is often firmly held in place by a metal wedge. The section in figure 26F shows how the hole is tapered both ways.

Files. The file is the most used hand cutting tool in the engineering workshop. It is made of hardened and tempered high carbon steel but the tang is left soft. The length of a file is measured from the tip to the shoulder and does not include the tang. Files are available from 100 mm to 400 mm long in a var-

FIG.27 TYPES OF CUT

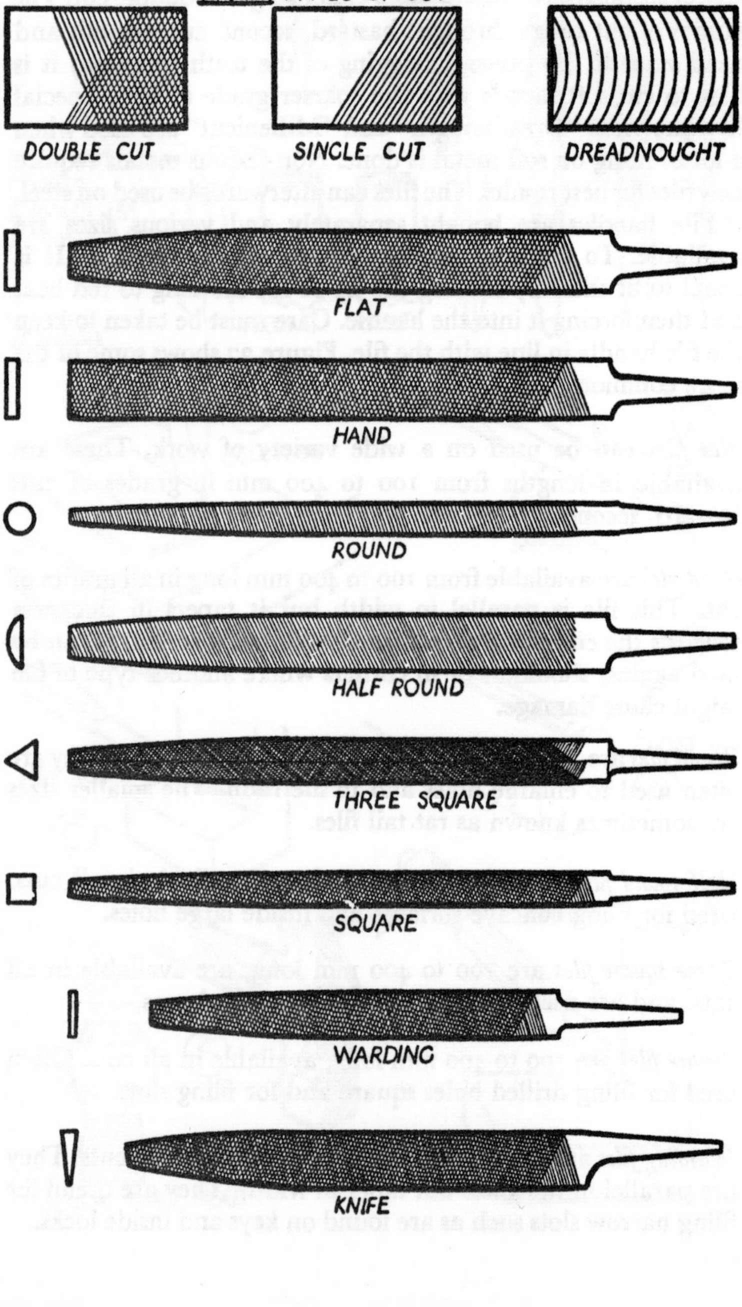

DOUBLE CUT   SINGLE CUT   DREADNOUGHT

FLAT

HAND

ROUND

HALF ROUND

THREE SQUARE

SQUARE

WARDING

KNIFE

Knife files are 100 to 300 mm long, available in all cuts, and are used for filing into sharp corners etc.

Needle or Swiss files are for fine work. These vary in length from 100 to 175 mm. They do not need a handle: the shaft is knurled to provide a grip. Finer cuts than smooth and dead smooth are made. A large number of shapes are available, one of which is shown (fig. 28).

Rifflers are used by engravers, die makers and silversmiths. They are usually double ended and scores of different shapes are available. One of these is shown (fig. 29).

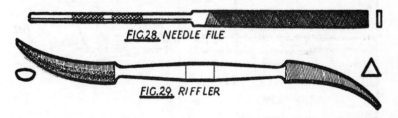

FIG.28. NEEDLE FILE

FIG.29. RIFFLER

Filing. Before commencing to use a file, make sure it is clean. This is best done by pushing a file pricker (fig. 30) a number of times across the teeth until it takes up the shape of the teeth and removes all the dirt and metal particles. The file pricker can be made from a thin piece of mild steel filed to a chisel end. Some people use a file card for this, but continued rubbing of the hard steel bristles on a file tends to spoil the edge of a file particularly when this is done almost as a habit in the school workshop.

The workpiece should be held securely and as low as possible in the vice and the edge to be filed held horizontally. The work should be at a comfortable height, but of course it is not possible to make the height of the vice suitable for all people. A right handed person should stand at the vice with feet apart—left foot foremost—more or less in the stance of a boxer. The file handle is held in the right hand with the right elbow close to the body. The tip of the file is held with the left hand. The weight of the body should supply the force and weight should be transferred from the right foot to the left on the forward stroke. It must be remembered that a file cuts only on the forward stroke.

On the return stroke the pressure is taken off the file, but it is not lifted from the work. Use the full length of the file and don't try to rush. The aim usually is to prevent rocking and to obtain a flat surface. For heavy filing more weight is put on the end of the file and the file is pushed diagonally across the work, first from one side and then from the other, thus removing the crests of the ridges made by the previous stroke. For light filing the tip is held lightly between the thumb and forefinger of the left hand.

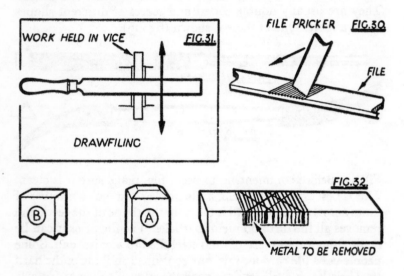

Drawfiling (Fig. 31) is a finishing process and if done properly gives a smooth flat surface. Chalk rubbed on the file helps to prevent pinning (the clogging of the teeth by small particles of metal) and gives a better finish to the work. Any oil or grease on the surface being filed makes the file cut less efficiently. Even perspiration from the fingers, when taking the last fine cuts, tends to make the file skid. For this reason avoid, as far as possible, touching the surface being filed. As the work nears completion it should be taken out of the vice and checked frequently with a try square or a rule, or both.

If a lot of metal has to be removed by filing, it is an aid to make criss-cross cuts in the metal first (fig. 32) either with a hacksaw or the edge of a file. Another method is to rough chamfer the work first as shown in figure 32A and then to file flat as at B.

Care of files. 1. Don't knock or rub files together. Remember they are hard and will damage each other.

2. Keep them in a rack slightly apart from each other.

3. Don't attempt to file hardened steel.

4. Avoid using a new file on the hard sandy skin of a casting—old files will do for this.

5. Don't throw away old files, they make good scrapers and hand turning and wood turning tools, but must be properly tempered otherwise they might break and cause injury to the user.

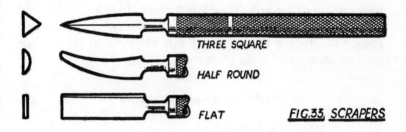

THREE SQUARE

HALF ROUND

FLAT

FIG.33. SCRAPERS

Scraping. Scrapers are made from hardened and tempered carbon steel and the edges are sharpened, after grinding, on a fine oil stone. Three scrapers are shown in figure 33. These are used for removing small amounts of metal usually when working on something which has to be accurate, e.g. when making a surface plate or scraping a bearing.

When scraping a flat surface it is usual to lightly coat a master flat surface, such as a good surface plate, with a thin coat of engineers blue. The work is then rubbed on the master surface or the master surface rubbed on the work, and any high spots which show blue scraped off. This is repeated as often as required until all the high spots are removed. Scraping, however, is a slow and therefore expensive process which has been largely superseded by surface grinding.

Taps and Tapping. Taps are used for making internal threads They are available in sets of three (fig. 34) made from high speed steel or carbon steel.

Before tapping a suitable hole must be drilled which is usually a little larger than the core diameter of the tap. (See chart at back of book.)

Start tapping with the taper tap which is held in either a bar or a chuck type tap wrench (figs. 34A and 34B). It is important to keep the tap in alignment with the hole and once the tap has started to cut it is advisable to reverse it a fraction of a turn periodically to break the chips. This tap is then followed by the second tap and then by the plug. If a shallow open ended hole is being tapped the taper tap alone will do the work. When tapping a blind hole the plug tap must be used finally and the chips knocked out of the hole from time to time. Taps are brittle and will break off in the hole if too much pressure is applied. To reduce the friction when tapping it is advisable to use a lubricant on all metals except brass and cast iron.

LUBRICANTS FOR THREADING

Material to be threaded	Lubricant
Aluminium	Paraffin
Brass	None
Bronze and copper	Paraffin or lard oil
Cast iron	None
Mild steel	Sulphur base oil

Broken Taps. A lot of time can be wasted in trying to remove a broken tap from a piece of work. Often it is quicker to discard the part and start again. However, there are several methods used for the removal of broken taps.

1. Use a tap extractor. These work better on the larger sizes. They have three or four prongs, according to the kind of tap being removed, which fit into the flutes of the broken tap.

2. Break out the tap using a small chisel and a hammer.

3. On an open ended hole it is sometimes possible to drive the tap out with a punch from the back.

4. If a carbon steel tap is broken in the hole it is possible to heat the tap and the surrounding metal with a blow pipe flame to cherry red and allow to cool slowly then centre punch and drill out. This is not possible with high speed steel taps because the temperature required is too high to be obtained with the blowpipe.

5. If the tap is broken in a blind hole, build a small wall of plasticine about 12 mm high all round the broken tap and carefully pour in concentrated nitric acid. This will etch away a little of the workpiece as well as part of the tap. Wash away every trace of the acid and unscrew the broken tap with a hammer and a small punch.

After a tap has been removed by any of these methods it is often necessary to drill and tap a size larger.

Dieing. Stocks and dies are used for cutting external threads. These are shown in figure 35. The dies are made from hardened and tempered steel and may be of the circular split die pattern or loose dies.

The circular split die is the one popularly used in school. There are three adjusting screws but the adjustment is only slight. The middle screw, which is pointed, forces the split open and the two side screws are for closing the die.

When starting to cut an external thread the die should be "open", i.e. with the centre screw tight; also the side screws must be screwed down to prevent any tendency for the die to twist. The end of the rod to be threaded should be slightly tapered to allow the die to start. The taper can be filed. Use a lubricant as for tapping and keep the die "square" to the rod. Reverse the die a little from time to time to break the chips. After the first cut try the thread in the tapped hole. If it is too tight take another cut with the dies after slackening the centre screw and tightening the outside ones.

Riveting. Rivets are mentioned in the chapter on joining metals and the more common kinds are shown there.

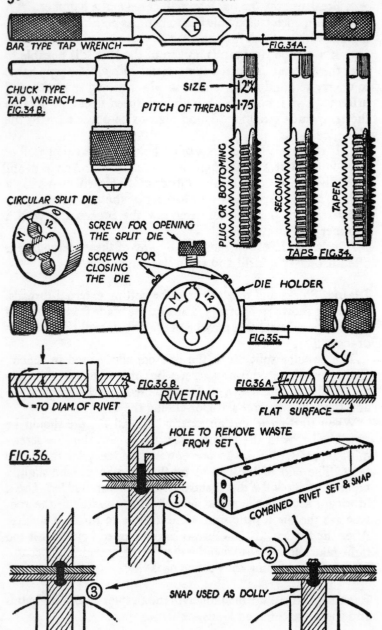

BAR TYPE TAP WRENCH — FIG. 34A.

CHUCK TYPE TAP WRENCH FIG. 34 B.

SIZE — 12%

PITCH OF THREADS — 1·75

PLUG OR BOTTOMING

SECOND

TAPER

TAPS FIG. 34.

CIRCULAR SPLIT DIE

SCREW FOR OPENING THE SPLIT DIE

SCREWS FOR CLOSING THE DIE

DIE HOLDER

FIG. 35.

FIG. 36 B.

=TO DIAM. OF RIVET

FIG. 36 A.

RIVETING

FLAT SURFACE

FIG. 36.

HOLE TO REMOVE WASTE FROM SET

COMBINED RIVET SET & SNAP

①

②

③

SNAP USED AS DOLLY

Riveting in school requires a ball pein hammer, a dolly and a set and snap (fig. 36). Before riveting the parts must be drilled with the right size drill. It is important that the rivet be a good fit in the hole otherwise it might bend when being hammered.

Countersunk-head rivets are often used in school work because they can be filed flush and make a clean job. When using a countersunk rivet, support the head on a flat surface such as the face of the anvil (fig. 36A). The length of the rivet depends on the depth of the countersink, but usually if the amount left for riveting is equal in length to the diameter of the rivet an adequate head can be formed leaving enough to clean off with a file (fig. 36B).

Snaphead rivets are supported underneath with a rivet snap held in a vice, which acts as a dolly (fig. 36 (1)). First the two pieces are set down to make sure the plates are properly together. This operation is important on large sheets which might be distorted. The head is first formed with a ball pein hammer (fig. 36 (2)) and finished off with the snap (fig. 36 (3)). The amount of rivet above the hole required for forming a snap head is usually equal to slightly more than the diameter of the rivet.

For special riveting jobs such as we meet when making model steam engines it is often necessary to make up special dollies.

Spanners and Screwdrivers (fig. 37). Nuts and bolts are loosened or tightened with a spanner. These are made to suit the various sizes of nuts and bolts available. It is important to use the right size spanner otherwise the nut or bolt head soon becomes badly worn at the corners. When using an adjustable spanner be sure that it is properly tight. Many kinds of spanners are available but the most popular ones are those shown

Screw Threads. I.S.O. (International Standards Organization) has recommended that British industry should adopt metric screw threads by 1975. This provides a 'coarse' and 'fine' series of screws, bolts and nuts (see table at back). However, the existing standard threads shown here will inevitably be still in use for some years.

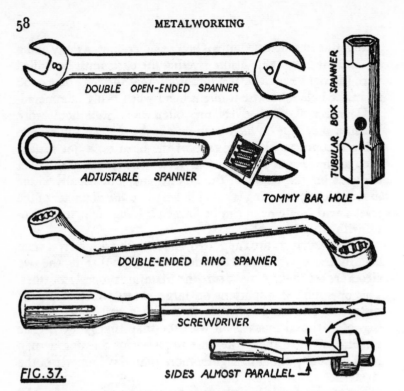

DOUBLE OPEN-ENDED SPANNER

TUBULAR BOX SPANNER

ADJUSTABLE SPANNER

TOMMY BAR HOLE

DOUBLE-ENDED RING SPANNER

SCREWDRIVER

FIG. 37.

SIDES ALMOST PARALLEL

British Standard Whitworth (B.S.W.) The BSW thread form was devised by Sir Joseph Whitworth and first used in 1841. This thread has been widely used since it was first introduced, but as engineering work has become more and more varied other standard threads have been introduced such as British Standard Fine and British Standard Pipe.

British Standard Fine (B.S.F.) and *British Standard Pipe (B.S.P.)*. These both use the Whitworth thread form but have a finer pitch. In the B.S.F. thread this fine pitch gives a larger core and thus more strength, except that the thread is a little weaker. But the nut is less likely to be loosened by vibration. For pipe work the thread needs to be fine otherwise it would break through the wall of the pipe.

British Association (B.A.). This is used often on threads below a quarter of an inch diameter. These threads have a fine pitch

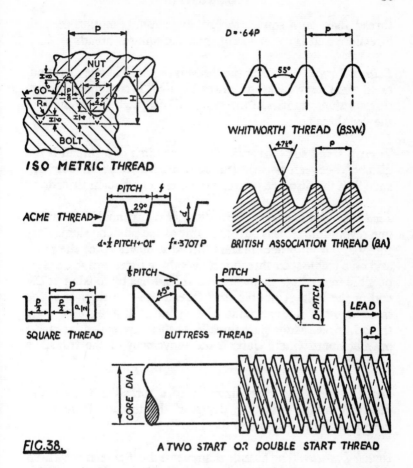

FIG.38.

A TWO START OR DOUBLE START THREAD

(metric) and the sizes are closely graded starting from O.B.A. which is the largest (see table at back). B.A. threads are used for delicate work.

Square Thread. This is used for transmitting motion in either direction such as on the cross slide of a lathe. There is less friction on this kind of thread than on the vee threads.

Acme Thread. This is often used on the lead screws of lathes because it is easier to engage the split nuts on this slightly vee'd thread than on a square thread. It transmits motion in both directions and is easier to cut than the square thread.

Buttress Thread. Wherever the thrust is required in one direction, as on some screw jacks, this thread is used. It combines the easy transmission qualities of the square thread with the strength of the vee thread.

Terms Used for Threads *Pitch.* The pitch of a thread is the distance between two threads measured axially; for convenience, it is the distance between the crests of adjacent threads.

Lead. The lead of a screw is the distance it advances in the nut in one revolution. This is only the same as the pitch on single start threads, but on a double start thread it moves twice the pitch and on a treble start thread it moves three times and so on. It is possible to see how many starts a thread has by looking at the end of the bolt. A double start thread has two threads of the same depth running round the cylinder and a three start thread, three. Multi-start threads, as these are called, are used on machinery where quick axial movement of the thread is required.

Core Diameter. The core diameter of a thread is the outside diameter minus twice the depth of the thread. It must be measured at right angles to the axis.

Outside Diameter. The outside diameter is the diameter measured over the crests of the threads. Screws, bolts etc. are known by this dimension, e.g. an M12 bolt has an outside diameter of 12 mm.

4
Methods of Joining Metals

Probably the oldest method of joining metals is by riveting. Over 4,000 years ago vessels were made by riveting together copper and bronze plates.

The craftsman of long ago must have worked under great difficulty using a very primitive drill to make his holes for riveting (fig. 1). Later when iron was used they found that joints could be made by forge or fire welding.

Joining metals by forge welding has been done for thousands of years but we are not sure when this method was first used. The swords used by the Vikings were made of plaited or twisted strips of metal which were heated to white heat and then hammered together, that is, they were forge welded (fig. 2).

The method of obtaining the heat was probably similar to that used today by the primitive Kikuyu people of Kenya. The

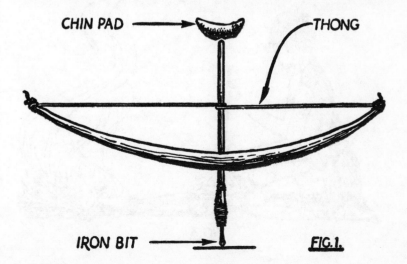

CHIN PAD ——→ THONG

IRON BIT ——→ FIG. 1.

furnace is a shallow hole in the ground lined with clay. A
charcoal fire is started and kept going with plentiful supplies of
charcoal. The blast comes from two bellows which consist of
"baggy" goat skins tied over specially made earthenware pots.
The loose skins are gathered up in the centre and bound on to
stocks in such a way that they can be moved up and down thus
increasing and decreasing the volume of air trapped inside. At
the bottom edge of each pot there is a tube which takes the air

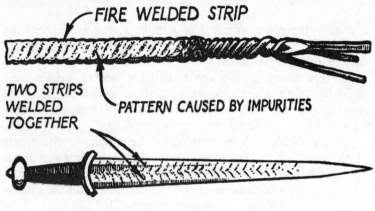

FIRE WELDED STRIP

TWO STRIPS
WELDED
TOGETHER

PATTERN CAUSED BY IMPURITIES

FIG.2.

FIG.3

to a tapered fireclay funnel (*tuyère*) which leads into the heart of the fire. There are no valves in these bellows. As one bellow is pumped down forcing the air into the fire, the other is brought up and the air comes in at the place where the tube enters the tapered funnel (fig. 3).

Today work is much easier for a craftsman and we have more methods of joining metals than were known by the ancient metalworkers. For convenience we can divide the methods of joining metals into two groups: 1. using heat, 2. working cold.

In group 1 we have:
   soft soldering
   silver soldering
   brazing
   welding

In group 2 we have:
   screws (this includes bolts, studs and nuts)
   rivets.

SOFT SOLDERING

This method of joining metals does not require a lot of heat nor expensive equipment. The solder is an alloy mainly of tin and lead.

Lead melts at 327°C and pure tin melts at 232°C but when they are alloyed together they start to melt, i.e. they become pasty, at about 183°C. The range of temperature over which they are pasty depends on the proportion of tin to lead, e.g. plumber's solder (tin 30% and lead 70%) has a long pasty range—necessary for wiping a joint—whereas tinman's solder (tin 65% and lead 35%) passes quickly from a liquid to solid state (see fig. 4). Solders with lower melting points are made by adding bismuth to the tin/lead alloy. These are often termed Low Melting Point (L.M.P.) solders.

PREPARATION OF JOINT

Before two surfaces are joined together by solder they must be cleaned mechanically, e.g. by filing, wire brushing, scraping

SOLDERS AND FLUXES FOR SOFT SOLDERING VARIOUS METALS

Work to be soldered	Flux	Type of solder
Brass Gilding metal Copper Gun metal	Zinc chloride. Paste flux. Resin. Solder paint (contains its own flux).	Any solder can be used but the choice of solder will depend on the type of work being done.
Electrical work	Resin cored solder. Resin.	Tin 60%, lead 40%.
Galvanised iron Zinc	Zinc chloride or very weak diluted hydrochloric acid.	Any solder with 40% or more tin.
Pewter Britannia metal	Glycerine to which one or two drops of hydrochloric acid is added. Resin, tallow, resin cored solder.	65% tin, 35% lead or pewter wire. For amateur use LMP solder = tin, lead and bismuth.
Lead	Tallow.	Tin 30%, lead 70%.
Aluminium	Cannot be soldered in the usual manner but there are many kinds of special aluminium solders and fluxes available. The difficulty is in removing the oxides, which form rapidly, from the surfaces of the metal. This is often done by melting the solder on to the fluxed surface and then scratch brushing underneath the layer of molten solder so that the solder can "take" without the aluminium being exposed to the air.	Proprietary brands usually containing only tin (no lead) with some zinc. Typically 90% tin, 10% zinc.
Cast iron	Tinning is slow: afterwards any flux can be used.	50% tin, 50% lead.
Chromium steel	Difficult to "tin" except by methods similar to those used on aluminium.	Any solder with 45% tin or more if pretinning has been successful.

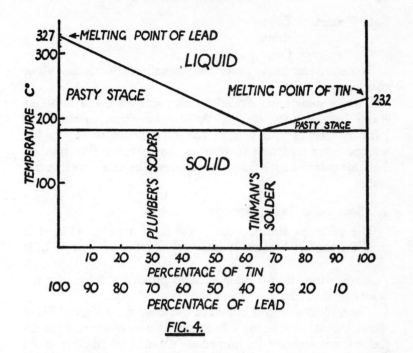

327 ← MELTING POINT OF LEAD
300
LIQUID
TEMPERATURE C°
PASTY STAGE
MELTING POINT OF TIN → 232
200
PASTY STAGE
PLUMBER'S SOLDER
SOLID
TINMAN'S SOLDER
100
10 20 30 40 50 60 70 80 90 100
PERCENTAGE OF TIN
100 90 80 70 60 50 40 30 20 10
PERCENTAGE OF LEAD

FIG. 4.

etc., but this is not enough. The remaining thin film of oxides must be removed chemically by using a flux.

FLUXES FOR SOFT SOLDERING

The fluxes are divided into two groups: active and safe.

Active fluxes. 1. Zinc chloride, also known as "killed spirit" is popularly used in workshops. It is made by adding scraps of zinc to hydrochloric acid until all the bubbling has stopped. It should be made in an earthenware or lead vessel in a place where the fumes are readily taken away, such as on a window sill. Then it should be filtered and about 50% water added. If necessary it can be cleared by adding a few drops of concentrated hydrochloric acid.

2. Paste fluxes containing either zinc chloride or ammonium chloride in petroleum jelly.

3. Ammonium chloride (Sal ammoniac).

Safe Fluxes. 1. Tallow
             2. Resin
             3. Oleic acid.

There are also many proprietary brands available, not all of them good.

Usually solders will "take" much more readily with active fluxes because they are slightly acid and tend to clean the joint by their etching action. The joint should be thoroughly washed after soldering to remove the corrosive flux residue. For this reason active fluxes should never be used on electrical work.

1. SOLDERING IRON METHOD

The soldering iron method is the most popular. Copper is used for the bit because it is a very good conductor of heat (fig. 5).

A soldering stove is often used to provide the heat for the soldering iron (fig. 5).

The soldering iron is heated in the stove until a green flame shows that it is hot enough. It should now be removed from the flame if not required for immediate use and rested close to the flame but not actually touching it. Oxides form very readily on the heated copper bit so it must be tinned before use. Once it has been tinned properly it should not need re-tinning for a long time. The common fault in schools is overheating. This results in the bit being burned. Directly after each heating the iron should be fluxed and given a fresh coat of solder. It is important to heat the whole of the bit not merely the tip otherwise it will not hold the heat long enough to do a satisfactory job.

Tinning is done by heating the bit in the stove until a green flame shows. Remove from the stove and briskly file the faces with a file which should be kept for this purpose. Don't overdo the filing. Now put the tip into a hollow in a sal ammoniac block in which there are small pieces of solder. By this method the whole of the tip can be covered with an even layer of solder at once. It is now tinned.

When the parts to be soldered have been properly prepared and fluxed the tinned soldering iron is taken from the stove, fluxed and recharged with solder. The flux can be in a small tin lid and the solder in another. The charged iron should be held against the pieces to be soldered for a moment to allow the heat to be transferred from the bit to the work and then gently moved along the joint. Often it is best to use the edge of the bit as this allows more heat to get to the work. Surplus solder can be picked up with the tip of the soldering iron.

Figure 5A shows a small electric soldering iron. Electric soldering irons are usually used for electrical work but can also be used where the ordinary soldering iron is used.

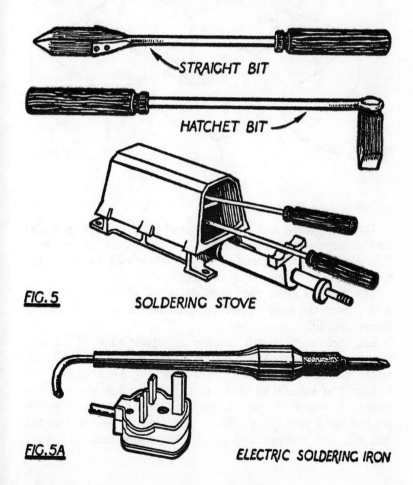

STRAIGHT BIT

HATCHET BIT

FIG. 5   SOLDERING STOVE

FIG. 5A   ELECTRIC SOLDERING IRON

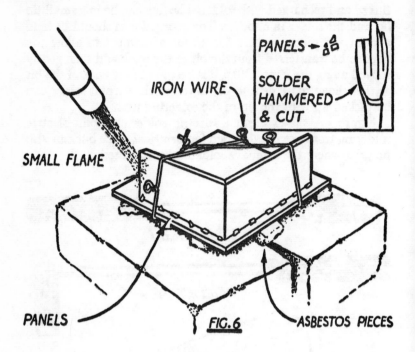

IRON WIRE

PANELS →

SOLDER
HAMMERED
& CUT

SMALL FLAME

PANELS

FIG.6

ASBESTOS PIECES

2. BLOWPIPE SOLDERING

This is a reliable method, particularly on heavy gauge metal and on large work where a soldering iron would be inadequate. It is not to be recommended for tin plate work because the tin surface can be damaged by the flame.

The method often used is to cut small pieces or panels of solder from the strip which has been hammered and cut as shown (fig. 6).

Lay these small panels of solder along the edges of the prepared joint. Usually killed spirits is used as a flux. The flame, which should be small, must be kept moving. First the flux will bubble and usually in doing so it will displace some of the panels. If any of the panels move too far they can be gently pushed back into place with a thin pointed rod—a pointed rod will not conduct too much heat away from the work (fig. 6A).

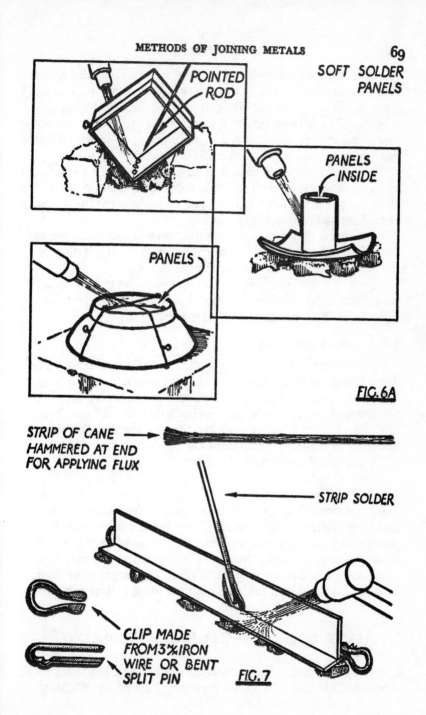

SOFT SOLDER PANELS

POINTED ROD

PANELS INSIDE

PANELS

FIG. 6A

STRIP OF CANE HAMMERED AT END FOR APPLYING FLUX

STRIP SOLDER

CLIP MADE FROM 3% IRON WIRE OR BENT SPLIT PIN

FIG. 7

When the melting point of the solder is reached, the solder will run into the joint. If the solder does not run into every part of the joint as required, it can be helped by quickly applying a little more flux to the parts where the solder has not run. This is best done with a small piece of cane which has been hammered to make the end fray (fig. 7).

Notice that flat work should never be laid flat on a fire brick or asbestos sheet, if it is it will take too long to heat up because the surface on which it is lying has to be brought up to the same heat as the rest of the work.

It is a good plan to support it either on a bed of small pieces of broken fire brick, or asbestos cubes, or small pieces of coke. By this means the flame can get under the work.

Panels of solder need not always be used. The strip of solder which has been suitably hammered at the end can be "fed" into the joint as the required heat is reached (fig. 7).

3. SOLDER PAINT METHOD

Solder paint is available in small jars and contains its own flux. The parts to be joined should be clean and well fitting. The solder paint is then applied to both pieces before they are positioned. Heat is then applied either with a small flame from the blowpipe or if convenient by pressing the flat face of a soldering iron against them until enough heat is transferred to make the solder paint melt.

4. SWEATING

By this method the parts to be joined are cleaned and fluxed and each surface is then tinned. These tinned surfaces are then put together and gently heated either by a soldering iron or the blowpipe. Sweating usually works better if slight pressure is applied to the parts to be joined. When a stronger joint than we can make with soft solder is required we use silver solder.

SILVER SOLDERING OR HARD SOLDERING

Silver solder is available in different grades. The temperature at which these melt can vary between 630°C and 830°C. Most

silver solders are made from alloying silver copper and zinc.
Here are some from the wide range available:

Easy-Flo melts at approx.   630°C
Easy Solder melts at approx.   723°C
Medium melts at approx.   765°C
Hard melts at approx.   778°C
Enamelling melts at approx.   800°C

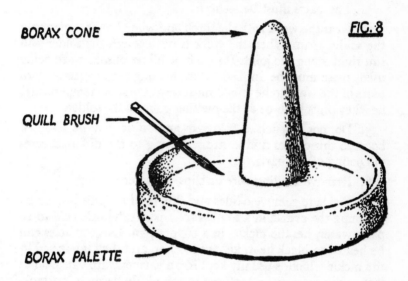

BORAX CONE

QUILL BRUSH

BORAX PALETTE

FIG. 8

Fluxes for Silver Solders

Most silver soldering can be done by using borax as a flux.
Borax may be bought in lump form (borax cone) (fig. 8) or in
powder. If the borax cone is used it is usual to use it in conjunction with the borax palette and a little water. The cone is
gently rubbed in the palette into which a few drops of water
have been placed. Soon the water will become cloudy and then
after a little more rubbing it will have the consistency of thin
cream. It is now ready for use as a flux.

If powdered borax is used it can be made into a thin paste and
then applied.

Other proprietary fluxes in powder form are available. In
many cases these are more suitable than borax particularly

when the makers of the solder make a flux to be used specifically with the solder.

SILVER SOLDERING METHOD

1. The parts to be joined must be well fitting and clean.

2. These parts must be fluxed properly particularly where you want the solder to run.

3. The parts must be secured.

4. Heat the work with the torch and when hot enough apply the solder strip. When the work is hot enough the solder will run right along the joint. If panels or filings of solder are being used, these must be applied before heating commences. Both parts of the work to be joined must be at the same temperature, i.e. they must both be at the melting point of the solder.

5. Do not quench a soldered joint if it can be avoided because this causes undue stresses owing to the different rates of cooling of the parts.

6. Remove binding wire or clips etc. after cooling.

7. Pickle to remove oxides and flux residue. This is done by warming the article in a solution of 1 part sulphuric acid to 10 parts water, i.e. the pickle, in a copper pan. Large articles can be heated to black heat, i.e. not red hot, and then immersed in the pickle which is usually kept in an earthenware vat. Do not leave soldered articles too long in the pickle because it attacks the zinc in the solder and makes the joint porous.

Sometimes it is necessary to silver solder a small part on to a much larger one. Owing to the length of time required to bring the larger part to the right temperature the flux is burnt away at the edges of the joint. This prevents the solder from running. One way to overcome this is to prepare the parts by drilling holes as shown in figure 9.

When the panels of solder and flux are in the hole the boss can be secured in its place with clips. Take care to properly flux the place where you want the solder to run. Now heat the work until the solder melts and you see the fine silver line of molten solder all round the joint. Allow to cool and clean in usual manner.

PUT IN SMALL
PIECES OF SOLDER
& FLUX WELL

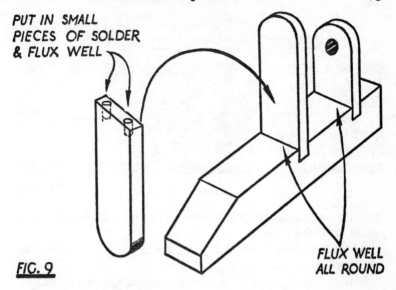

FIG. 9

FLUX WELL
ALL ROUND

How Solder Joins Metals

When sufficient heat is applied to the solder it melts and combines at the point of contact with the metals it is joining. This of course applies only to well-fitting, properly cleaned and fluxed metal (fig. 10).

This combining of the solder and the metals to be joined happens not only in soft soldering but also in silver soldering and brazing. The intermetallic compound is usually only a few thousandths of an inch deep.

BRAZING

This is similar to silver soldering: in fact silver soldering is sometimes known as silver brazing. To be precise brazing is the joining of metals with brass. Brass is an alloy of copper and zinc.

A higher temperature is required and a stronger joint is made by brazing than by silver soldering.

The brazing alloy is called brazing spelter. Spelter is obtainable in rod, powder, granulated or in ribbon form. If used in

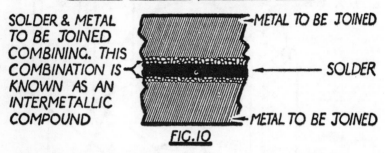

ENLARGED
SECTION THROUGH SOLDERED JOINT

SOLDER & METAL
TO BE JOINED
COMBINING. THIS
COMBINATION IS
KNOWN AS AN
INTERMETALLIC
COMPOUND

METAL TO BE JOINED

SOLDER

METAL TO BE JOINED

FIG.10

powder or granulated form it is usually mixed with flux and
water to make a paste.

There are several grades but these are three popularly used
and known as:

Soft   50% copper 50% zinc melts at approx. 870°C
Medium 54% copper 46% zinc melts at approx. 880°C
Hard   60% copper 40% zinc melts at approx. 900°C

FLUX FOR BRAZING

Borax can be used for most purposes but there are several
made up powders available.

BRAZING METHOD

Prepare as for silver solder. In the school workshop the
biggest enemy to brazing is heat loss. This causes the operator
to take too long on the work and this in turn causes excessive
oxidation. Often this is owing to insufficient care being taken
in packing firebricks or asbestos round the parts to be joined.
Also brazing is reserved for the larger pieces which conduct the
heat from the joint very readily. Figure 11 shows a well packed
joint to be made on a gate frame.

If a brazing rod is being used it helps if the tip of the rod is
heated and then dipped in the tin of dry flux. This causes the
flux to adhere to the end of the rod. When the parts to be
brazed are hot enough, this flux on the end of the rod will help
the flow of molten brass when it is touched on to the joint.
Remember the heat to melt the rod must come from the work

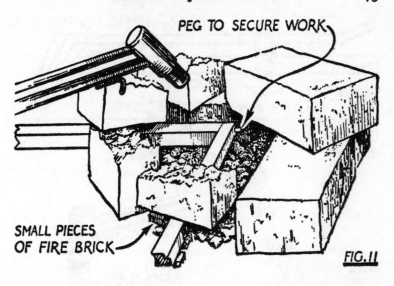

PEG TO SECURE WORK

SMALL PIECES
OF FIRE BRICK

FIG. 11

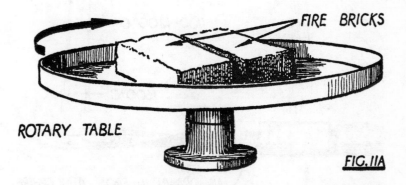

FIRE BRICKS

ROTARY TABLE

FIG. 11A

and not the flame. Important too is the fact that brazing should be done at one heat, i.e. the torch should not be taken off the work once having started until the brazing operation is completed; otherwise excessive oxidation takes place.

For circular work a rotary table is very useful. This can be used for soldering as well as brazing (fig. 11A).

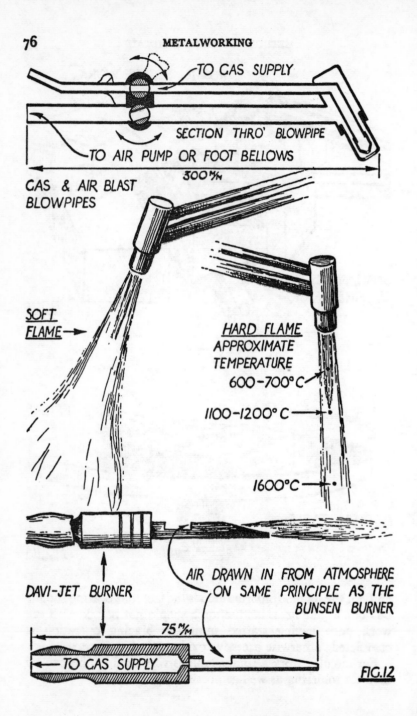

TO GAS SUPPLY

SECTION THRO' BLOWPIPE

TO AIR PUMP OR FOOT BELLOWS

300 m/m

GAS & AIR BLAST BLOWPIPES

SOFT FLAME →

HARD FLAME
APPROXIMATE
TEMPERATURE

600–700° C

1100–1200° C

1600°C

DAVI-JET BURNER

AIR DRAWN IN FROM ATMOSPHERE
ON SAME PRINCIPLE AS THE
BUNSEN BURNER

75 m/m

← TO GAS SUPPLY

FIG.12

CLEANING THE JOINT AFTER BRAZING

The makers of the flux will usually give their recommendations. Hot water is often mentioned for the removal of flux residue. Small work can be boiled in a solution of water and alum.

Figure 12 shows a blowpipe in section. The soft flame shown is used for obtaining an "all over" heat on a piece of work. It is made more fierce (hard flame) by either increasing the air blast or cutting down the gas for the purpose of concentrating the heat on a smaller area.

At the bottom of figure 12 is shown a Davi-jet burner. This is useful for soft soldering particularly on pewter ware. The intensity of the flame is adjusted merely by turning the gas tap.

WELDING*

ELECTRIC ARC AND RESISTANCE WELDING

Arc welding is done by using a coated metallic electrode, which makes an electric arc with the job being welded, or two carbon electrodes. The parts are joined by fusion. The metallic electrode is actually a metal filler rod coated with a fluxing agent. This coating also contains a material which gives off a gas as it burns therefore excluding the atmosphere from the joint being made.

Resistance welding is not unlike the old process of forge welding. A heavy electric current is passed (by means of two electrodes) between the parts to be joined until the fusion temperature is reached. These parts are then held under pressure for a brief moment until fusion at that point is complete.

---

* The interested student can read fully on welding from the book: *Welding* by A. C. Davis.

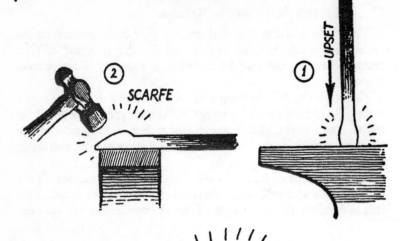

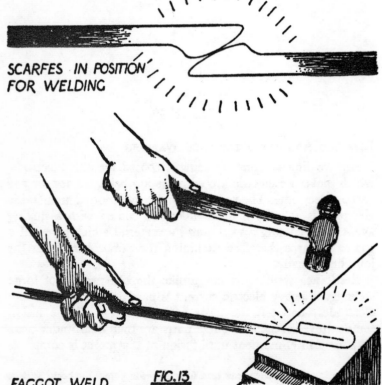

FAGGOT WELD   FIG. 13

Oxy-acetylene Welding

In this process, unlike silver soldering and brazing, the parent metals are melted. The oxy-acetylene flame melts the edges of the parent metal into pools to which a filler rod of the same material is melted.

Forge Welding

Forge welding, or fire welding, uses the blacksmith's hearth. Before a fire-welded joint can be made it is essential to have a clean clinker-free fire and the parts to be joined must be upset and scarfed (fig.13). The scarf must have rounded faces so that they touch in the centre; thus the molten scale is driven out during hammering. It is usual to have an assistant for fire welding. The parts to be joined are heated to a creamy white heat and removed from the fire and tapped on the edge of the anvil to shake off the dirt. Care must be taken to ensure that the scarfs are in proper relationship to each other before the first blow is struck in the centre of the work. It must now be repeatedly hammered, working from the centre, to drive out the molten scale. It may be necessary to reheat for the weld to be completed.

A properly fire-welded joint cannot be detected from the parent metals. A beginner will do well to start by making a faggot weld as an exercise. This does not require an assistant nor a pair of tongs (fig. 13).

Some skilled blacksmiths can fire weld* without using any flux but others always use a flux. Silver sand, burnt borax, laffite welding plate or a powder sold by The Amalgam Co. of Sheffield can be used.

SCREWS

This is a broad term which includes: bolts, studs, set screws, grub screws, thumb screws, socket head cap screws, Phillip screws etc.

* Full details regarding fire welding may be obtained from The Rural Industries Bureau publications on forge work.

Usually these are used to secure two or more pieces together except where a bolt or screw is used as a hinge pin.

BOLTS

These are as shown. They always have a nut and usually a washer too (fig. 14).

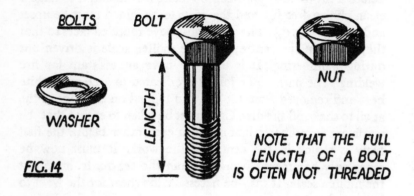

BOLTS   BOLT   NUT

WASHER   LENGTH

FIG. 14   NOTE THAT THE FULL LENGTH OF A BOLT IS OFTEN NOT THREADED

SCREWS

These have no nut (see top of fig. 15).

GRUB SCREWS OR SET SCREWS

Often used to secure pulleys to shafts (bottom of fig. 15).

THUMB SCREWS

These are used where easy removal is desired (bottom of fig. 15).

STUDS

They have no head and no nut. They are sometimes used in place of bolts. It is easier to replace a worn stud than to re-drill and tap a hole after the thread is worn or stripped. A good example of the use of studs can be seen on the cylinder block of a car (fig. 16).

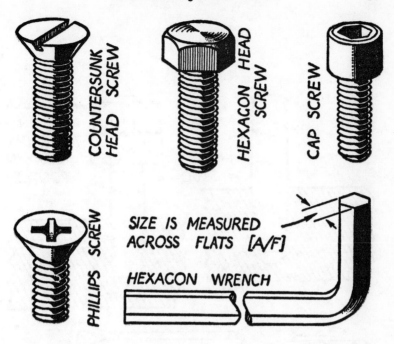

COUNTERSUNK HEAD SCREW

HEXAGON HEAD SCREW

CAP SCREW

PHILLIPS SCREW

SIZE IS MEASURED ACROSS FLATS [A/F]

HEXAGON WRENCH

END OF PHILLIPS SCREW DRIVER. AVAILABLE IN FOUR SIZES

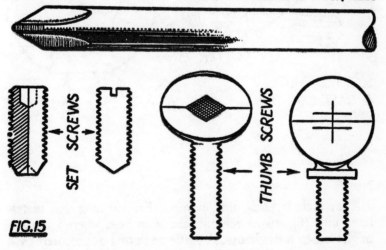

SET SCREWS

THUMB SCREWS

FIG.15

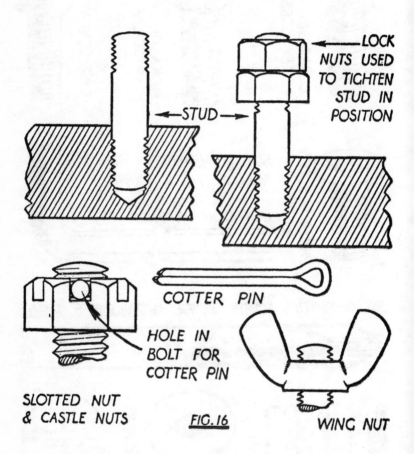

LOCK NUTS USED TO TIGHTEN STUD IN POSITION

←STUD→

COTTER PIN

HOLE IN BOLT FOR COTTER PIN

SLOTTED NUT & CASTLE NUTS

WING NUT

FIG. 16

NUTS

They include wing nuts, hexagon-headed nuts and castellated nuts (fig. 16). Lock nuts are often used where vibration might loosen a single nut. A castle or slotted nut secured by a cotter pin is similarly used to prevent loosening by vibration.

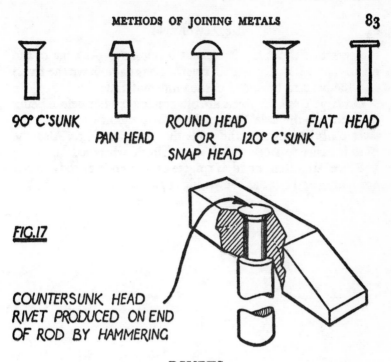

90° C'SUNK

PAN HEAD

ROUND HEAD
OR
SNAP HEAD

120° C'SUNK

FLAT HEAD

FIG.17

COUNTERSUNK HEAD
RIVET PRODUCED ON END
OF ROD BY HAMMERING

RIVETS

Metal parts or plates can be joined by rivets to make a permanent joint or, if a single rivet is used it can be as a pivot or hinge.

Those commonly used are shown in figure 17.

Rivets are classified by the shape of the head, their length, diameter and the metal from which they are made.

The diameter of the rivet used must be related to the thickness of the plates being riveted. In school we often use our own judgement when selecting rivets for a piece of work, but it is common practice when riveting plates between 1.5 mm and 12 mm thick to use a rivet the diameter of which equals twice the thickness of the plates being riveted. Plates thicker than 12 mm should have a rivet $1\frac{1}{2}$ times the thickness of the plate. When riveting plates of unequal thickness the calculation is based on the thinner plate.

The distance between the centres of two rivets in the same row (pitch) should not be less than 2 × diameter of rivet and the centre of the rivet should not be closer to the edge of the metal than $1\frac{1}{2}$ × diameter of rivet. It is usual to have the rivets and the parts to be joined of the same material.

On large work the rivets are often made red hot before being inserted into the hole. This makes a better joint because as the rivet cools it contracts and pulls the plates together. Also the rivet is easier to work as it is more plastic when red hot.

Rivets are often made as spigots on the ends of rods which are hammered over as shown (fig. 17).

5
Casting

Casting is done in a foundry where molten metal is poured into cavities in sand left by a pattern. Foundry work in school is usually done in a part of the workshop set aside for this purpose.

The metal is melted in a crucible pot which is heated in an insulated crucible furnace. Crucibles are made of plumbago but zinc-based alloys and aluminium alloys can be melted in a cast iron pot (fig. 1).

The patterns are popularly made of soft close-grained wood, a good example being jelutong which is close-grained and easy to work. Wherever possible internal corners are radiused by applying wax or leather fillets or by using plastic wood so that no fragile corners will be left in the sand when the pattern is removed. The pattern is also suitably tapered or drafted. $\frac{1}{8}''$ per foot is sufficient, but for school work a greater draft is often allowed. This drafting is to facilitate easy removal from the sand. The pattern is finished with glass paper and varnished or painted. Figure 2 shows the pattern for a small vice. Allowance must be made for machining and for the metal shrinking when it cools.

Patterns which do not have one large face, as in figure 2, can be made as split patterns. These are often easier to manage if mounted on a board as in figure 3. If a board is not used, the halves of the pattern can be accurately located by dowel pins as shown in figure 4. When a pattern is made for use by an outside foundry, the various parts must be coloured to indicate to the foundryman where to allow the better metal to be for subsequent machining. These colours are specified in the British Standards No. 467: 1957. Red, for parts to be left as

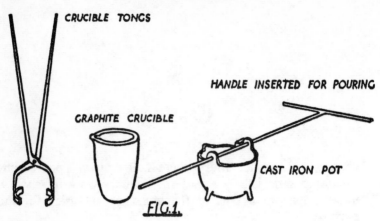

CRUCIBLE TONGS

GRAPHITE CRUCIBLE

HANDLE INSERTED FOR POURING

CAST IRON POT

FIG.1.

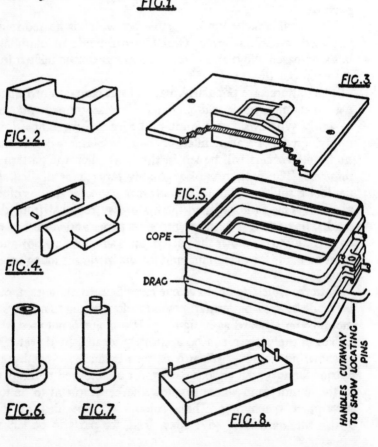

FIG. 2.

FIG. 3

FIG. 5.

COPE

DRAG

FIG. 4.

FIG. 6.   FIG. 7.

FIG. 8.

HANDLES CUTAWAY TO SHOW LOCATING PINS

cast; black for core prints; yellow where machining is to be done etc.

FLASKS OR MOULDING BOXES

These are usually made of steel, cast iron or aluminium alloy (fig. 5). The top half is called the cope, the pins of which locate into the sockets of the lower half known as the drag.

SAND

Oilbonded sand such as Petrobond is excellent for beginners because there is no need to worry about the correct moisture content; but it is more expensive than the popular Mansfield, Erith or Belfast sands which are natural sands and are made damp with water.

These natural sands are a mixture of sand grains and clay particles. They are refractory so that the hot metal does not bake or melt them, and they are more or less porous thus allowing the escape of steam and gases. The moisture content must be right. This can be judged by squeezing a handful, which should remain unbroken when the hand is opened and yet break when it is thrown down.

CORES

Cores are used where it is required that parts of the casting should be hollow. Figure 6 shows a hollow casting and figure 7, the pattern. The core prints are for making cavities in the sand in which to place the core. The core is made from sand bonded with oil to give cohesion. The core must be permeable to allow the gases to escape, and strong enough to stand handling, yet sufficiently brittle to crumble when the metal contracts. Cores can be made in a core box (fig. 8) or in metal piping.

For school work the core can be made of beach sand (sharp sand) bonded with linseed oil and baked in an oven until hard.

The linseed oil is mixed, a little at a time, into the sand until a handful squeezed does not exude oil and yet holds together. The core can be baked in an improvised biscuit-tin oven over a soldering stove, or in an old domestic oven, to a temperature of about 200°C. It will first go lighter in colour as the oil dries and then start turning brown. When it is a little darker than when first put in the oven, the baking is finished. Figure 9 shows the core in place in the mould resting in the cavities made by the core prints.

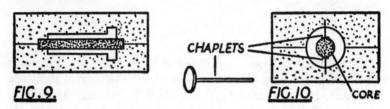

FIG. 9.   CHAPLETS   FIG. 10.   CORE

CHAPLETS

Chaplets are small supports for the core (fig. 10) made of the same metal as the casting. When the metal is poured these fuse into the casting. Although seldom used in school work, they are found necessary in industry where intricate cores are used.

MOULDERS' TOOLS

A few of these are shown in figure 11. The large rammer is made of wood and the small one of metal. These are used for ramming the sand all round the pattern. The water brush is soft and comes to a point. It is used for damping the mould where small repairs are made (usually to the edges). The taper trowel is one of the many shaped trowels moulders use to make the sand flat where desired. The spoon tool is often used to make gates. The gimlet is screwed into the pattern and tapped in all directions just above the thread with a metal rod while the handle is held. This is known as rapping. It loosens the pattern in the sand so that it can be withdrawn easily. Bellows are used for blowing out particles of sand from the mould. The

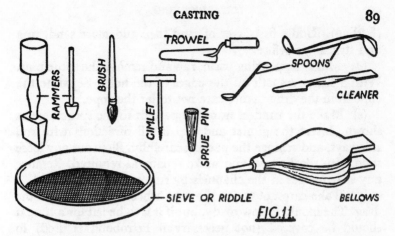

FIG.11

sieve or riddle is used for sifting the facing sand over the pattern. Sprue pins are round tapered pieces of wood used for making the runners and risers.

THE MOULDING PROCESS

For simplicity let us consider preparing the mould from the pattern for a small vice shown in figure 2 (p. 86).

(*a*) Choose a flask which allows at least 50 mm spare round the pattern. Open the flask and turn over the drag on to a flat surface, preferably a flat board (turn-over board) and place the pattern as shown in figure 12. The parting powder, which can be French chalk or a proprietary make, is held in a cotton bag and dusted over the pattern. This prevents the pattern from sticking in the sand.

(*b*) Riddle sand over the pattern (Petrobond does not need riddling) until it is covered, then add unsifted sand and ram down using the peen end of the rammer. Fill to the top with sand and ram with the butt end of the ram and make level (strickle) by drawing a firm straight edge across the top of the drag.

(*c*) Turn over the drag and fit the cope. Sprinkle with parting powder. Press the sprue pins into the sand. Their position is determined by experience—this takes into account the flow of the metal and the removal of excess metal afterwards (fettling). Riddle first layer of sand then add more sand, ram and strickle as before.

(*d*) Make the pouring basin, rap and remove the sprue pins. With a finger smooth off the edges of the holes. Separate the cope from the drag taking care not to jar the cope.

(*e*) Make the runners from the pattern to the sprue hole as shown. Insert the gimlet and rap in all directions with rod sideways, and remove the pattern carefully. Blow out any loose sand with the bellows and make repairs as required. Remove any sharp edges in the channels by running a finger round.

(*f*) Take care not to jar the cope when replacing it on the drag. The mould is now ready, but if it is to be left for a time it should be covered (not necessary if Petrobond is used) to prevent loss of moisture.

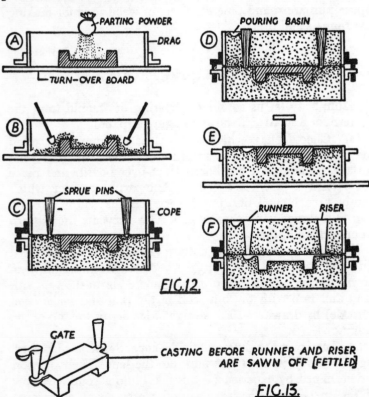

FIG. 12.

CASTING BEFORE RUNNER AND RISER
ARE SAWN OFF [FETTLED]

FIG. 13.

Odd-side Boxes

If the pattern does not have a flat back an odd-side box has to be made by placing the cope on the turn-over board with its locating pins upwards. Ram the cope with sand and then cut out the sand to take the pattern to half its depth. Then ram the sand round the pattern and strickle. Dust with parting powder and fit the drag, fill with sand, ram and strickle flat. Lift the drag with care and turn over. Knock out the sand in the cope (odd-side). With the pattern in the drag, place the empty cope in position, dust with parting powder, position sprue pins, fill with sand, ram and strickle. Rap and remove spruce pins and continue as for previous mould.

Pouring the Metal

Directly before the metal is poured the dross must be removed with a skimmer (fig. 14). Keep the crucible close to the pouring basin and pour in a continuous unbroken stream, as fast as the mould will take it, until the metal appears at the riser. When the metal has cooled and the casting been removed, it will be as in figure 13. This shows the relative size of the gate. The process of melting the metal prior to pouring must be properly done otherwise faulty castings result.

Melting the Metal

In school aluminium alloys and zinc alloys are widely used.

Aluminium alloys melt at about 600°C
Zinc alloys melt at about 390°C

These metals can be melted either in a plumbago crucible or a cast iron pot.

Furnaces for schools usually use gas and air. There are various types available, but whichever kind is used the makers' instructions must be followed regarding the lighting.

Small pieces of metal charged into the crucible will melt more quickly than large pieces. However, once the first charge is molten larger pieces can be added. The metal should never be heated much above its melting point and it should be poured promptly after skimming. Overheated metal results in the

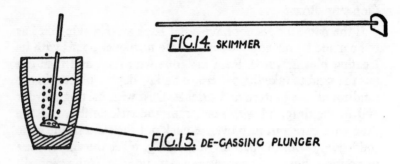

FIG.14. SKIMMER

FIG.15. DE-GASSING PLUNGER

following typical faults: poor quality casting; excessive shrinkage and tearing of the metal.

When melting aluminium, fluxing and degassing are sometimes necessary.

FLUXING

A small amount of powdered flux (proprietary make) is applied to the charge as it becomes pasty. This melts on the surface and protects the metal from the atmosphere.

DEGASSING

If porous castings are being constantly obtained, degassing should be carried out before pouring. For school work it is convenient to use tablets which are plunged to the bottom of the melt with a domed tool (fig. 15).

6

Blacksmithing

THE HEARTH

There are various types of hearth available for school use but the two most popular ones have back blasts, i.e. the air blast comes from the back. One has a water cooled tuyère and the other a dry tuyère. The type with the water cooled tuyère is the better one because those with dry tuyères tend to burn away at the blast hole and require frequent replacement of the tuyère or tue iron. Figure 2, shows a part-section through the hearth. The hearth tools are shown above figure 1.

FUEL

Some smiths use coal and others coke breeze. The choice depends upon local custom. However, good blacksmith's coal is hard to obtain. The beginner is well advised to use coke breeze. This must be good smithy breeze, free from dust; a suitable size is known as "beans". Crushed or broken-up boiler coke or furnace coke is not suitable for forging.

The following points should be remembered:

1. Keep the fire in a small area. This is achieved by keeping the blast to a workable minimum.

2. Prevent the fire from burning hollow. The heat of the fire must be in the middle, just below the piece of metal being heated (see fig. 1). A hollow fire allows the blast air to oxidise the metal or may even burn it.

3. Remove clinker periodically. When clinker is cold it looks like crude black glass and makes a characteristic "clink

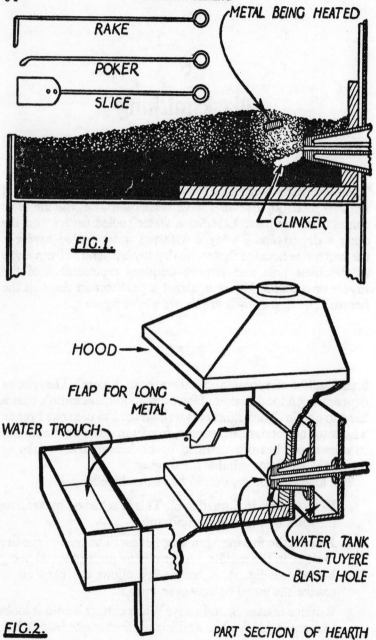

RAKE

POKER

SLICE

METAL BEING HEATED

CLINKER

FIG.1.

HOOD →

FLAP FOR LONG METAL

WATER TROUGH

WATER TANK
TUYERE
BLAST HOLE

FIG.2.

PART SECTION OF HEARTH

clink" sound when touched with the fire tools. It is formed by the combination of oxygen and the impurities in the fuel.

The clinker forms just below the blast hole. The blast blows it on to the metal being heated to which it sticks, thus making forging difficult and dangerous because the clinker spurts out under the hammer blows. To remove the clinker turn off the blast for a few minutes to allow the clinker to solidify. It can then be hooked out in one piece with the poker which should be flattened and curved for the purpose (fig. 1). Knowing just where to find clinker and how to remove it without disturbing the fire too much is an art.

THE ANVIL

The London pattern anvil is the one most used and is shown in figure 3. Anvils for school work should not weigh under 50 kgms nor over 125 kgms. (They are sold by weight.) The body of the anvil is usually made from wrought iron or mild steel with a top facing of hardened carbon steel. Smiths often like to stand the anvil on an elm trunk. This reduces the noise a little and gives it a certain amount of resilience. In school they are nearly always on stands. Some resilience can be obtained by using the plywood pad shown in figure 3.

TOOLS

HAMMERS

A 0·5 kg ball pein hammer is a good size for most boys. The bigger boys can manage a 1 kg hammer providing the haft is shortened. A 3 kg sledge hammer for heavy striking is needed occasionally.

SWAGE BLOCK

This is a useful tool although good work can be done if one is not available. A useful size is about 300 mm × 300 mm × 150 mm. These are used on a stand (fig. 3). It can be used in the vertical position or horizontally as shown by the dotted lines for shaping and swaging.

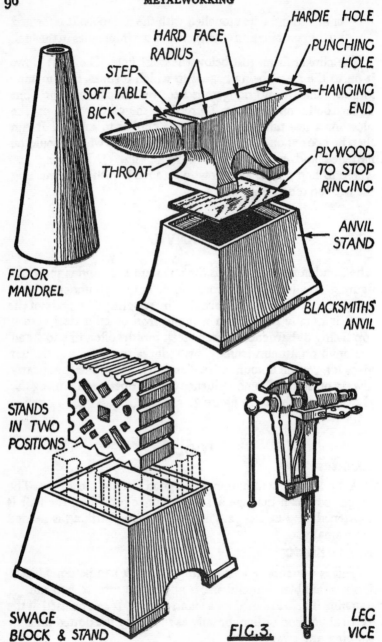

FLOOR MANDREL

HARDIE HOLE
PUNCHING HOLE
HARD FACE
RADIUS
STEP
SOFT TABLE
BICK
HANGING END
THROAT
PLYWOOD TO STOP RINGING
ANVIL STAND
BLACKSMITHS ANVIL

STANDS IN TWO POSITIONS

SWAGE BLOCK & STAND

LEG VICE

FIG.3.

FLOOR MANDREL

These are available in a number of sizes and are made from cast iron. They are useful for round work like rings and hoops (fig. 3).

LEG VICE

Although inferior in its gripping action to the engineer's parallel jaw vice, it is useful for heavy bending and withstands hammering (fig. 3).

TONGS

These are selected to suit the work. Traditionally a blacksmith makes his own tongs, but for school use they are bought ready made. A useful selection is shown in figure 4. Closed mouth tongs are used for thin metal. Usually these have a vee groove along the inside of the jaws for holding small section, round or square, metal.

Open mouth tongs are used for holding flat strip metal.

A tong ring can be slipped over the end of the tongs to keep the work gripped. This is useful when forging the end of metal

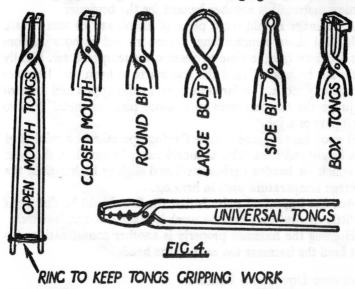

OPEN MOUTH TONGS CLOSED MOUTH ROUND BIT LARGE BOLT SIDE BIT BOX TONGS

UNIVERSAL TONGS

FIG. 4.

RING TO KEEP TONGS GRIPPING WORK

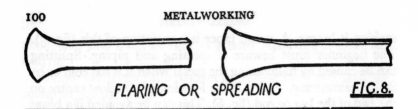

FLARING OR SPREADING   **FIG.8.**

FIG.9

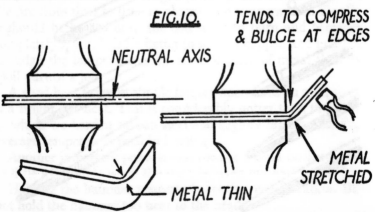

FIG.10.   TENDS TO COMPRESS
& BULGE AT EDGES

NEUTRAL AXIS

METAL
STRETCHED

METAL THIN

OUTSIDE OF BEND STRETCHES. THE INSIDE TENDS TO
COMPRESS. THE AXIS REMAINS CONSTANT.

BENDING

This can be done in the leg vice or on the anvil, or with bending horns and a wrench.

Small section metal can be bent in the leg vice but it is essential to work quickly, before the jaws have taken too much heat from the metal.

A centre punch mark on the metal will show where to hold it in the vice (fig. 10). Blacksmiths make up their own bending jigs and tools for more complicated work, particularly where a number of units are required.

These methods cause the metal to stretch on the outside of the curve and so become thin (fig. 10).

Bending without thinning can be done as shown in figure 9 on the anvil.

First a centre punch mark must be made. Then heat and bend to 45°, as shown. Next upset. Then complete the right angle as shown.

The bending of an eye as on the handle of a poker needs a little consideration. The length of metal needed to form the eye must be estimated. One method is shown in figure 11 (1). The dotted line shows the length of metal required.

The metal is then heated and bent at right angles as shown in figure 11 (2). Now reheat the metal and withdraw from the fire and quench the metal at the bend by dipping in the trough or with water poured from a can (fig. 11 (3)). Now bend on the bick as shown in figure 11 (4). Next reverse the work and continue shaping as shown in figure 11 (5). Close up the eye by tapping lightly round the outside of the eye (fig. 11 (6)). A good eye should be circular and should have its centre over the centre of the shaft.

HORNS AND WRENCH

These are used for scrolls or other gentle curves. The metal is heated and the work is bent as shown in figures 12 and 13.

TWISTING

This is a form of decoration often used on square metal, but metal of other sections can be twisted. The type of twist is

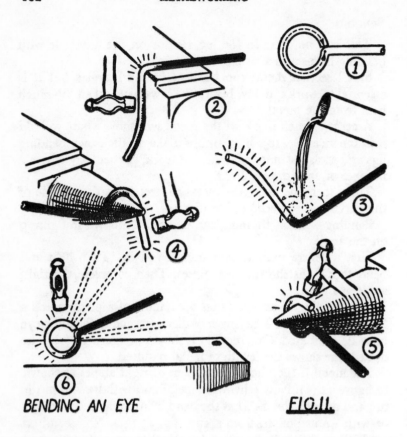

BENDING AN EYE   FIG. II.

influenced by the heating. A good red heat over a long length will give a long gradual twist, but if the bar is heated more intensely over a short length a short sharp twist is produced.

Twisting should be done at one heat because it is difficult to obtain an even twist if the metal has to be returned to the fire. Care must be taken to keep the metal straight. For long bends or double twists a tube can be put over the metal as a sleeve. This must be an easy fit otherwise when the metal is twisted it is difficult to remove. This method is used by beginners. It is not wholly satisfactory because the actual twisting cannot be observed. Another method of obtaining a long even twist is to have an assistant who pours a little water on to those parts that are twisting too quickly. Long twists can also be kept in alignment by using a rest as shown in figure 12A.

SCROLLS

These are usually in the form of a "C" or an "S". It is usual to make these by using a scroll tool which should be made after having gained experience in making a scroll by hand. The method of making a scroll by hand is shown in figure 12. First draw the metal down, keeping the width the same over the entire length. Next start the bend as shown.

When the metal needs reheating remember to heat the part which needs bending. Continue to bend the scroll using the close spaced horns as shown. A small scroll often needs a number of heats when being made by a boy.

SCROLL TOOL

These can be made in the same way as the scroll just mentioned except that they are made from stouter metal—18 mm × 10 mm is a good size. The end is flared on one side only. This is so that the centre of the scroll tool is higher than the rest of the tool to allow the first part of the bend to be made in the scroll as shown in figure 13.

Scrolls made on the scroll tool are started off as in figure 12. Then they are put on the centre of the scroll tool and held with

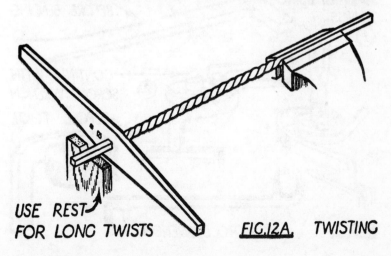

USE REST FOR LONG TWISTS   FIG.12A.   TWISTING

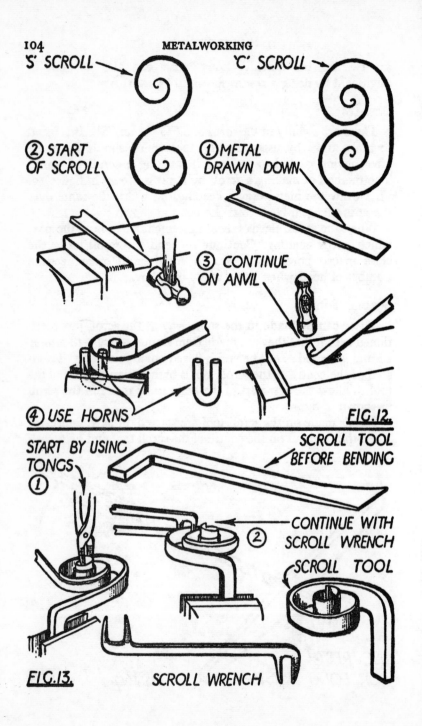

'S' SCROLL

'C' SCROLL

② START OF SCROLL

① METAL DRAWN DOWN

③ CONTINUE ON ANVIL

④ USE HORNS

FIG. 12.

START BY USING TONGS ①

SCROLL TOOL BEFORE BENDING

CONTINUE WITH SCROLL WRENCH ②

SCROLL TOOL

FIG. 13.

SCROLL WRENCH

round nose pliers and bent round. They are finished by using a wrench (fig. 13). Finally the scroll should be placed on the flat face of the anvil and lightly tapped to make it level.

UPSETTING OR JUMPING UP

This is the reverse of drawing down. A good heat is needed; a slightly higher temperature than that used for simple forging operations. The process is made easier for boys if the end of the metal is prepared as shown in figure 14 before upsetting, particularly on small section metal, as this allows the thrust of the blow to be central. (This applies only to metal to be upset at the end.)

The upsetting can be done by striking the end of the metal on the face of the anvil as at A, or on the side (B), or on a chipping block on the floor (C), or with a hammer on the anvil if the work is short enough (D).

Any bend that occurs must be straightened out at once. The metal must then be reheated and the process continued. It helps if the tip of the bar is quenched before continuing with the upsetting. This allows the thickening to take place away from the very end. If the thickening is required in the middle of the bar then that part must be heated. The metal on either side of the area to be upset can be cooled by water poured from a can.

SWAGING

This is usually a process of finishing the cross section of the work to size and shape. Top and bottom swages are usually used as shown in figure 15. For larger work the swage block can be used (fig. 3, p. 96).

FULLERING

This process can be used for thinning down the metal by making grooves or hollows across it. This is usually done by using top and bottom fullers as shown in figure 15. If the thinning is required on one side only the top fuller can be used on its own with the work resting on the anvil.

UPSETTING ON END OF METAL   FIG. 14.

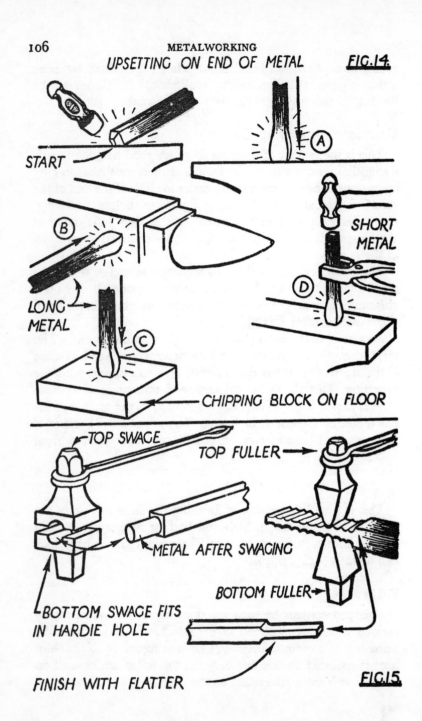

START

(A)

SHORT METAL

(B)

LONG METAL

(C)

(D)

CHIPPING BLOCK ON FLOOR

TOP SWAGE

TOP FULLER →

METAL AFTER SWAGING

BOTTOM SWAGE FITS IN HARDIE HOLE

BOTTOM FULLER →

FINISH WITH FLATTER

FIG. 15

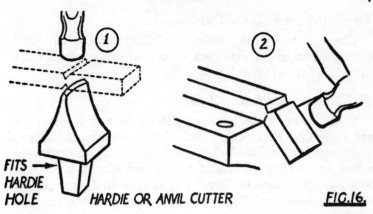

FITS
HARDIE
HOLE   HARDIE OR ANVIL CUTTER   FIG.16.

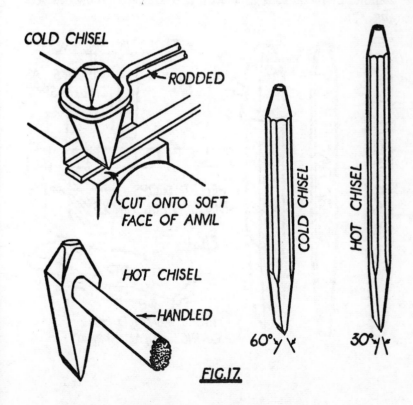

COLD CHISEL

RODDED

CUT ONTO SOFT
FACE OF ANVIL

HOT CHISEL

HANDLED

COLD CHISEL

HOT CHISEL

60°〵〳   30°〵〳

FIG.17

THE HARDIE OR ANVIL CUTTER

This is used in the hardie hole. The metal is cut partly through from either side then tapped with the hammer over the edge of the anvil to break it (fig. 16).

HOT CHISEL AND COLD CHISEL

These are known as hot or cold depending on whether they are used to cut hot or cold metal. Hot chisels are not hardened and tempered because the heat from the metal being cut would soften them. They are ground to a cutting edge of 30° and are long enough to keep the hand well away from the hot metal as shown in figure 17. Cold chisels are hardened and tempered and ground to 60°.

For large work the chisels are fitted with either wooden handles or metal rods as shown, and are often known as sets (fig. 17).

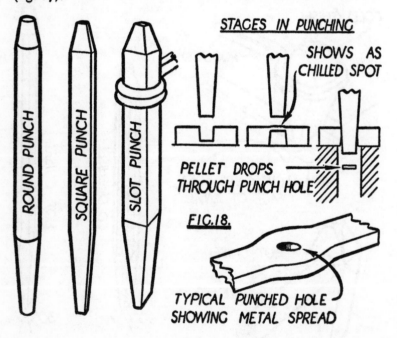

STAGES IN PUNCHING

SHOWS AS CHILLED SPOT

ROUND PUNCH

SQUARE PUNCH

SLOT PUNCH

PELLET DROPS THROUGH PUNCH HOLE

FIG.18.

TYPICAL PUNCHED HOLE SHOWING METAL SPREAD

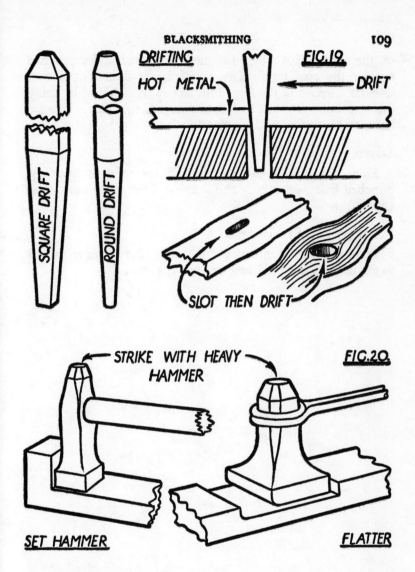

DRIFTING   FIG. 19.

HOT METAL ←   → DRIFT

SQUARE DRIFT   ROUND DRIFT

SLOT THEN DRIFT

STRIKE WITH HEAVY HAMMER   FIG. 20.

SET HAMMER   FLATTER

PUNCHES FOR HOT WORK

These can be round or square or any shape. They should be long enough to keep the hand away from the hot metal. Large ones can be rodded. Figure 18 shows a punch being used. The punch is first driven into the metal then removed and quenched. The metal is then turned over and punched from the other side on the chilled spot where the metal has been under pressure against the cold anvil. The billet shown should drop out. Greater strength of the forged metal can be obtained by using first a slot punch then a drift as shown (fig. 19). This is because less metal is removed with a slot punch.

DRIFTS

These are similar to punches and are used to open up punched holes, smoothing and shaping them at the same time (fig. 19).

FLATTERS AND SET HAMMERS

These are used to smooth out the work after hammering and to get into sharp or radiused corners (fig. 20).

7

Heat Treatment of Steel

PART ONE

HARDENING

We are here dealing with the kind of heat treatment normally done in the school workshop for which we need only use the brazing hearth and torch.

More information regarding the structure of steel is given in Part II. Although this is kept in simple terms it is probably best understood as a subject if done in conjunction with the science laboratory where there are suitable microscopes and possibly some testing equipment.

For hundreds of years such small tools as chisels, punches, knives, shears etc, have been hardened and tempered by metalworkers using similar methods to those mentioned here.

Many special alloy steels are available but these have to be treated as advised by the manufacturers. We are considering only plain carbon steel.

Steels may be roughly classified as follows:
Mild Steels 0·1—0·33% carbon. Medium carbon steels 0·34—0·60% carbon. High carbon steels 0·60—0·90%C and tool steels 0·90%—1·3% carbon.

For small tools we use steel with a carbon content of between 0·8—1·3% carbon. Files fall into this category and for this reason small tools are often made from old files.

If we heat a piece of carbon steel with the brazing torch until it is red hot and then plunge it quickly into cold water we find that it has become "dead" hard. This can be tested with the heel of a file, i.e. the part of the teeth nearest the handle, so as not to spoil the working part of the file.

The primary problem in hardening is judging the correct temperature at which to plunge the steel into water. This temperature is commonly known as "cherry red" and it is best judged in a shady corner away from direct sunlight or bright electric light.

If the steel to be hardened is heated with the torch the temperature will rise slowly until it reaches "cherry red" but then although the torch is kept on the steel it will cease to rise in temperature for a few seconds. This is known as the change point; the heat from the torch on the steel is now latent, that is "hidden", because it is used to bring about changes in the structure of the steel. This taking in of heat is called decalescence (see fig. 1), and it occurs between 700°C and 900°C approximately, depending on the carbon content.

It is at this temperature that we plunge the steel into the water and in so doing we arrest it in its changed state.

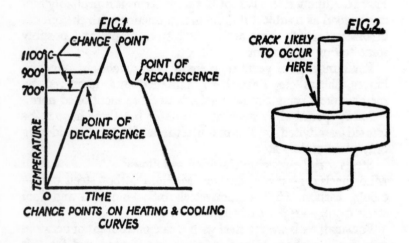

CHANGE POINTS ON HEATING & COOLING CURVES

A way of showing this change at red heat is to heat the metal well above "cherry red" and then allow it to cool slowly in a darkened corner of a room. As the temperature slowly drops to the change point it will be seen to glow suddenly. This is caused by the latent heat being given out. This is called recalescence (fig. 1). However, this is only for demonstration purposes and it must not be used as a method for arriving at the temperature at which to quench the steel. The best results are obtained if the steel is slowly brought up to the change point and then plunged; that is, it is best plunged on a rising temperature.

The hot metal is usually plunged into clean water which is at room temperature. It is essential that the quenchant (the liquid in which the hot metal is quenched) takes the heat away quickly in order to arrest the steel in its changed state. If the cooling needs to be more drastic, cooking salt can be added to the water to make it into a saturated solution. This is best judged by adding the salt to the water until a slice of potato will float in it. This, however, increases the possibility of cracking. Cracks might occur even when using clean water. If this is happening it is often because the steel is being overheated, but it might be because the quenchant is taking the heat from the steel too rapidly.

If soap is added to clean water it will make it less severe as a quenchant. An even less drastic quenching medium is high flash paraffin and a slower one still is mineral oil.

It will also be noticed that cracks occur on steel where there are deep scratches or small grooves such as those left by a turning tool. To avoid this it is best to remove the rough surface and polish the steel before hardening.

Be careful when quenching long thin tools such as chisels, gravers or knife blades, that they are plunged into the liquid vertically and that they are moved up and down, not from side to side, otherwise distortion might take place. If they are plunged horizontally the side entering the water first will contract first, thus causing the steel to be badly distorted. It is good practice to stir the liquid vigorously just before plunging any piece of steel as this helps the liquid to conduct the heat quickly and evenly.

As previously mentioned cracks occur in steel, particularly large pieces, if they have been taken to a temperature too far above the change point and then quenched. This is owing to the fact that when steel reaches the change point it is also at its state of least density. In other words, when it is at this temperature of change it has expanded to its maximum.* If it is quenched

* To be precise, further expansion does actually take place at higher temperatures.

above this temperature it undergoes cooling contraction, the skin becoming hard and rigid. The inner portion has not yet felt the quenching effect and is still red hot. An instant later the quenching effect is transferred to this portion, which as it passes through the change point must expand, thus causing cracks on the outside.

For this reason large tools or tools which have a drastic change of section (fig. 2) should be heated to a temperature just approaching "cherry red" and, depending on the carbon content, dipped in oil or high flash paraffin.

Completely hardened steel is usually too hard and brittle for normal use and so we have to reduce the hardness by a secondary process known as tempering.

TEMPERING

Tempering reduces the hardness of the steel and increases the toughness, i.e. the capacity to withstand shock. The degree of toughness required is determined by the kind of job the tool has to do. Tools for turning brass, scrapers and engraving tools have to be much harder than repousse punches and these in turn must be harder than a screw driver which is just soft enough to be filed and yet tough enough not to be deformed when a twisting force is applied.

To temper a piece of hardened steel, polish the hardened portion with clean dry emery cloth (avoid using oil as this leaves a thin film) and let a small flame play on the metal a short distance from the part to be tempered (fig. 3A). Soon you will see the bright metal near the flame turn light yellow and then straw to middle-straw and then light brown to dark red brown to purple and then to blue. As the heat is conducted along the metal these colours which are in fact oxides will move along in bands. The lightest colour will be the one furthest from the source of heat. When the right colour has reached the part to be tempered, the steel is quenched in clean water. The lighter the colour (best seen in daylight) at which the steel is quenched, the harder the metal will be.

TEMPERING CHART

	°C	
Light blue	315	Too soft for cutting edges.
Blue	300	Springs, saws for wood, screwdrivers.
	290	Carving knives, fine saws, saws for bone and ivory.
	285	Needles, gimlets, axes, adzes, augers.
Purple	270	Flat drills for brass, cold chisels for light work, wood borers.
Dark straw or red brown	260	Wood chisels, plane irons, stone cutting tools, axes.
	250	Flat drills, reamers, taps, screwing dies, shears, punches, chasers.
Middle straw	240	Pen-knives, circular cutters for metal, boring cutters.
	235	Milling cutters, lathe tools, wood engraving tools.
Pale straw	230	Surgical instruments, razors, hammer faces, ivory cutting tools.
Pale yellow	220	Steel engraving tools, scrapers, light turning tools.

If a uniform temper is required along the whole length of the steel it can be held in light tongs in a tube which is heated on the outside (fig. 3B) or held over a heated plate (fig. 3C).

Beginners often have failures with tempering because they misjudge the colour at which to quench. It must be remembered that if in tempering, the steel is heated beyond the proper colour the whole process of hardening and tempering must be repeated. If, however, after quenching the temper colour is not dark enough it will do no harm to re-polish the tool and re-temper until the darker colour is reached then quench.

ONE HEAT HARDENING AND TEMPERING

This is the method often used by blacksmiths usually on the end or point of tools.

The steel is heated at one end to cherry red and the tip only is quenched. It is moved up and down slightly to reduce the possibility of cracking at the water line. Then it is taken from

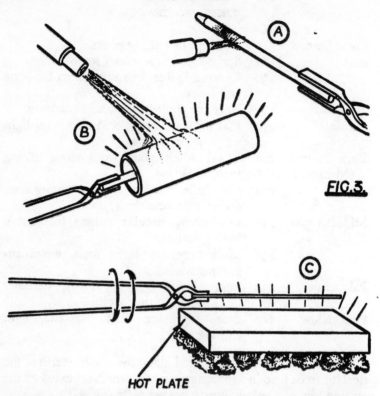

FIG.3.

HOT PLATE

the water and the end is briskly rubbed with an old piece of carborundum stone or something similar so a portion of the tip is bright. After a few moments the heat from the unquenched part is conducted to the tip thus showing the usual bands of colour. When the correct colour reaches the tip it is completely quenched.

CASE HARDENING

This is a method of hardening mild steel by adding carbon to the "skin" or "case" of the steel and then quenching it as if it were a high carbon steel.

The work to be case hardened is put in a shallow steel tray or shallow open box and a powder rich in carbon (usually "kasenit", which is a proprietary brand) is sprinkled on top to cover the work. With a brazing torch the work is made red hot. This causes the carbon to be absorbed by the steel. The longer the work is kept at cherry red the deeper the carbon will go. It should be kept at cherry red in the kasenit for at least 15 minutes and then quickly removed and quenched in clean water. Beware of the loud "bang" it makes. If tested with the heel of a file it will be found to be hard. Usually, in school, because of the time factor it is not possible to make the hard case any more than about 0·2 mm deep.

Case hardening is excellent for such things as spanners where a hard surface and a tough core are essential.

SOFTENING STEEL

To make steel as soft as possible it must be heated to just above the change point and then quickly buried 150-200 mm deep in slaked lime or vermiculite which should first be heated. Slaked lime and vermiculite are very poor conductors of heat and they allow the steel to lose its heat very slowly, thus allowing the change to the soft state to be gradual. This process is known as annealing.

The easier workshop method which makes the steel soft though not quite as soft as by annealing is done without slaked lime or vermiculite. The steel is heated to the change point and it is left to cool on the edge of the hearth or on a fire brick. This is known as normalising.

The purpose of both of these processes is usually to make a hard piece of steel soft enough for it to be machined, filed, sawn, bent or twisted.

Softening relieves the internal stresses. Any tool which has to be re-hardened should first be softened to relieve the stresses set up by the first hardening. This helps to prevent cracking.

PART TWO

We have mentioned the workshop methods in Part 1. In this section we are looking a little deeper into the heat treatment processes and the structure of steel.

Steel is basically an alloy of carbon in iron, although other elements may be present either in residual amounts or as intentional additions to give specific properties.

CARBON IN STEEL

Carbon forms a chemical compound with iron of the formula Fe_3C (containing 6·68% C) which is known as cementite and may appear in steel either individually as the compound or intimately mixed with virtually pure iron to form pearlite. The latter contains 13% of cementite and 87% of the nearly pure iron called ferrite. Under a microscope pearlite is seen to consist of thin plates of ferrite interleaved with thin plates of cementite. Pearlite is so named because under certain conditions it has a pearl-like lustre.

IRON

Iron (Fe) may exist in different physical forms, even though its chemical properties do not alter. This characteristic is known as allotropy, and is common to other elements, such as sulphur.

Metallurgists name the different forms of iron after Greek letters, i.e. alpha α, beta β, gamma γ, and delta δ.

Iron in the cold state is known as α iron and it remains so up to 768°C when it changes to β iron, where only a magnet change takes place. At 910°C it transforms to γ and then at 1400°C to δ.

These are changes in the arrangement of the atoms, but the important change so far as the hardening of steel is concerned, is the change from γ, known as austenite, on cooling below 723°C.

The change from α to β occurs at 768°C and above this temperature the iron is non-magnetic.

The change to γ iron at 910°C on heating is accompanied by a marked contraction.

The austenitic (γ) form of iron *can* hold carbon in solid solution up to approximately 2%, whilst ferrite (α) can retain only about 0·002%.

In steel the existence of carbon up to a maximum content of 0·87%* dissolved in γ iron is able to depress the temperature at which the change from γ to α occurs and the resulting precipitation of cementite commences. Beyond this critical content however, the change temperature rises again. This can be seen more clearly if we plot the level of change-point temperatures against

* This figure varies with the purity of the iron.

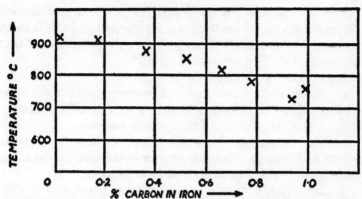

HOW THE START OF THE γ–α CHANGE TEMPERATURE IS DEPRESSED BY INCREASING CARBON CONTENT FIG.4.

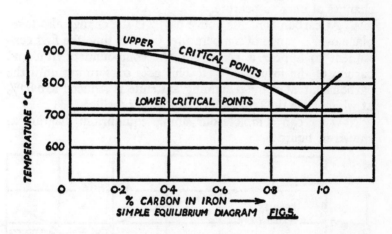

SIMPLE EQUILIBRIUM DIAGRAM FIG.5.

carbon content in steel as shown in figure 4. This diagram shows that as the carbon content increases to 0·87% so the temperature of change drops from 910°C to 723°C. Above the 0·87% carbon content, however, the temperature at which the change begins starts to rise again.

Figure 5 is a similar diagram to figure 4, but the individual points have been joined and the line so formed is labelled the "upper critical line". A horizontal line is also drawn through the minimum transition temperature reached and this is called the "lower critical line". Thus we have a simple version of what is known as an "equilibrium diagram".

From figure 5 we can see:

1. At all temperatures and carbon contents above the upper critical points the carbon is held in γ iron in solid solution, a form of alloy known to metallurgists as austenite.

2. The minimum possible transformation temperature occurs with 0·87%C, the change from γ to α iron throws all the carbon out of solution at once to form pearlite.

3. The change from γ to α iron takes place over a wider range of temperature as the carbon content is reduced below 0·87%. This range is indicated as the difference between the upper and lower critical points. The first constituent to appear is ferrite and this goes on appearing until the carbon content of the remaining γ iron has been enriched to 0·87%C, then this changes at once to pearlite.

4. At carbon contents above 0·87%C the change also takes place over a range of temperature, but this time the first constituent to appear is cementite, the compound of iron and carbon of the formula Fe_3C. This goes on forming until the carbon content of the remaining austenite is reduced to 0·87% at which time the remainder changes to pearlite.

Now we can complete our simple equilibrium diagram as shown in figure 6.

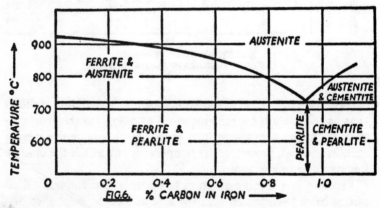

FIG.6.   % CARBON IN IRON →

CARBON CONTENT AND ITS EFFECT ON HARDNESS, TOUGHNESS AND DUCTILITY

Ferrite is almost pure iron. It is soft and ductile. Steel containing a lot of ferrite will have a low tensile strength and will be tough and ductile.

Pearlite is a hard material mainly because of its intricate laminated structure of thin plates of ferrite and the extremely hard plates of cementite. As the carbon content increases up to 0·87% so does the hardness of the metal as a whole, but the toughness and ductility decrease.

Cementite. It is very hard and brittle. Steels containing more than 0·87% carbon have free cementite at the crystal boundaries. This causes extreme hardness in the metal as a whole and care must be taken with the heat treatment. It is used where great hardness is required, such as in ball-bearings, ball races and tools.

THE CRYSTALLINE STRUCTURE OF STEEL

The crystal structure of steel can be seen under a microscope but the metal must first be prepared. The piece to be examined is first ground flat. Then it is polished with successively finer grades of emery paper and finished on soft cloth impregnated with alumina powder or diamond paste. The polished surface is then etched with dilute acid which attacks the different constituent parts differentially, thus revealing the crystalline structure. The four diagrams shown give an idea of the appearance of steels when seen through a microscope, but of course, no two pieces ever look exactly alike.

1. Ferrite or pure iron is as shown in figure 7.
2. Steel containing less than 0·87% carbon, figure 8.
3. Steel containing 0·87% carbon (eutectoid steel), figure 9.
4. Steel containing more than 0·87% carbon, figure 10.

RATE OF COOLING AND ITS INFLUENCE ON STRUCTURE

Annealing. Annealing as previously mentioned is done to produce the maximum softness in metal. A piece of say 0·5% carbon steel is heated to just above the upper critical tempera-

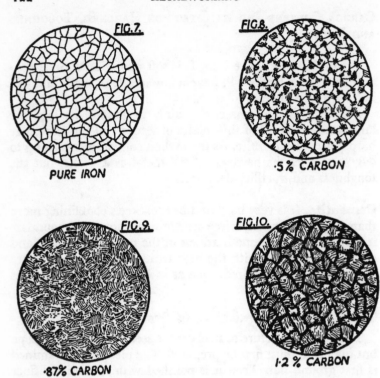

FIG.7.
PURE IRON

FIG.8.
·5% CARBON

FIG.9.
·87% CARBON

FIG.10.
1·2% CARBON

ture and then allowed to cool very slowly in the furnace, i.e. the furnace is switched off and the metal cools at the same slow rate as the furnace.

As the temperature falls ferrite is precipitated first forming new crystals of this nearly carbon-free constituent around the original austenite crystal boundaries. As more ferrite comes out it will form a series of large new crystals. At the same time the remaining austenite will be enriched in carbon until it contains 0·87% carbon. When the temperature drops through the lower critical point the remaining austenite will change at once to pearlite (fig. 11).

In annealing the slow cooling ensures that the carbon is allowed time to diffuse into the austenite as the ferrite appears along the crystal boundaries. This gives annealed steel a comparatively coarse crystal structure.

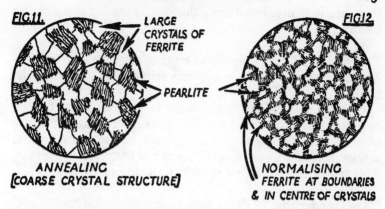

FIG.11.   LARGE CRYSTALS OF FERRITE   FIG.12.

PEARLITE

ANNEALING
[COARSE CRYSTAL STRUCTURE]

NORMALISING
FERRITE AT BOUNDARIES
& IN CENTRE OF CRYSTALS

AUSTENITE DIMINISHES ON COOLING TO FORM PEARLITE

Normalising. Normalising is similar to annealing except that the rate of cooling is faster, the metal being allowed to cool in still air. Draughts may cause it to cool too quickly.

The metal is heated in the same way as for annealing, but because the cooling is quicker the carbon does not have time to diffuse so easily through the metal and small crystals of ferrite appear both round the crystal boundaries *and* in the centres of the original crystals as in figure 12. Normalised steel has a finer crystal structure than annealed steel and is slightly harder.

Low carbon steels from which boiler plate and some girders are made are usually normalised.

Quenching. When steel is quenched the cooling is so rapid that carbon does not have time to diffuse through the mass. Instead the metal is "frozen" and the carbon is prevented from precipitating as iron carbide (cementite) below 723°C and will remain in super-saturation until the temperature drops to a value where an instantaneous transformation will take place to form a product known to metallurgists as martensite. This product has a characteristic needle-like structure (fig. 13) which is extremely hard and brittle due to distortion of the ferrite crystal lattice by carbon. This brittleness must be reduced before the steel can be successfully used in service and therefore it is usual to follow the quenching by a tempering treatment.

Tempering. Tempering allows some of the carbon to redistribute itself as iron carbide and this reduces the stresses in the steel.

Only a relatively low temperature is required (up to 650°C) to permit this redistribution to take place, producing a structure of iron carbide finely dispersed in ferrite, in the past known as sorbite, but now more correctly known as tempered martensite. This tempered steel is less hard but much tougher (fig. 14).

Case Hardening. In Part 1 we mentioned case hardening mild steel using "kasenit". A piece of mild steel after being heated to just above the critical range for about one hour in "kasenit" and allowed to cool slowly would appear as in figure 15.

MARTENSITE [QUENCHED]

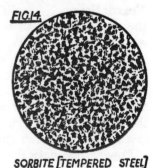

SORBITE [TEMPERED STEEL]

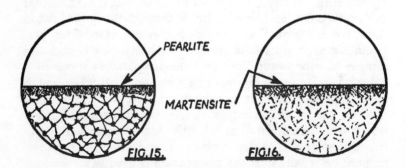

PEARLITE

MARTENSITE

FIG.15.   FIG.16.

Notice that the body of the mild steel contains a very small amount of carbon, but not enough to affect the hardness.

If the same steel is rapidly cooled from just above the critical temperature by plunging it in water, the outside or case would become martensitic but the core, not containing enough carbon, would be soft. It would appear as in figure 16.

Low carbon steels can be case hardened to great advantage. Because the case contains more carbon than the core the upper critical point of the case is lower than that of the core. The steel is quenched from the high carburising temperature thus making both the core and the case martensitic. Next it is re-heated to a temperature which will just turn the case (higher carbon content) austenitic but only hot enough to temper the core (lower carbon content). When quenched from this temperature the case will be martensitic and therefore hard and the core sorbitic and therefore tough.

There are various other methods of case hardening such as: sorbitising. This is not unlike the blacksmith's "one heat" hardening and tempering mentioned in Part 1. The red hot steel is taken from the rolling mill and the surface sprayed with water thus making it martensitic. The heat from the interior of the steel as it slowly cools then turns the martensite into sorbite thus giving a tough outside and a less hard centre.

For further reading see list of books at back.

HEAT TREATMENT OF NON-FERROUS METALS

In the school workshop we use copper, brass, gilding metal, aluminium, aluminium alloys and, less often, zinc and nickel silver.

All the above mentioned metals work harden, i.e. the crystal structure becomes distorted with bending and hammering. They can be softened in the brazing hearth using the torch for heating.

Copper. To soften heat to dull red and either allow to cool in air or quench in water. Quenching in dilute sulphuric acid will soften and clean the surface (see Chapter 9).

Brass. Soften by heating to dull red and allowing to cool in air. Quenching can cause some brass to crack.

Gilding Metal. Soften as copper.

Aluminium. Soften by heating and quenching in water, but take care not to overheat. The temperature can be judged by rubbing a piece of wood on the surface of the metal. When the wood leaves a black charred streak the aluminium is hot enough to plunge into cold water. This will make it quite soft. The correct heat can also be judged by rubbing streaks of soap on the cold metal. Heat until the soap turns brown and then quench. Another method is to put oil on the surface. Heat until the oil burns, then quench. In schools the first method has been found to be the most reliable.

Aluminium Alloys. Soften as aluminium.

Zinc. This can be made workable by placing in boiling water.

Nickel Silver. Soften as brass. Never quench.

8

Sheet Metalwork

This work includes, apart from tinplate, the use of sheet aluminium, brass, copper and galvanised iron, also sheet steel and terne plate. Industrially these metals are formed into useful articles by machines which can stamp, bend and form the sheet metal as required. In school we use hand processes usually on tinplate. Sometimes terne plate is used and more rarely galvanised iron.

Galvanised iron is in fact galvanised steel and is mostly used out of doors because of its rust-resisting property. It is mild steel coated with zinc. Terne plate is sheet mild steel coated with an alloy of lead and tin. Tin plate is sheet mild steel coated with tin. It varies in thickness between 0·254 mm and 0·52 mm. We often refer to the thickness of tin plate in decimals, but tin plate manufacturers have their own method of indicating the thickness (see metricated version of B.S. 2920).

SETTING OUT

Before a tinplate article is bent or formed into shape, the tinplate must be cut to the correct size and shape. This shape, before it is formed, is known as the development.

Simple developments can be drawn directly on to the tin plate with a hard pencil or copper scriber. The lines to be cut, or parts to be hidden by a joint, can be scribed. It is important not to mark with a scriber any part of the job which will be exposed, because this allows rust to form where the mild steel has been exposed. Care should also be taken to prevent the surface of the tin from being scratched: for this reason it is

JOINTS

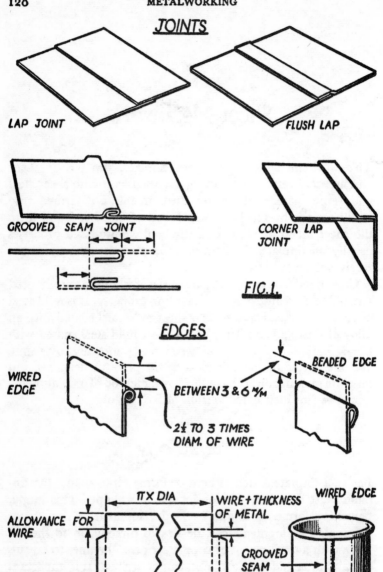

LAP JOINT

FLUSH LAP

GROOVED SEAM JOINT

CORNER LAP JOINT

FIG.1.

EDGES

WIRED EDGE

BETWEEN 3 & 6 ᵐ/ₘ

2½ TO 3 TIMES DIAM. OF WIRE

BEADED EDGE

π × DIA

WIRE + THICKNESS OF METAL

WIRED EDGE

ALLOWANCE FOR WIRE

ALLOWANCE FOR CAPPED ON BOTTOM

GROOVED SEAM

CAPPED ON BOTTOM

1× GROOVED JOINT

2× GROOVED JOINT

 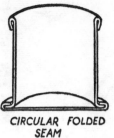 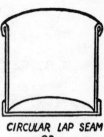

KNOCKED UP BOTTOM   CIRCULAR FOLDED   CIRCULAR LAP SEAM
                           SEAM   OR
        FIG. 2.   CAPPED ON BOTTOM

advisable to put newspaper on the bench on which to lay the tin plate.

Complicated developments are often drawn on paper and carefully cut out. By this means it is possible to see how the finished article will look and also to check the dimensions. With care this paper development can be used as a template, i.e. it can be laid on to the tinplate and drawn round with a sharp pencil or copper scriber. The parts to be cut must be carefully checked with a rule and then scribed. Another method is to stick the pattern on to the tinplate.

Allowances must be made for joints and seams. Figure 1 shows the allowances for joints and seams, also for the beaded edge and wired edge. Figure 2 shows the allowances for a circular lap seam, a circular folded seam and a knocked up bottom.

Tools (fig. 3)

Bench Shears. There is usually one bench shearing machine bolted to a bench in each metalworkshop. The blade is curved so that it presents the same cutting angle in all positions. Any size sheet can be cut and there is a hole at the side of the blade into which a rod can be inserted for shearing. The fixed blade can be adjusted and locked in position by the screws provided.

Snips. Two kinds are shown: the universal snips can cut inside and outside curves and straight lines. The straight snips are to cut straight lines or outside curves. Curved snips are also available. These are for cutting inside curves.

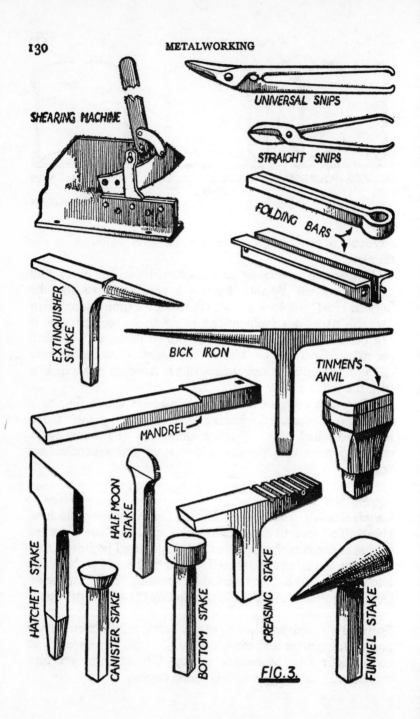

SHEARING MACHINE

UNIVERSAL SNIPS

STRAIGHT SNIPS

FOLDING BARS

EXTINQUISHER STAKE

BICK IRON

TINMEN'S ANVIL

MANDREL

HATCHET STAKE

HALF MOON STAKE

CANISTER STAKE

BOTTOM STAKE

CREASING STAKE

FUNNEL STAKE

FIG. 3.

Folding Bars. These are for bending and folding. The sheet metal is inserted up to the line where the bend is required and then the folding bar is gripped in the vice. The work is now firmly held and can be bent over using a mallet, or a piece of wood can be held against the sheet and this tapped with a hammer.

Extinguisher Stake and Bick Iron. These are useful for making conical work. The flat top and the square end are often used for box making.

The Mandrel. This is about four feet long. It is made of cast iron and has a rounded top at one end and a flat top at the other. There is a square hole at the flat end in which small stakes can be held. Sheet metal workers often use the mandrel on large work.

Tinmen's Anvil. The top surface is flat and one edge is curved. It can be held in a special socket or in the hardie hole of a large anvil.

Hatchet Stake. Used for bending straight edges beyond a right angle.

Half Moon Stake. Used for bending curved edges.

Canister Stake. Used on the bottom of a canister for "getting in" to the corners as in making a knocked up bottom.

Bottom Stake. Similar in use to the canister stake but the sides can be used for truing up the side of a canister.

Creasing Stake. The grooves are used for finishing off wired edges and other similar operations. The square end is usually cut back slightly so that it can get into the corner of a box.

Funnel Stake. Used for large conical work such as funnels which were once made by hand by tin-smiths.

Mallets (fig. 4). These are used on tinplate to avoid damaging the surface. The tinman's mallet has a head of boxwood or lignum vitae and a handle of cane. The bossing mallet, used for hollowing, also has a boxwood or lignum vitae head and a cane handle. The rawhide mallet has a hickory handle.

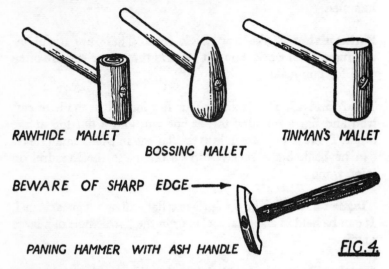

RAWHIDE MALLET   TINMAN'S MALLET

BOSSING MALLET

BEWARE OF SHARP EDGE ⟶

PANING HAMMER WITH ASH HANDLE   FIG. 4

Paning Hammer. Sometimes used for tucking in joints and wired edges. Care must be exercised in its use because it can easily damage the surface of the metal.

METHOD OF MAKING JOINTS

Flush Lap Joint. First make a lap joint then solder the joint. Now set the joint down on to a flat surface using a piece of hardwood and hammer as shown in figure 5.

Corner Lap Joint. Bend lap using folding bars and mallet as shown in figure 6 then solder.

Grooved Seam Joint. The size for this is usually stated on the drawing. For school work it is normally between 3 mm and 7 mm inclusive. The allowance for this joint is twice the joint size

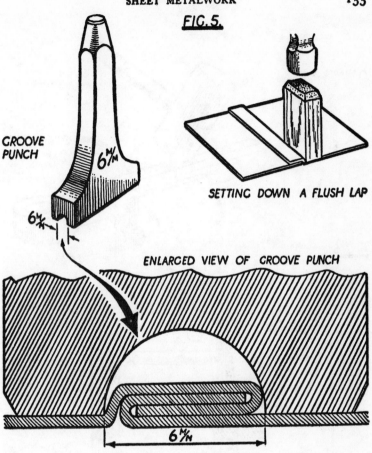

FIG. 5.

GROOVE PUNCH

6 M/M

6 M/M

SETTING DOWN A FLUSH LAP

ENLARGED VIEW OF GROOVE PUNCH

6 M/M

on one side and only once on the other (fig. 1). However, to allow the grooving tool (fig.5) to fit over the joint, slightly less than the width of the joint must be bent over. Figure 5 shows this clearly. A reliable way to find out exactly how much to bend over for a particular thickness of metal is to make a trial joint using two small pieces of the same metal (see fig. 7 (1), (2), (3), (4), (5)). The grooving tool is offered up as shown in figure 8 and then set down using a hammer on the grooving tool. Finish off the joint by tapping down with a mallet along the top of the joint as in figure 9. For a good joint it is important that the bend in both pieces is parallel.

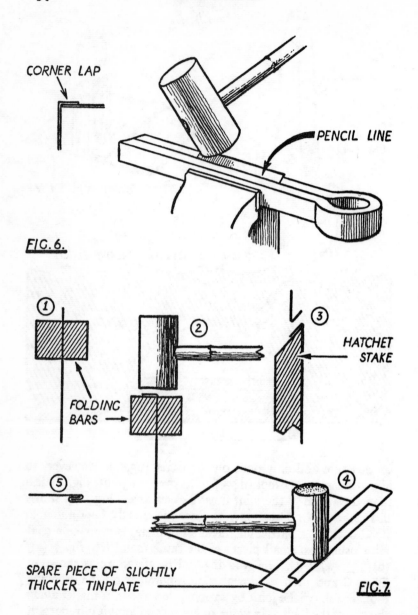

CORNER LAP

PENCIL LINE

FIG. 6.

① FOLDING BARS

②

③ HATCHET STAKE

⑤

④

SPARE PIECE OF SLIGHTLY THICKER TINPLATE

FIG. 7.

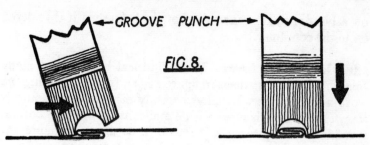

FIG. 8.

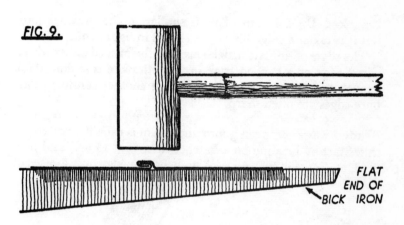

FIG. 9.

FLAT
END OF
BICK IRON

Capped On or Circular Lap Seam. Cut the disc for the bottom making allowance for the "turn up". Carefully set down on a canister stake with a mallet. Do not try to set down too much at each blow. The disc must be continually rotated using only light blows making sure all the time that the bend is occuring on the pencilled circle (fig. 10). An alternative way is to have a disc or former of metal of the right diameter and a backing disc. (This is not always possible in school owing to the large number of discs of different sizes that would be needed.) The tinplate circle is positioned centrally between these whilst they are held in a vice (fig. 10). Care must be taken not to lose the position of the tinplate when it is rotated in the vice. Any small wrinkles can finally be removed by tapping with a mallet on a bottom stake. When the bottom is finished it is soldered on to the container.

Circular Folded Seam. The cylindrical body is first made then the flange is made as in figure 11 (1), (2), (3), rotating the work anti-clockwise. Usually the body distorts at the joint as shown at A. Tap this true with a mallet as shown. The bottom is made as in figure 10 and set down as shown in figure 12. Care must be taken to avoid hammer contact with the sides of the vessel particularly when using the paning hammer.

Knocked Up Bottom. This is similar to the previous joint but it is taken a stage further as shown in figure 13.

The edges of tinplate articles are usually finished either with a wired edge or a beaded edge because tinplate is seldom thick enough to withstand damage. Safety is another consideration: bare edges are often sharp.

Beaded Edge. Between 3 mm and 6 mm is usually allowed for this. Start by bending on a hatchet stake (fig. 14 (1)) and proceed, as shown in figure 14 (2), to bend the edge over a piece of

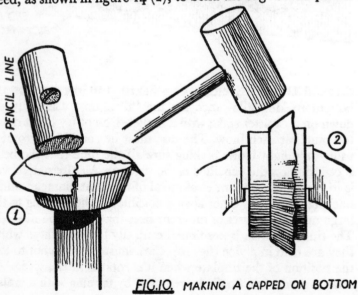

PENCIL LINE

① ②

FIG.10. MAKING A CAPPED ON BOTTOM

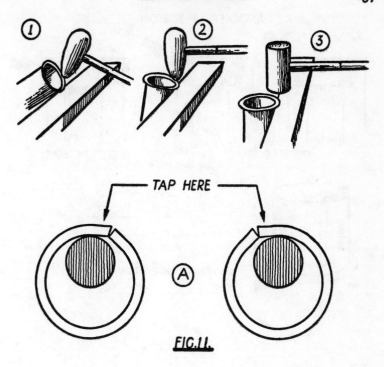

TAP HERE

Ⓐ

FIG.11.

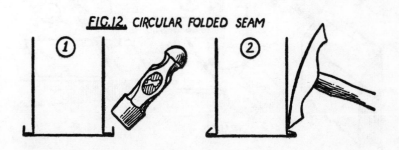

FIG.12. CIRCULAR FOLDED SEAM

KNOCKED UP BOTTOM

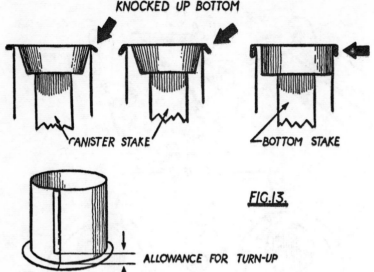

CANISTER STAKE

BOTTOM STAKE

FIG.13.

ALLOWANCE FOR TURN-UP

BEADED EDGE

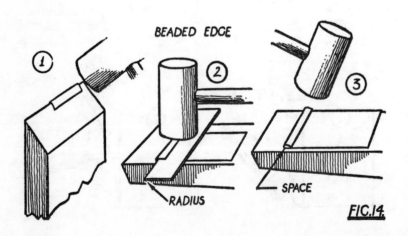

① ② ③

RADIUS

SPACE

FIG.14.

WIRED EDGE

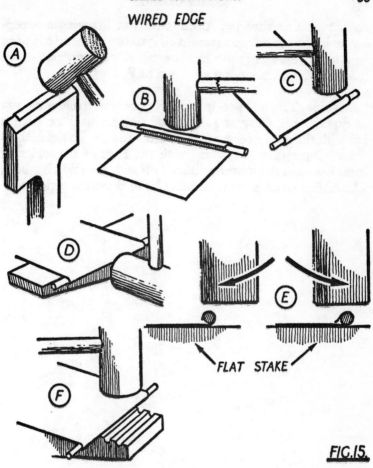

FIG. 15.

metal which has a radiused edge. Finish with a mallet as in figure 14 (3). Never flatten the edge completely otherwise it will lose its rigidity.

Wired Edge. Allow between two and a half to three times the diameter of the wire for this. Start by bending to the pencil line on a hatchet stake, figure 15A, then lay the wire in and tap down until the wire is trapped (B). Next, true the edge on a bick iron or similar stake as shown at C and D. If the tin plate does not enclose the wire, "dress" with a mallet using a sweeping action to one side as shown at E. If too much metal has been bent over, "dress" in the other direction. The edge can then be finished on a creasing iron as shown at F.

Soldering. This is almost invariably done with a soldering iron as explained in Chapter 4. On good tinplate work no edge is left with the mild steel exposed as this will rust. To finish these "raw" edges they are tinned with the edge of the soldering iron. Excess solder must be "lifted" off with the soldering iron. The surface of tin plate must never be filed or emery-clothed.

9
Silversmithing

The silversmithing operations are usually carried out in the school workshop in copper and gilding metal owing to the high price of silver.

The operations are the same and when sufficient skill has been gained using base metals the student can at a later date try working in silver. It is customary to have silver articles hall marked, but it is not compulsory if they are not to be sold. Hallmarking is carried out at the Goldsmith's Hall in London or in Sheffield, Birmingham, Edinburgh or Glasgow. The address of the Goldsmiths' Hall, from which full particulars are available, is given at the back of this book.

MATERIALS

COPPER

This is a little easier to work than silver, but unless it can be finally workhardened by planishing it remains soft after the heat required for silver soldering.

GILDING METAL

Gilding metal is really a kind of brass having a composition of between 95% copper and 5% zinc, and 80% copper and 20% zinc. It is known as gilding metal because of its golden colour. Its working properties are very much like those of silver. It does not become too soft after soldering, and for this reason gilding metal is most used for the silversmithing operations in school.

PENCILLED CIRCLES

SOFT WOOD

HOLLOWING BLOCK

BOSSING MALLET

BLOCKING HAMMER

SAND BAG

SINKING

RAISING

250GRM RAISING HAMMER

PENCILLED LINES

SCRIBED LINES

RAISING MALLET

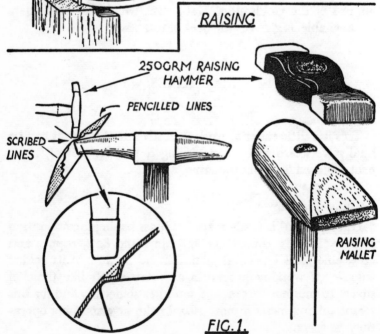

FIG. 1.

NICKEL SILVER

This resembles silver in colour but it is harder to work. It can however be used on work which does not require a lot of forming.

CLEANLINESS

It is essential that all the tools and materials be spotlessly clean. Any speck of dirt, such as a metal filing, if left either on the tools or the sheet of metal will damage the surface of the metal if hammered. A slight burr on a hammer or a stake will also make nasty marks on the work and these are difficult to remove. Therefore all stakes and hammers should be kept polished and lightly oiled when not in use.

STAKES AND HAMMERS

The silversmith's most important tools are his stakes and hammers. Often special stakes have to be made to suit a particular job. These are sometimes forged from mild steel or they can be cast in iron from a wooden pattern. The bought stakes are often made of cast iron but some are made of steel. The working surface of a stake should be true and well polished. The raising stake and raising hammer are shown in figure 1, also the bossing mallet. The cylindrical mallet which is so often used for truing and removing dents etc. is shown in figure 3. The head is made from boxwood or lignum vitae and the handle is of cane.

Figure 2 shows some of the more common stakes. The treblet is used for truing rings and large conical work. It stands on the bench and is often about two feet tall. Mushroom stakes are mostly used for planishing. The two arm stake can be used for raising or planishing. The bottoming stakes can be used for truing the bases of canisters and boxes. The horse and crank are very useful because they can hold a wide variety of stake heads. The three arm mandrel is used in much the same way as the treblet but for work on a smaller scale. The large tray hammer

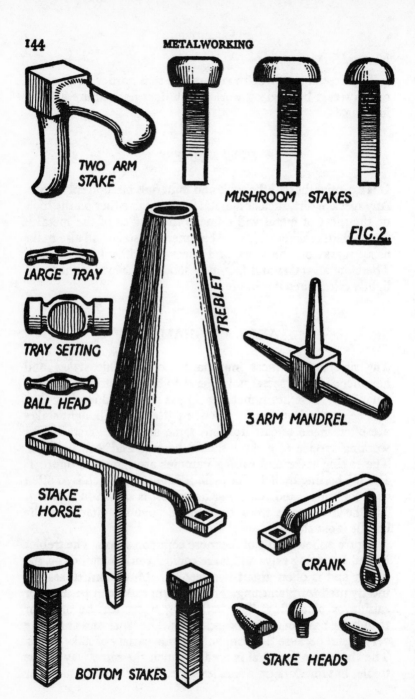

TWO ARM STAKE

MUSHROOM STAKES

FIG. 2.

LARGE TRAY

TRAY SETTING

BALL HEAD

TREBLET

3 ARM MANDREL

STAKE HORSE

CRANK

BOTTOM STAKES

STAKE HEADS

has oval faces of two different sizes for sinking and smoothing curves. The ball head hammer can be used for planishing inside curves of such things as ash trays. The tray setting hammer weighs about 1·1 kgm and is used for flattening large trays.

PROCESSES

HOLLOWING

This is the process used when making bowl shapes. It can be done with a bossing mallet using a hollowing block or a leather sandbag. Hollowing blocks can be made from beech or similar hard wood with the hollow on the end grain as shown in figure 1, or they can be made by gouging out hollows in the end grain of a tree stump which can stand on the floor.

To make a simple bowl shape first cut out a circle of metal with snips. Usually between 0·9 and 1·3 mm is used, but on larger diameters 1·6 mm is more suitable. The roughness is taken off the edges by filing (fig. 1) and the disc is softened by heating to dull red and quenching in water or dilute sulphuric acid, which is usually kept in an earthenware trough under a sink or near a water tap. This dilute sulphuric acid is known as "pickle". It is made by adding approximately 1 part acid to 9 parts water. Remember always add the acid to the water, not the water to the acid, otherwise it splutters and can be dangerous. If the disc has been plunged in water it will be soft but the oxides will still be on the surface and they must be removed by rubbing with pumice powder on a rag. If the disc has been plunged in the pickle it will be free of oxides but should be rinsed in water to remove any trace of acid and dried.

When starting to hollow keep the centre mark from which the circle is scribed on the convex side. The centre for the other side should be found with a pencil compass and concentric circles drawn at about 12 mm intervals. Now place the disc over the hollowing block or leather sandbag and with the pencilled lines uppermost gently tap with the bossing mallet slowly rotating the work and keeping the blows in concentric circles (fig. 1). It is usually better to start with the outside circle and slowly work inwards. If the work becomes too hard it should be softened from time to time as required.

The diameter of the disc will alter very little and the edge will remain at the same thickness; but where the metal has been stretched into the hollow it will have become thinner. If we wish to retain the thickness of the metal and make a deeper vessel we do it by raising.

SINKING

This is similar to hollowing except that a flat rim is left on the work as on a small tray. Often a blocking hammer is used instead of a mallet.

One method is shown in figure 1. The edge of the disc is kept against the pins (3 mm diameter steel is suitable for these) and the work is slowly rotated as it is being hammered. After each time round it should be inverted on a flatting plate and the rim trued using a block of wood and a hammer. The bottom can also be kept flat by this method.

Note. Flatting plates may be bought. Actually they are nothing more than a sturdy surface plate. For school work an old surface plate can be used, but it should be painted round the edge with a distinctive colour so that it will not be confused with the surface plates used for marking out.

RAISING

This is the process of making a hollow vessel by hammering or malleting from the outside.

The disc is best prepared from 0·9 mm sheet. Only slight hollowing is required, about 25 mm deep on a 175 mm diameter disc.

Now a raising stake and raising hammer or mallet must be used. The raising hammer is the more suitable tool because a mallet, owing to its softness, needs continual re-shaping at the face. This means that a new mallet will be required from time to time.

The raising hammer is shown in figure 1. It is important that the shape is as shown. Most raising hammers when bought need filing or grinding to the proper shape.

The stake can be made from 50 mm diameter mild steel about 400 mm long and held in a sturdy vice or a bought cast iron stake can be used. Ideally the bought stake should be held in a heavy stake block, but it may be held in a heavy vice.

Before starting to raise you should have a sketch of the vessel you intend to make. The size of the blank can be estimated by adding the average diameter of the vessel to the height. This will give you the approximate diameter of the blank. Experience is needed to estimate the blank accurately, particularly since some people tend to stretch the metal more in hammering than others.

Start by making the base circle with a pair of dividers. It is better to have this circle scribed with dividers because a more precise base can be obtained in this way. Now make concentric circles with a pair of compasses on the outside of the work about 8mm apart starting from the scribed circle. These are guide lines for raising.

Place the disc over the stake as shown so that the scribed circle is just over the edge of the stake (fig. 1). Start hammering. Be sure that the face of the hammer makes a flat mark on the work. The hammer must bring the metal down to the stake but don't hit too hard otherwise stretching will result. Usually about three blows are necessary before the metal is properly down to the stake. The work is then turned about 12 mm and the next flat made. Continue until you have completed the first circle, then start on the next one 8 mm up. When this is done go on to the next and so on until you reach the last one. At this last circle the metal is usually wrinkled. It is better to tap these wrinkles hard down on to the stake using a cylindrical mallet. If a hammer is used stretching might occur at the edge. The diameter of the disc is now about 6 mm smaller than before. Now soften, rinse and dry the work. Draw the concentric circles with the pair of compasses. The scribed circle should still show. Continue as before. The work will need softening at the end of each raising.

From time to time check the work to see that the sides are going up evenly. For this a cardboard template may be used (fig. 3). The work can be trued with the raising hammer on the stake but, instead of working right round, the raising is kept in short rows on the side which is protruding. Figure 3 shows how

RAISING

1ˢᵀ RAISING

CARDBOARD TEMPLATE

STAGES IN RAISING

SURFACE PLATE

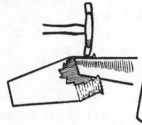

SEAMED & RAISED VESSEL

PLANISHING

COLLET HAMMER

280 GRM. PLANISHING HAMMER

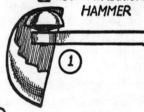

①

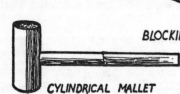

BLOCKING HAMMER→

③

CYLINDRICAL MALLET

FIG. 3.

the shape alters with raising. Figure 4 shows a teapot which has been raised.

Often to save time tall vessels like coffee pots and vases are first developed and seamed using hard solder (the enamelling grade is too hard) and then finished by raising (fig. 3).

When raised work has reached the desired shape it can be planished to remove the raising hammer marks.

PLANISHING

This is the process of making the work "plain", but in fact the planishing hammer leaves small facets on the work which can be attractive if done regularly.

Before starting to planish, be sure the stake is highly polished, also the work and the hammer.

On hollow work the stake must have a slightly smaller radius than the work so that when the hammer strikes the work it is trapped between the stake and the hammer (fig. 3 (1)) and makes a clear ringing sound. Often a different stake and hammer are needed for different parts of the job. A simple bowl as shown in figure 3 (1) could be done using one stake.

Before starting to planish work similar to figure 3 (1) draw concentric circles about 3 mm apart and start planishing from the centre. If the work and the hammer are polished it is difficult to see the hammer marks, but this can be overcome by rubbing the hammer backwards and forwards on a piece of 3/0 blue back emery paper. This gives the hammer a very fine satin-like surface which shows as a fine matt surface on each of the facets. When the planishing is finished this slightly matt surface is easily polished using crocus or rouge block on a soft mop such as a "swansdown".

Each facet in planishing should overlap the previous facet and each row should overlap the previous row. After planishing the work is hard. Sometimes to remove the raising marks the job has to be planished two or three times.

Some planishing has to be done with a collet hammer (fig. 3 (2)) or a blocking hammer (fig. 3 (3)). A 280 gms planishing hammer is shown (fig. 3 (1)) but for small work a 140 gms hammer can be used.

FIG. 4.—RAISED TEAPOT IN BRITANNIA SILVER
Designed and made by the author

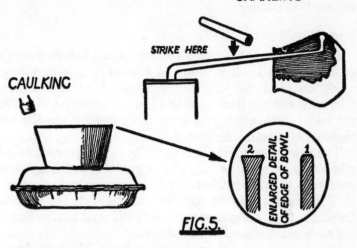

SNARLING

STRIKE HERE

CAULKING

2 1 ENLARGED DETAIL OF EDGE OF BOWL

FIG.5.

Planishing does three things:
1. It makes the work hard.
2. It spreads the metal slightly.
3. It makes the metal a little thinner.

SNARLING

This is the process of striking a blow (usually on the inside of a container) by utilising the rebound of a long slender tool, one end of which is gripped in a vice (fig. 5). By this means it is possible to alter the shape or remove the dents from deep awkward shaped vessels.

CAULKING

Caulking is a method of thickening the edge of a piece of work by hammering as shown in figure 5. It is done for strength and appearance.

Start by slightly chamfering the edge as at figure 5 (1). Then hammer round and round three or four times, keeping the blows close together, until a thick edge is obtained as at figure 5 (2). The hammer marks and any burrs can be removed with a water of Ayr stone. Water of Ayr stones have a mild abrasive quality. They are available in sticks about 95 mm long ranging in size from 3 mm square section to 25 mm square section. They are used with water.

BUILT UP WORK

Often a hallowed or raised bowl requires a base or foot. One of the simplest kinds is shown in figure 6A. The base ring is made first and the joint soldered with hard or enamelling solder. Notice the little spacing pieces of iron wire to prevent the solder from running on to the binding wire; also the extra loops for tightening the wire.

The ring is next soldered on to the body using easy or easy-flo solder. To be sure the base ring is properly positioned it is a good plan to make stitches with an engraving tool as shown at B. This ensures that the base will not move during soldering. Be sure to keep the graver sharp or it will tend to slip. Engraving tools are discussed in Chapter 10.

Wires can be applied on rims or on bases. These can be held in place with bent cotter pins as shown at C.

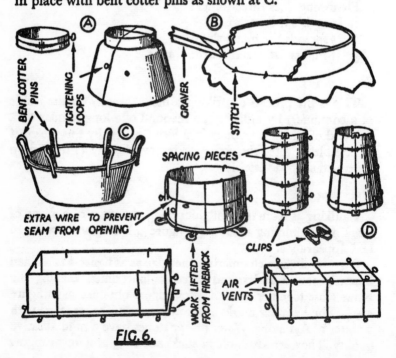

FIG. 6.

BOXES AND SEAMED WORK

Figure 6D shows the method of using iron binding wire on several seamed jobs. The clips shown are made from 0·9 mm annealed mild steel. These are particularly useful for large work on which the edges tend to come out of alignment on heating.

When finally soldering the cover on a box, air vents must be made, as shown, usually by starting to saw at the joint line of the box and the cover.

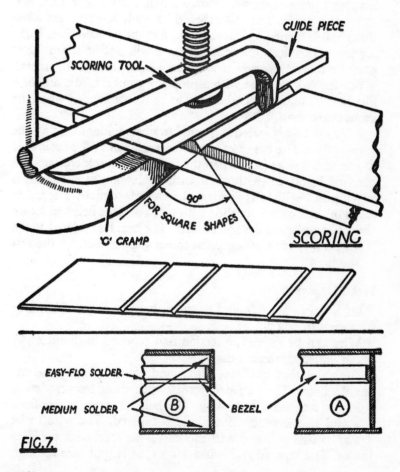

GUIDE PIECE

SCORING TOOL

FOR SQUARE SHAPES 90°

'C' CRAMP

SCORING

EASY-FLO SOLDER

MEDIUM SOLDER

BEZEL

B

A

FIG. 7.

When soldering the bottom on to a box it must be lifted from the firebrick slightly to allow the flame to heat the bottom. The circular box is shown on cotter pins and the rectangular box on 3 mm diameter iron wire.

Rectangular boxes are developed from a flat sheet and "V" grooves are made where the sharp bends are required.

"V" grooves are usually made with a scoring tool (fig. 7). This can be made from silver steel which is then hardened and tempered to light straw. The edge should have an angle of 90° for rectangular boxes, 60° for hexagonal and 45° for octagonal shapes. A piece of metal is clamped beside the line to be scored to act as a guide. The score should be made so deep that when the metal is turned over it shows as a slightly raised line. If the scoring is not deep enough, the bend will not be sharp. Care must be taken, however, not to score right through the metal.

Scoring can be done with a properly ground cold chisel or a file, but the filing method is only to be recommended when the grooves are short.

After the box is folded it is usual to silver solder along all the folded joints. The base can be mitred as shown at B, or soldered flat on to the sides (A). When the top has been soldered on and the box finally sawn through with a piercing saw, the sawn edges must be filed flat and tested on a surface plate. The inside edges of the box are finished with a bezel. This helps to locate the cover and gives the box rigidity. The bezel is soldered to the box with a lower melting point solder than is used for the rest of the joints.

Wire Drawing

Often wires are required to strengthen the edges of bowls or for bezels in boxes.

Wire can be altered in section and reduced in diameter by being pulled through a drawplate.

Drawplates are available with round, square, oblong and tri-angular holes. They are made from hardened and tempered steel.

Figure 8 shows a drawplate. The holes progress in size from one end to the other. Each hole is tapered. The wire to be drawn is first softened and the end is tapered with a file as shown. The tapered end is inserted in the largest hole through

WIRE DRAWING

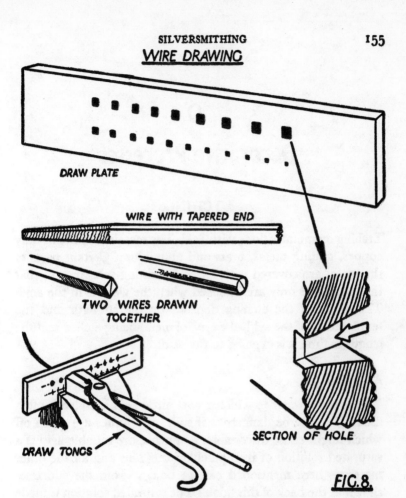

DRAW PLATE

WIRE WITH TAPERED END

TWO WIRES DRAWN TOGETHER

SECTION OF HOLE

DRAW TONGS

FIG. 8.

which the untapered part of the wire just cannot pass. The drawplate is held in a vice and the wire is oiled or rubbed with beeswax or soap and then the tapered end which is protruding through the hole is gripped with the tongs and pulled through. It is then drawn through the next hole. Drawing causes work hardening so the wire must be softened often. To do this, coil it up so all the coils are touching each other, otherwise stray coils will become burnt before the others have reached the annealing temperature. Clean and lubricate the wire before continuing with the drawing. With care two wires can be drawn through the plate together as shown.

10

Decorative Processes

ETCHING

Etching on metal is done with acid. The metals used are usually copper, gilding metal, brass and aluminium. Certain parts of the metal are covered with an acid resisting substance so that the bare parts only are attacked when the work is in the acid. The depth of the etching depends on the strength and the temperature of the acid, the type of metal being etched and the length of time it is exposed to the acid.

Acids

Four parts water to which 1 part nitric acid is added is often used. This can be dangerous if spilt, also fumes are given off which might cause discomfort. A much more reliable acid is a saturated solution of iron perchloride. (This and all the other materials here mentioned can be bought from the addresses shown at the back of this book.) The saturated solution is made from lumps. No fumes come from this and it is relatively harmless if splashed on to the skin. However, as a precaution against staining, always wash your hands after using it.

Cleaning the Metal

Before any acid resist is applied the metal should be degreased with fine pumice powder or whiting and water to which a few drops of ammonia have been added. This can be mixed in a saucer and vigorously rubbed on with cotton wool. A good detergent can be used instead of ammonia.

RESISTS

For convenience we can put these into three groups but there are of course other ways such as dusting with powdered resin etc.

Applied resists. These are applied in the form of cut out shapes of plastic material known by the trade names "Fablon" and "Contact", which have a strong adhesive on one surface.

Figure 1 shows a small dish on which a cut shape has been stuck. Be sure that the plastic shape is pressed well down at all the edges.

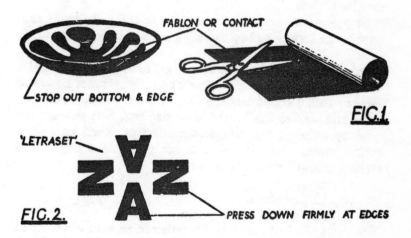

FABLON OR CONTACT

STOP OUT BOTTOM & EDGE

FIG. 1

'LETRASET'

FIG. 2.

PRESS DOWN FIRMLY AT EDGES

"Letraset," which is the proprietary name for sheets of transfer letters and motifs which are available in scores of different sizes and type faces, may be used as acid resists. The sheets may be purchased from most artists colourmen and the letters can be stuck on to the metal either in the form of a pattern or as lettering for wall plaques etc. Providing they are well stuck down very accurate lettering can be produced by this means (fig. 2).

Painted Resists. The best known of these is quick drying stopping-out varnish which can be bought or made in the following ways:

(a) 1 part benzine or benzol $\left.\right\}$ by volume
   1 part asphaltum powder

This must be made in a screwtop jar. The asphaltum powder should soon dissolve. Always screw the lid on after use. If benzine or benzol are not available petrol may be used as a substitute.

(b) 114 gms asphaltum
   0·25 litre turpentine

The asphaltum and turpentine is put in a jar which should be stood in a saucepan of water and heated until thoroughly dissolved.

Stopping-out varnish is painted on to the parts to be protected; this includes, of course, the back and edges of the work.

Dabbed Resist. This is also known as "dabbed ground" and it can be bought. It is in a small box and is sometimes known as etching ball. Do not buy the "soft ground" which looks the same and is often sold in the same size box. Soft grounds are used by etchers for obtaining the effect of pencil lines on a copper plate. This method does not concern us here. Solid etching ground can be made as follows:

28 gms beeswax
28 gms asphaltum
14 gms Swedish brown pitch

The wax and pitch are melted together in an enamel saucepan and the asphaltum powder gradually added while stirring with a glass rod. The whole is allowed to simmer for 20 minutes more or less (depending on the quality of the pitch) and then poured into lukewarm water and rolled into balls. This mixture is applied to the work with a dabber which is made in the following way. A disc of cardboard about 50 mm in diameter is cut; a bunch of rag is placed on this and a wad of cotton-wool over all. A piece of pure silk being placed over the wadding, the bunched ends are held firmly in the left hand and whipped with string beginning next to the fingers and working towards the card. This gradually strains the silk tighter and tighter over the cotton-wool (which must be worked into shape) so that no folds are left over the front surface of the pad (fig. 3).

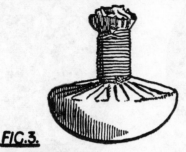

FIG.3.

The work is warmed on a hot plate to such a heat that the etching ball will start to smear on the article as it is stroked across. At this heat it can just be held in the fingers. With the dabber, carefully start dabbing the smears of ground evenly over the article. Do not overheat! Ideally it should feel tacky when being dabbed. The thickness of the ground should be such that it is slightly translucent. When the article is evenly covered it should be returned to the hot plate and moved about until the whole surface becomes glazed. It can then be stood against a vertical surface, face inwards, so that the dust will not settle on the surface while it is cooling.

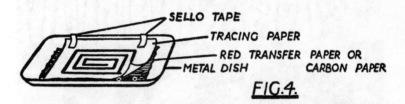

SELLO TAPE
TRACING PAPER
RED TRANSFER PAPER OR
METAL DISH   CARBON PAPER
FIG.4.

The design is transferred from tracing paper on to the metal using red transfer paper or carbon paper (fig. 4). When the design is transferred on to the ground it can be scratched through with a needle or for broad areas a small knife blade. Remember that clean sharp edges will remain sharp during etching, but ragged lines will become more ragged.

Ideas for designs can often be developed from natural forms. Figure 4A shows six sketches taken from nature and from much

FIG. 4ᴬ

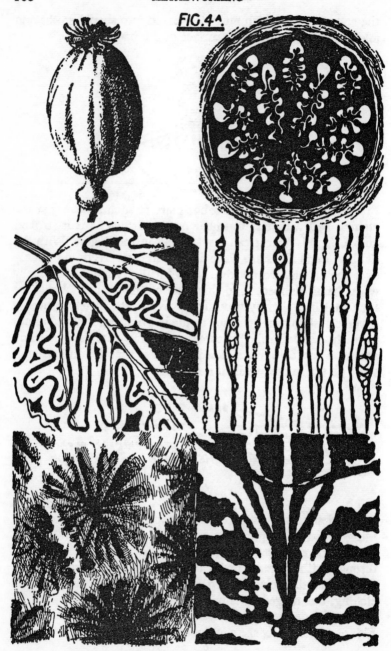

---

enlarged photographs of details of natural forms. However, natural forms should not be copied slavishly but used as a basis for designs.

USE OF ACID

When using nitric acid the work is either immersed in the acid which can be in a porcelain, glass or plastic container, or if the work piece to be etched is deep enough, such as a bowl, the acid can be poured in. Nitric acid works vigorously forming bubbles which should be brushed off with a feather every few minutes whilst the work is being etched. If this is not done ragged lines can result.

Work done with iron perchloride should be bitten either face down or on edge in the acid because the sediment which forms tends to "choke" the effect of the acid if done face up. If the work is such that it must be done face up then the acid must be agitated with a feather every few minutes to remove the sediment.

To see how deep the acid is biting, remove the work from the acid (avoid putting your fingers either in the iron perchloride or the nitric acid) and wash under a tap. Dab with a soft cloth to dry. If it has to be returned to the acid check to see if the acid resist, front and back, needs "touching in" with stopping out varnish. This is sometimes necessary because small "pin holes" can develop in the ground.

REMOVAL OF THE RESIST

The plastic applied sheets can of course be peeled off. The other grounds can be removed with a soft cloth and turpentine.

Never buff etched work as this ruins the characteristic sharp edges of the etching. Use a soft hand brush with metal polish or whiting and methylated spirit. Finish with a soft polishing cloth.

ENAMELLING

Enamelling is the process of fusing glass on to a metallic base. The glass is usually crushed and it can be coloured or clear, opaque or translucent. The metallic base, for school work, is almost always copper, although gold, silver and steel can be enamelled.

The art of enamelling has been known for centuries. The earliest examples were found in Cyprus in the form of enamelled gold rings dating back to the thirteenth century B.C.

Enamelling is a fascinating art and there are many different techniques. The interested reader should refer to the bibliography at the back of this book. However, here is a simple enamelling technique which can be used readily in school with the minimum of equipment.

Requirements: small slightly hollowed copper dishes (to be enamelled)

   pumice powder and ammonia
   powdered enamels
   fine mesh coffee strainer
   gum tragacanth made up in liquid form (from any chemist)
   a water colour brush
   heavy gauge wire mesh
   small cover bent from 0·8 mm stainless steel
   blow torch
   brazing hearth and fire bricks
   carborundum slip 150 mm × 12 mm × 12mm.

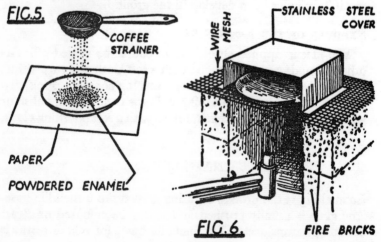

FIG.5.
COFFEE STRAINER
PAPER
POWDERED ENAMEL

WIRE MESH
STAINLESS STEEL COVER
FIG.6.
FIRE BRICKS

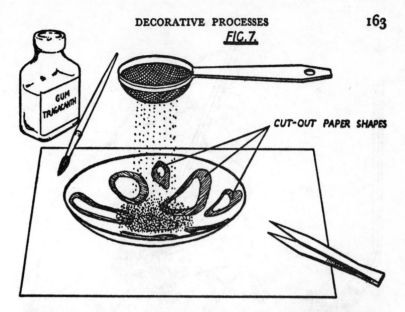

FIG. 7.

CUT-OUT PAPER SHAPES

Method: Clean the copper dish as for etching. Rinse thoroughly and brush on gum tragacanth. Lay the dish on a piece of clean white paper and sieve your chosen enamel evenly over the surface (fig. 5). Do not leave any bare patches and be sure the enamel goes right to the edge of the dish. The layer of enamel should be about 0·75 mm thick. Carefully place the dish on the wire mesh for firing (fig. 6). Any enamel left on the paper after the dish is removed should be returned to the enamel container.

Start firing with a very small soft flame to dry off the enamel, then heat evenly to cherry red with a large intense flame. When the enamel has fused allow to cool slowly on the mesh.

The first coat is now on the dish. Paint with gum tragacanth as before and stick into place the cut-out paper shapes (fig. 7). The second layer of enamel is then dusted over the dish as before. With a pair of tweezers carefully remove the cut-out shape thus leaving the original fired surface free of powdered enamel. Fire as before. Now we have a dish in two colours. This could be quite satisfactory at this stage, but if further dustings, possibly with transparent colours, are required they can be done.

Finish the dish by carefully stoning the edge with the carborundum slip and water. Clean the back with fine emery cloth. Take care not to distort the work or the enamel will fracture.

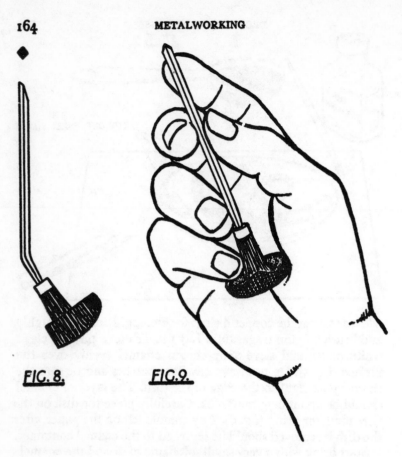

FIG. 8. FIG. 9.

ENGRAVING

There are many different tools available for engraving, but the one most used is the square graver (fig. 8). It should fit the hand as in figure 9. This graver can be made from 3 mm square silver steel. The tang is filed and bent and the tip hardened and tempered to light straw—do not go beyond light straw. The point is stoned as in figure 10, first on a medium India stone and then finished with a circular motion on an Arkansas stone (fig. 11).

Professional engravers often test the sharpness of the graver by touching the point at an angle against the thumb nail. If the tip catches and does not slide, it is sharp.

TRANSFERRING THE DESIGN TO BE ENGRAVED

1. For highly polished surfaces. Trace the drawing. Rub Russian tallow or plasticine on the back of the tracing paper, then lay it on the article to be engraved and with a blunt scriber transfer the drawing. This will leave a copy of the design on the metal. The fine lines of Russian tallow or plasticine on the metal can then be gone over with a scriber to prevent them from being rubbed off. The metal is now ready to be engraved.

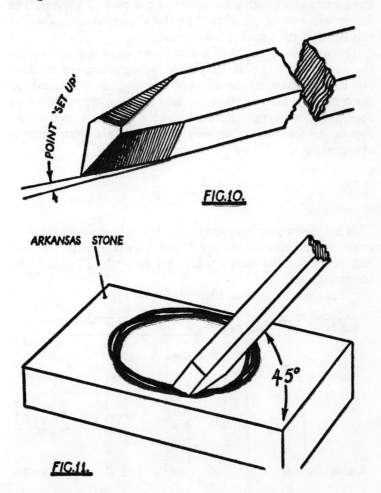

POINT 'SET UP'

FIG.10.

ARKANSAS STONE

45°

FIG.11.

2. Rub plasticine or beeswax all over the area to be engraved and then dust with whiting. Now with a sharp pointed piece of hardwood draw the design. This can be corrected as many times as you wish. Finally, lightly scratch in with a scriber and engrave.

3. To reverse the design. Trace the design on transparent acetate sheet (0·25 mm thick works well) with a scriber. Rub pencil lead into the tracing. Now lay this (in reverse) on the metal which has been rubbed with beeswax. Rub the back of the acetate sheet with a burnisher or the back of a spoon. The design will now be transferred on the work in reverse. Go over this lightly with a scriber before engraving.

The work to be engraved is usually rested on a sand bag and the engraving tool point is pushed gently along the marked-out lines—lightly for the first cut—turning the work and not the tool at the curves. Make the lines deeper where required by re-entering with the engraving tool and taking more cuts. Figure 11A (*designed and engraved by the author*) shows an example of engraving.

REPOUSSÉ

This is a method of decorating a sheet metal article by means of raised or indented motifs, made with punches (these are blunt and never cut the metal) whilst set in pitch. The tools and materials used are:

Punches made from silver steel (fig. 12)

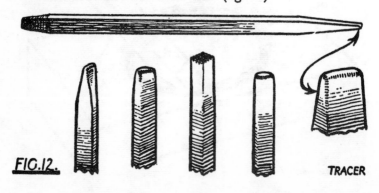

FIG. 12.

TRACER

FIG.13.

Repoussé or chasing hammer   (fig. 13)
Pitch
Cast iron pitch bowl and leather ring stand (fig. 14)
(A shallow metal tray will suffice for most school work.)
Blow pipe

THE PITCH

This must be tough enough to support the work and yet
resilient enough to allow the metal to be driven in by the
punches.

A good recipe for pitch is as follows:

    3 kilos Swedish pitch
    3 kilos Plaster of Paris
    227 gms tallow

The pitch is melted, the tallow added and the plaster stirred in
a little at a time. Before the work is set into this pitch it should
be lightly greased to facilitate cleaning after removal from the
pitch.

METHOD

Assume we are starting with a flat piece of 0·8 mm (this is
probably the best gauge for repoussé work) soft copper. Have
the pitch in a 25 mm deep metal tray about 25 mm larger all
round than the workpiece. Warm the surface of the pitch with a
soft flame and press the copper sheet on to the surface so that the
pitch just comes over the edges. Be sure there are no air bubbles
under the copper. Allow to cool. Trace the design on the copper
using carbon paper. Remove the carbon paper and lightly
scratch through the design with a scriber. Hold the tracing
punch in the left hand at such an angle to the work that when it

is struck repeatedly with the chasing hammer it moves towards you making a smooth indented line following the lines of your traced design. A little practice is necessary before this can be achieved. When you have finished with the tracing punch, warm the surface of the work with the blowpipe and remove. Clean with rag and paraffin. The design now shows in the form of raised lines on the back. Set the work in the pitch as before but face down this time. The parts to be embossed are now punched down with suitably shaped punches. The work may be reversed as many times as required until the desired effect is obtained. Figure 15 shows a part sectioned piece of repoussé work. Figure 14 shows the cover of a circular box set in pitch. Cast iron is used for the pitch bowl because it is heavy and withstands the effect of the punching.

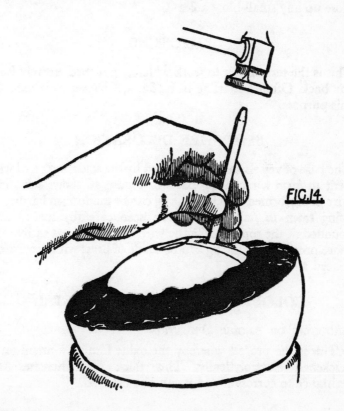

FIG. 14.

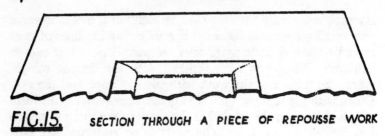

<u>FIG.15.</u>   SECTION THROUGH A PIECE OF REPOUSSE WORK

CHASING

Chasing is often not unlike repoussé work in appearance and it is done with similar punches, but it is done from the outside of the work—not from both sides. Castings can be chased with fine corrugated punches which produce a matt surface and also close up any small blow holes.

EMBOSSING

This is the term given to work which is punched entirely from the back. Often a snarling iron (fig. 5, Chapter 9) is used for this purpose.

BENT WIRE DECORATION

The base of vessels can be decorated by the soldering on of wire bent to form a repeating pattern. Figure 16 shows soft brass wire being formed on a jig. The jig can be made from hardwood using sawn-off nails which have been carefully spaced and rounded at the top to allow the wire to be removed easily. For more precise work the jig can be made of brass with accurately spaced steel pins.

COLOURING AND FINISHING METAL

ANODISING OR ANODIC OXIDATION

This is the process whereby the oxide film on aluminium is thickened electrolytically. This thick film increases the resistance to corrosion and it can also be dyed.

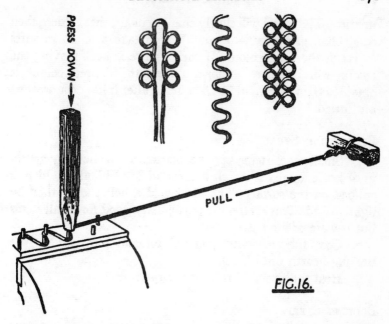

PRESS DOWN

PULL

FIG.16.

The aluminium is first de-greased. The most common electrolyte is dilute sulphuric acid which is in a lead lined bath (cathode). The aluminium article becomes the anode. After 30 to 60 minutes the article should be taken out, thoroughly rinsed and dyed if required.

The Aluminium Development Association publishes a booklet for schools on this subject in which full instructions are given.

COLOURING OF COPPER, BRASS AND GILDING METAL

There are various colouring agents which can be bought and many recipes available, particularly in some of the older books. However, many of these recipes are not reliable. A good mixture which will colour these metals chemically can be made as follows:

photographer's (plain) hypo	10 parts by weight
sugar of lead (lead acetate)	1 part by weight
citric acid	1 part by weight
water	40 parts by weight

Clean and de-grease the work to be coloured. Dip in the

mixture. The metal will slowly change colour, first golden, then rose, blue, grey-green to grey. It will take 5 to 10 minutes to reach the final colour. If the mixture is kept moving the colour will be more uniform. When the desired colour is obtained the work should be lacquered after it has been washed and dried.

BLACKENING STEEL

1. Small steel items can be blackened by heating gently until hot enough to scorch a piece of wool blanket which is rubbed on the surface. The blackened article should then be lightly oiled. This method is particularly good for small items but beware of the nasty smell!

2. Coat the steel with mineral oil and burn off on the brazing hearth until black.

3. Heat the steel and rub with saltpetre.

BLUEING STEEL

Polish the work with fine emery cloth avoiding oil and grease. Heat to blue as for tempering, quench in paraffin and polish with beeswax.

BURNISHING

This is the process of polishing soft metals, such as gold, silver and copper, by rubbing with a hard smooth tool made from agate, bloodstone or hardened steel. Various shaped burnishing tools are used and soapy water is a popular lubricant. The polish obtained by an expert can be remarkable. The action is one of pressing down the minute surface irregularities so that the surface becomes consolidated.

MOTTLING

This is a finish obtained on small pieces of engineering work by means of carborundum paste and 6 mm diameter dowel rod held in a drilling machine chuck. As the rod spins the end is pressed against the work causing the carborundum to make polished circles on the surface. If the circles are kept in neat rows this type of finish can enhance the surface, but it should be used with restraint.

ELECTROPLATING

This is a process whereby a thin layer of metal is deposited on another by means of an electric current passing through a solution of metallic salts.

It is possible by this means to deposit gold, silver, nickel, chromium, cadmium and copper. There is a mistaken belief among some students that plating will hide blemishes in their work. It will not: plating emphasises blemishes.

LACQUERING

Lacquering is done to protect metals from the atmosphere. It is a clear varnish (often with an amyl-acetate base) to which colouring matter is sometimes added. It is applied to thoroughly cleaned metal by brushing, dipping or spraying. In school, lacquer is usually applied with a brush; for best results a good quality camel hair brush should be used. Care must be taken to ensure that every part of the surface is covered, otherwise the uncovered parts will oxidise and show later as streaks. Badly applied lacquer must be removed using the solvent recommended by the manufacturer and then re-lacquered.

PAINTING

Iron and steel work which is to be exposed to the weather should be protected, unless it is stainless steel. Paint is the commonest protector. Before painting the work should be free of rust, oil or grease.

The paint may be brushed or sprayed. Several thin coats are better than one thick coat. Cracks often occur on a thick layer of paint because the outside of the paint dries first and contracts, whilst the layer of paint nearest the metal is still soft and cannot "anchor" the top layer to the metal.

If castings are to be painted any blow holes must be filled with a filler which suits the paint to be used and rubbed down between coats of paint with wet and dry emery paper.

PLASTIC COATING

This gives a durable and attractive finish to metal articles such as draining board racks or shoe racks which are never quite satisfactory when painted.

The article is heated in an oven to about 200°C then covered with a layer of a proprietary powder which is then fused on to the metal by reheating. Take care to follow the maker's instructions. (See information at the back of this book).

11
Safety

Strangers entering a school workshop are often amazed that there are so few accidents involving personal injury.

It would seem that in a busy school workshop the stage is set for a drama in which all sorts of dreadful accidents will occur from decapitation to being burnt alive!

The vigilance and good common sense of our handicraft masters, in no small measure, make the workshop a safe place in which to work.

However, here is some general information for the prevention of accidents.

Clothing. When starting to work take off your jacket; roll up your sleeves and tuck your tie into your shirt so that i. does not hang loose. Wear either an overall or an apron which should not be loose fitting. In the forge area wear a leather apron if one is available. Wear shoes with stout soles. Do not wear gym shoes: a sharp piece of bent metal on the floor can easily pierce these, or a hot piece of coke from the forge can burn through them.

Hair. Beware of hair that is too long. This can easily be caught up on a drilling machine or on the end of the horizontal milling machine arbor.

Oil or Grease on the Floor. If any oil or grease gets on the floor see that it is cleaned away and if possible put sawdust down to prevent people from slipping.

Never Run in the Workshop. Walk wherever you go and if you are carrying a tool or a piece of metal, have proper regard for anyone who might accidentally step into your path.

Safety Stop Switches. School workshops are usually fitted with these to enable anyone to stop all the machinery in case of emergency. You should know where these are in your workshop and how and when to use them.

Fire Blanket. This is often kept in a red cylindrical container hung on a wall, usually by the brazing hearth or forge area. Should anyone's clothing catch fire this asbestos blanket is used for the purpose of smothering the flames.

Acids. When putting hot work into dilute sulphuric acid (pickle) do it at arm's length to avoid being splashed and don't drop the work in. Avoid inhaling the fumes as far as possible.

Acids are best kept near a water tap so that if anyone is splashed they can quickly wash away the acid.

Electrical Faults. If you suspect that any machine is electrically faulty report it at once to the master in charge of the workshop.

Blacksmithing. Do not leave hot work where anyone might stand on or touch it. Beware of hot scale when hammering white hot metal.

TOOLS

Hammers. Report loose hammer heads to your teacher. Never strike two hammer heads together because it might cause a splinter of steel to fly off one of them.

Files. Always use a file with a properly fitting handle.

Cold Chisels. Take care when cutting through metal on a chipping block because often this causes the small pieces you are cutting off to be shot away at great speed. To prevent this stand up another chipping block or something similar in the path of these flying pieces. Report to your teacher any undue mushrooming of the chisel top.

Bench Shears. If you are guiding the metal into the bench shear be sure that it is *your* hand that is operating the handle. Do not let someone pull the handle down while your fingers are near the blades. The handle itself is in fact as dangerous as the cutter, so keep clear when metal is being cut.

MACHINE TOOLS

Do not talk to, or otherwise distract, a person who is using a machine tool.

If you leave a machine, switch it off.

Drilling Machine. When using this machine be sure the work is properly held in a vice and also be sure that there is a bolt or something similar to prevent the work and the vice from spinning round should the drill get caught. Never hold small work in your fingers.

Lathe. Make sure the work is firmly held in the chuck before starting the machine. Never leave the chuck key in the lathe chuck. Do not open the guard which covers the gear trains at the end of the machine unless the isolating switch is off. Never try to remove swarf whilst the machine is in motion. Remember the swarf nearly always has razor-like edges and it is often hot. Do not try to use your hands as a brake on the chuck. Never try to clean or polish work with a rag whilst the machine is revolving. When brushing the lathe down after work beware of the sharp tool.

Shaper. Do not bring your eye down level with the work being cut and in line with the ram. The chips are flicked away at the end of the cut and can cause eye injury. If you want to see how near to the line you are cutting, stop the machine. When setting up work be sure the isolator switch is off.

Milling Machine. Keep your hands away from the cutter when it is in motion. Do not remove any guard which has been fitted to the machine for your safety. Switch off the isolator when setting up work. Never try to apply soluble oil to the work with a brush when the cutter is revolving. Do not sweep the table with your hand because milling chips are often like needles.

Grinding Machine. Always use the eye guard or goggles. Be sure the gap between the rest and the wheel is not more than about 2 mm. If this is not so, small work can be dragged down into the gap.

Power Hacksaw. Do not press down on the top weight in order to speed the cutting. This often causes the blade to break and the sharp fragments shoot in all directions. Be sure there is enough metal for the vice to hold, otherwise it might be wrenched out when the machine is set in motion, thus causing the blade to break.

Finally, always report any accident to the teacher in the workshop.

12

Drilling

The drilling machine, because of its simplicity and the early need for drilled holes, is usually the first machine to be used by boys in the metalwork room.

When starting to drill the following hints will be useful:

1. Check that you have the correct drill and be sure the chuck is properly tightened.

2. Secure the work either in a hand vice or a drilling vice.

3. Take precautions against drilling into the vice or drilling machine table when (a) using a hand vice by resting the work

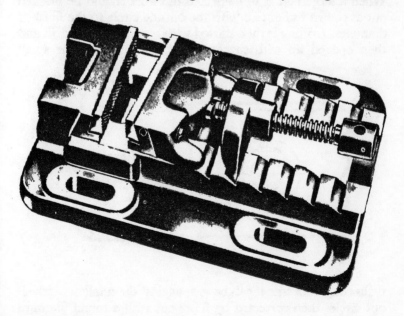

on a piece of accurately planed hardwood or, (b) by using
packing strips when using the machine vice. A typical machine
vice is shown in figure 1. A hand vice is shown in Chapter 3,
figure 21.

4. Check that the speed is correct for the drill and the material
you are drilling.

5. Bring the drill down to the centre punch mark and press
hard enough to start the drill cutting and keep it cutting—do
not let it rub, as this overheats the drill tip and makes it blunt.
Ease off the pressure when the drill is about to break through
because at this stage it tends to "grab" the work.

6. Use a coolant if applicable to the material you are drilling.

CENTRE PUNCHING

This must be done accurately on the marked out cross lines.
When a large hole is to be drilled the work should be marked
out as shown in figure 2 with the outside circle to the finished
diameter. Drilling is then started with a small "pilot" drill and
then opened up with successively larger drills. If the small

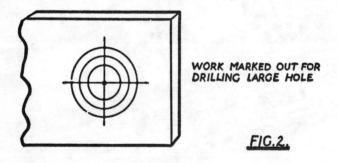

WORK MARKED OUT FOR
DRILLING LARGE HOLE

FIG. 2.

drills run out of true it can be seen against the smallest marked-
out circles then corrected by filing out with a round file until
finally the largest drill just splits the dot punches on the outside
circle.

FIG. 3—HAND DRILL

FIG. 4—ELECTRIC HAND DRILL

HAND DRILLS

Hand drills (fig. 3) are used for making holes up to 8 mm diameter. They are useful for making holes in work which cannot be taken to the drilling machine.

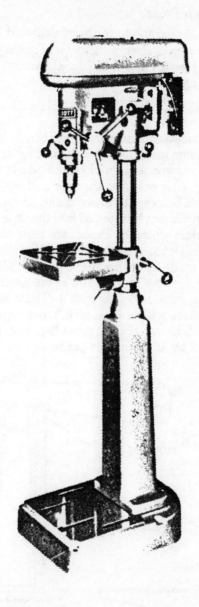

ELECTRIC HAND DRILLS

These do a similar job to the hand drill and have maximum capacities between 6-12 mm diameter. Figure 5 shows a stand on which an electric hand drill (fig. 4) can be held for use as a sensitive drilling machine.

DRILLING MACHINES

In the school workshop these are either bench drilling machines or pillar drilling machines. Bench drilling machines have a capacity up to 12 mm and should stand on a sturdy bench. The pillar drill (fig. 6) is bolted to the floor and has an intermediate table which can be raised or lowered and on some models tilted. Taper shank drills can be inserted into the taper socket spindles of these machines when the chucks are removed (fig. 7). If the taper shank drill is too small for the spindle socket the difference in size can be made up with a sleeve (fig. 7). These are made in single steps, e.g. 1 to 2, 2 to 3, and so on. Others are available which step up from 1 to 3 or 1 to 4. These sleeves should be tapped into place with a hide mallet and removed by lightly hammering a drift into the slot provided. The speed of the drill can be altered by adjusting the position of the vee belt on the pulleys.

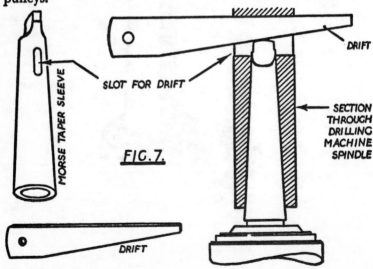

FIG. 7.

TWIST DRILLS

Twist drills are available in H.S.S. or carbon steel. Carbon steel drills are cheaper than H.S.S. but must be run at half the speed. However, the smaller sizes of these, with proper use, will last almost as long as the H.S.S. kind.

The speed of the drill should be calculated in the same way as for turning and the coolants recommended for turning also

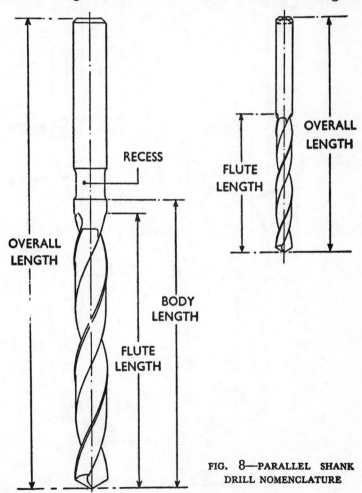

FIG. 8—PARALLEL SHANK
DRILL NOMENCLATURE

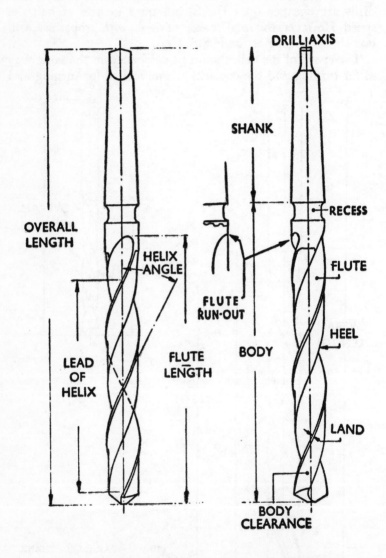

FIG. 9—MORSE TAPER SHANK DRILL NOMENCLATURE

FIG. 10.

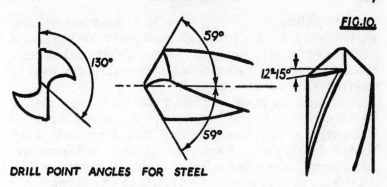

DRILL POINT ANGLES FOR STEEL

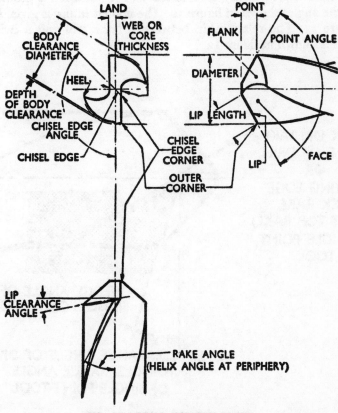

FIG. II—DRILL NOMENCLATURE

apply to drilling.   It is important to know
whether a drill is made from high speed steel or carbon steel if
it is to be run at its proper speed. Often drills are marked either
H.S. or C.S. but if no such marking is visible the sparks must be
observed when it is being ground.

Twist drills are made with either parallel or taper shanks.
Sizes up to about 12 mm have parallel shanks and above this
morse taper shanks. Straight shank drills are usually called
"jobbers drills". Figures 8 and 9 show the twist drill nomenclature in accordance with the British Standards Institution.

Drills are made in sizes from 0·5 mm to 65 mm. diameter.

The drill commonly used in the school workshop is ground
to the angles shown in figure 10. The nomenclature is given in
figure 11. The relationship between a lathe tool and a twist
drill is shown in figure 12.

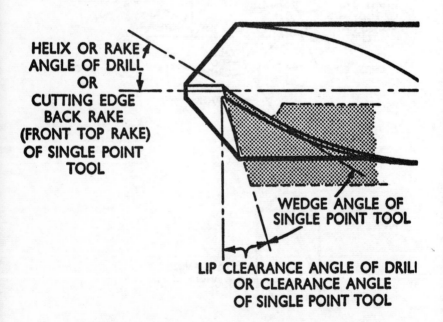

HELIX OR RAKE
ANGLE OF DRILL
OR
CUTTING EDGE
BACK RAKE
(FRONT TOP RAKE)
OF SINGLE POINT
TOOL

WEDGE ANGLE OF
SINGLE POINT TOOL

LIP CLEARANCE ANGLE OF DRILL
OR CLEARANCE ANGLE
OF SINGLE POINT TOOL

FIG. 12—RAKE AND LIP CLEARANCE ANGLES

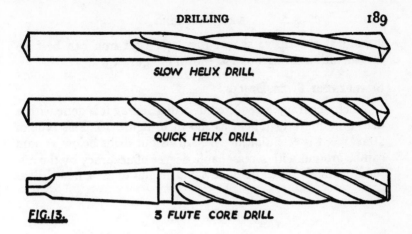

SLOW HELIX DRILL

QUICK HELIX DRILL

FIG.13. 3 FLUTE CORE DRILL

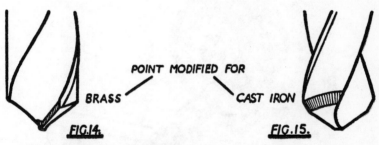

POINT MODIFIED FOR

BRASS

CAST IRON

FIG.14. FIG.15.

Special drills are available (fig. 13):

Slow Helix drills used for brass, gunmetals and phosphor bronze (the rake angle is decreased).

Quick Helix drills used for soft metals such as aluminium and copper (the rake angle is increased).

Multi-flute Core drills may have 3 or 4 flutes and are used for enlarging existing holes, particularly cored holes in castings. These drills are strong because the flutes are not deep and therefore the web or core is relatively thick.

In the school workshop these special drills are seldom used, but the tip of an ordinary twist drill can be modified to a certain extent to suit the material being drilled. When drilling brass almost no rake is needed and the drill helix angle is ground at the tip as shown (fig. 14). Cast iron can best be drilled with a drill ground as shown in figure 15.

Sharpening Twist Drills

When accuracy is required in drill grinding it is done with a drill grinding attachment as shown in figure 16. This type of attachment is essential for large drills but drills below 12 mm can be ground with a reasonable degree of accuracy by the offhand method. When doing this it is helpful to use a new drill as

UNEQUAL LIP
ANGLES

FIG.17.

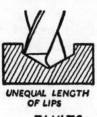

UNEQUAL LENGTH
OF LIPS

FAULTS

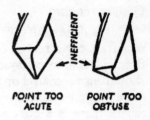

POINT TOO
ACUTE

POINT TOO
OBTUSE

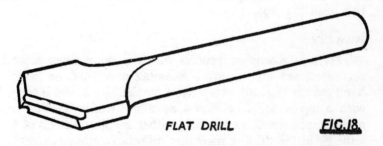

FLAT DRILL   **FIG.18.**

a model in order to obtain the correct angles and clearances:
but practice is necessary to achieve proficiency in this type of
freehand grinding. Some faults in drill grinding are shown in
figure 17.

FLAT DRILLS (figure 18)

These can be made from silver steel or carbon steel in the
school workshop. They must be hardened and carefully tempered usually to a light straw.

PROCESSES

COUNTERSINKING

This is done with a countersinking cutter (fig. 19).

COUNTERBORING

This is done with a counterboring cutter (fig. 19) to accommodate a cap screw or cheese head screw. Counterbores made from H.S.S. may be bought or they may be turned in the workshop from silver steel or plain carbon steel, and the flutes filled. Care must be taken with hardening as cracking may occur where there is a change of section. Temper to a mid-straw colour and sharpen with a slip stone.

SPOT FACING

This is done with a counterboring cutter on rough or uneven surfaces, but only deep enough to provide a square seating for a bolt head (fig. 19).

REAMING

This is a secondary process which is done when smooth accurate holes are required. Reaming may be done using a hand reamer (fig. 20) which has a parallel shank and is turned with a tap wrench, or with a machine reamer which has a morse taper shank and is held either in the tailstock of the lathe or in the drilling machine. Adjustable reamers (fig. 21)

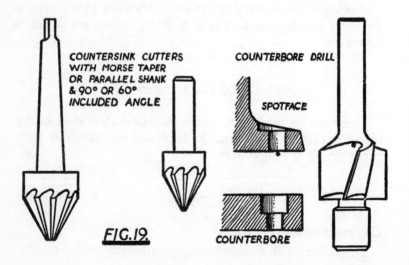

COUNTERSINK CUTTERS WITH MORSE TAPER OR PARALLEL SHANK & 90° OR 60° INCLUDED ANGLE

COUNTERBORE DRILL

SPOTFACE

COUNTERBORE

FIG. 19.

FIG. 20—HAND REAMER
Courtesy of Firth Brown Tools Ltd.

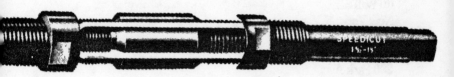

FIG. 21—ADJUSTABLE REAMER
Courtesy of Firth Brown Tools Ltd.

can be slightly enlarged after each pass through the hole until the correct size is obtained.

Whichever reamer is used care must be taken not to turn them backwards but keep them rotating in the cutting direction both in entering and withdrawing, otherwise the swarf tends to become wedged behind the cutting edges causing them to chip. Reaming should be done slowly and cutting fluid used when applicable. Holes to be reamed should be drilled out to about 0·125 mm to 0·25 mm below size for holes up to 12 mm and between 0·3 mm and 0·6 mm below size for larger holes.

Where to Buy Tools and Materials

Acli Metal & Ore Company
110 Wall St.
New York, N.Y.

Aluminum Co. of America
200 Park Ave.
New York, N.Y.

Daub Steel & Metals
230 Park Ave.
New York, N.Y.

Phillip Brothers
299 Park Ave.
New York, N.Y.

Precious Metals Co.
20 Exchange Place
New York, N.Y.

Index

© Drake Publishers Inc. , 1971

Published in 1972 by
Drake Publishers Inc.
381 Park Avenue South
New York, N.Y. 10016

ISBN: 87749-020-1

Printed in the U.S.A.

TABLE OF CONTENTS

PREFACE

What prompted the author to prepare this book was the oft-repeated question, by blacksmiths and mechanics of all kinds, as well as farmers: "Is there a book treating on this or that?" etc., etc. To all these queries I was compelled to answer in the negative, for it is a fact that from the time of Cain, the first mechanic, there has never been a book written by a practical blacksmith on subjects belonging to his trade. If, therefore, there has ever been such a thing as "filling a long-felt want," this must certainly be a case of that kind.

In medecine we find a wide difference of opinion, even amongst practitioners of the same school, in treating diseases. Now, if this is so where there is a system, and authority for the profession, how much more so must there be a difference of opinion in a trade where every practitioner is his own authority. I shall, therefore, ask the older members of the blacksmith fraternity to be lenient in their judgment if my ideas don't coincide with theirs. To the apprentice and journeyman I would say: do as I do until you find a better way.

The author has been eminently successful in his practice, and his ideas have been sought by others wherever he has been, blacksmiths coming even from other States to learn his ways.

This little book is fresh from the anvil, the author taking notes during the day while at work, compiling the same into articles at night.

CHAPTER I

THE SHOP AND TOOLS

In building a shop care should be taken in making it convenient and healthy. Most of the shops are built with a high floor. This is very inconvenient when machinery of any kind is taken in for repairs, as well as in taking in a team for shoeing. Around the forge there should be a gravel floor. A plank floor is a great nuisance around the anvil. Every piece cut off hot is to be hunted up and picked up or it will set fire to it. I know there will be some objection to this kind of floor but if you once learn how to keep it you will change your mind. To make this floor take sand and clay with fine gravel, mix with coal dust and place a layer where wanted about four inches thick. This floor, when a little old, will be as hard as iron, provided you sprinkle it every night with water. The dust and soot from the shop will, in time, settle in with it and it will be smooth and hard. It will not catch fire; no cracks for small tools or bolts to fall through; it will not crack like cement or brick floors. If your shop is large, then make a platform at each end, and a gravel floor in the center, or at one side, as in Fig. 1. This floor is cool in summer and warm in winter, as there can be no draft. The shop should have plenty of light, skylights if possible. The soot and dust will, in a short time, make the lightest shop dark. The shop should be whitewashed once a year. Have plenty of ventilation. Make it one story only if convenient to do so, as an upper story in a blacksmith shop is of very little use. The shop is the place where the smith spends most of his time and he should take just as much care in building it, as a sensible housekeeper does in the construction of her kitchen.

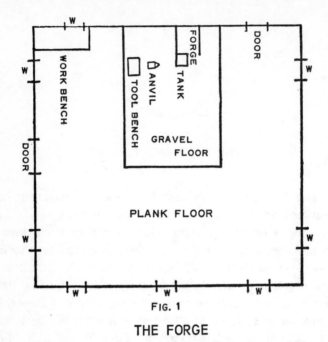

FIG. 1

THE FORGE

The forge can be made either single or double, square or round. The square is the best as it can be placed up against the wall, and you will then have more room in front of it. The round forge will take more room, if it is placed in the center of the floor there will be no room of any amount on any side and when the doors are open the wind will blow the fire, cinders and smoke into the face of the smith. This is very uncomfortable. The smokestack, if hung over the fire will sometimes be in the way. Of course the hood can be made in halves and one half swung to the side, but it will sometimes be in the way anyhow, and it seldom has any suction to carry away the smoke and cinders.

THE ANVIL

The anvil should not be too close to the forge, as is often the case in small country shops. Make it six feet from center of fire to center of anvil. The anvil should not be placed on a

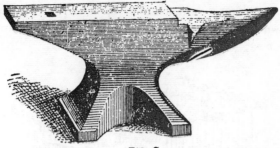

FIG. 2

butcher block with the tools on, but on a timber the same size as the foot of the anvil. Set the timber down in the ground at least three feet. For heavy work the anvil should stand low in order to be able to come down on it with both hammer and sledge with force. When the smith has his hands closed the knuckles of his fingers should touch the face of the anvil and it will be the right height for all-around blacksmithing.

COAL BOX

Close to the forge under the water tank or barrel should be a coal box 18 × 24 × 16 inches, this box to be dug down in the ground and so placed that one end will protrude from under the barrel or tank far enough to let a shovel in. This opening can be closed with a lid if the tools are liable to fall into it. In this box keep the coal wet. In Fig. 1 a plan is given from which you can get an idea of a shop and how to place the tools and different articles needed.

TOOL TABLES

On the right hand of the anvil should be a tool bench or tool table 20 × 20 inches, a little lower than the anvil. Outside, on three sides and level with the table, make a railing of 1¼ inch iron, about 1½ inch space between the table and railing, this makes a handy place for tools and near by. Many blacksmiths have no other place than the floor for their tools, but there is no more sense in that than it would be for a carpenter to throw his tools down on the floor all around him. There ought to be "a place for every tool and every tool in its place."

FIG. 3 TOOL TABLES

THE HAMMER

When a lawyer or a minister makes his maiden speech he will always be in a great hurry on account of his excitement. The sentences are cut shorter, broken, and the words are sometimes only half pronounced. After a few years practice he will be more self-possessed and the speech will be changed from unintelligible phrases to logical oratory. When the carpenter's apprentice first begins to use the saw, he will act the same way—be in a great hurry—he will run the saw at the speed of a scroll saw, but only a few inches of stroke; after some instructions and a few years practice the saw will be run up and down steady and with strokes the whole length of the blade. When the blacksmith's apprentice begins to use the hammer he acts very much the same way. He will press his elbows against his ribs; lift the hammer only a few inches from the anvil and peck away at the speed of a trip hammer. This will, in most cases, be different in a few years. He will drop the bundle — that is, his elbows will part company with his ribs, the hammer will look over his head, there will be full strokes and regular time, every blow as good as a dozen of his first ones. Some smiths have the foolish habit of beating on the anvil empty with the hammer, they will strike a few blows on the iron, then a couple of blind beats on the anvil, and so on. This habit has been imported from Europe, free of duty, and that must be the reason why so many blacksmiths enjoy this luxury.

THE SLEDGE

In Europe great importance is laid upon the position taken by the apprentice and the manner he holds the sledge. The sledge is held so that the end of it will be under his right armpit, when the right hand is next to the sledge, and under his left arm when the left hand is nearer the sledge. In this unnatural position it is next to impossible to strike hard and do it for any time. This is another article imported free of duty, but few Americans have been foolish enough to use it. In this country the apprentice will be taught to use the tools in a proper way.

The end of the sledge-handle will be to one side; at the left, if the left hand is at the end of the handle, and at the right if the right hand is at the end of the handle; and be down between his feet when the handle's end must be low. The apprentice should stand directly in front of the anvil.

In swinging, the sledge should describe a circle from the anvil close down to the helper's feet and up over his head and down to the anvil; this is a perpendicular circle blow. Be sure not to give it a horizontal start; that is, with one hand close to the sledge the apprentice starts out either in the direction of the horn or the butt end of the anvil, and then up while both hands should clasp the extreme end of the handle close together the sledge should be dropped down to the feet then up. The hold taken should not be changed, but the hands held in the same place.

For ordinary use a nine-pound sledge is heavy enough, a large sledge will give a bump, while a small one will give a quick good blow, it is only occasionally and for special purposes a large sledge is needed, even an eight-pound sledge will do. Try it, and you will be surprised how nice it works.

With these preliminary remarks we shall now begin to make a few tools. We will begin with the blacksmith's tongs. I shall only give an idea how to forge the jaws, and every man that needs to make them has seen enough of this simple tool to know what kind is needed, and what he has not seen will suggest itself to every sensible smith.

BLACKSMITH'S TONGS

Take a piece of one-inch square Swede iron, hold the iron diagonally over the anvil, with your left hand a little toward the horn, the end of the iron to reach out over the outside edge of the anvil. Now strike so that the sledge and hammer will hit half face over the anvil and the other half of the sledge and hammer

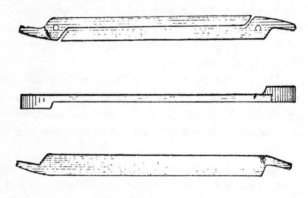

FIG. 4

outside of the anvil. Hammer it down to about three-eighths of an inch thick. Now pull the iron towards you straight across the anvil, give it one half turn toward yourself so that this side which was up, now will be towards yourself; the end that first was outside the anvil now to rest over the inner edge of the anvil, push the jaw up against the anvil until it rests against the shoulder made in the first move. Now hammer this down until it is the thickness of the jaw that is desired. Next, turn it over, with the bottom side up or the side that was down, up; push it out over the outside edge of the anvil again so far that the shoulder or set down you now have up, will be about an inch outside and over the edge of the anvil, now give a few blows to finish the jaw, then finish the shanks and weld in half inch round iron to the length desired. The jaws should be grooved with a fuller, if you have none of the size required take a piece of round iron and hammer it down in the jaws to make the groove. Tongs grooved this way will grip better. Next, punch a hole in one jaw, place it over the other in the position wanted when finished, then mark the hole in the other jaw, and when punched rivet them together, the jaws to be cold and the rivet hot. The following story will suggest to you how to finish it. An apprentice once made a pair of tongs when his master was out, and when he had them riveted together could not move the jaws. As he did not know how to make them work he laid them away under the bellows. At the supper table the apprentice told his master the following story: An apprentice once made a pair of tongs and when he had them riveted together he could not move the jaws, and as he did not know what to do he simply threw them away, thinking he must have made a mistake somehow. "What a fool," said the master, "why didn't he heat them." At the next opportunity the apprentice put his tongs in the fire and when hot they could be worked very easily.

HOW TO MAKE A HAMMER

Take a piece of tool steel 1¼ inches square, neat it red hot. Now remember here it is that the trouble begins in handling tool steel. If, in the process, you ever get it more than red hot, it is spoiled, and no receipt, or handling or hammering will ever make it good again. The best thing in such a case is to cut off the burnt part in spite of all proposed cures. This must be remembered whenever you heat tool or spring steel. If the burnt part cannot be cut off, heat it to a low heat, cool it in lukewarm water half a dozen times, this will improve it some, if you can hammer it some do so. Now punch a hole about two inches from the end with a punch that will make a hole $1\frac{1}{8} \times \frac{3}{8}$. If the punch sticks in the hole, cool it off and put a little coal in the hole that will prevent the punch from sticking. This is a good thing to do whenever a deep hole is to be punched. Be sure that the hole is made true. Next, have a punch the exact size of the hole wanted when finished, drive it in and hammer the eye out until it has the thickness of about $\frac{3}{8}$ of an inch on each side and has a circle form like No. 2, Fig. 5.

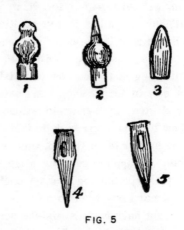

FIG. 5

In order to do this you may have to heat the eye many times, and upset over it with the punch in the eye. This done put in the bottom fuller and with the top fuller groove it down on each side of the eye, like the cut referred to. Now dress down the face then the peen-end. When finished harden it in this way: Heat the face-end first to a low red heat, dip in water about an inch and a half, brighten the face and watch for the color. When it begins to turn blue cool off but don't harden the eye. Wind a wet rag around the face end and heat the peen-end, temper the same way. With a piece of iron in the eye, both ends can be hardened at the same time, but this is more difficult, and I would not recommend it.

For ordinary blacksmithing a flat peen hammer is the thing, but I have seen good blacksmiths hang on to the machinist's hammer as the only thing. See No. 1, Fig. 5. This hammer is more ornamental than useful in a blacksmith shop. The hammer should be of different sizes for different work, light for light work, and for drawing out plowshares alone the hammer should be heavy.

For an ordinary smith a hammer of two up to two and one-half pounds is right. Riveting hammers should be only one pound and less. No smith should ever use a hammer like No. 3, Fig. 5. This hammer I have not yet been able to find out what it is good for. Too short, too clumsy, too much friction in the air. I have christened it, and if you want my name for it call it Cain's hammer. It must surely look like the hammer used by him, if he had any.

HOW TO MAKE CHISELS

A chisel for hot cutting, see Fig. 5, No. 4. This chisel is made of 1¼ square tool steel. Punch a hole 1⅛ × ¼ × ½ about three inches from the end, the eye should be narrow in order to leave material enough on the sides to give it strength. When eye is finished, forge down below it, not on the head-end, with top and bottom fullers, like cut. This gives the chisel a better shape. Now dress down the edge, then heat to a low cherry red, and harden, brighten it and when the color is brown cool off.

COLD CHISELS

Use same sized steel as above referred to, make it like No. 5, Fig. 5. To distinguish it from the hot cutting chisel, and to give it more strength, in hardening this chisel, draw the temper until it is blue. This is the right temper for all kinds of cold chisels.

SET HAMMER

One might think that anybody knows how to make a set hammer, if every smith knows it, I don't know, but I do know that there are thousands of smiths who have never had a set hammer nor know its use. To make one: Take a piece of tool steel

1¼ × 1¼ inches, punch a hole about two inches from the end, the hole to be 1¼ × ⅜. Now cut off enough for head. Make the face perfectly square and level, with sharp corners, harden and cool off when the temper turns from brown to blue. This is a very important little tool and for cutting steel it is a good deal better than the chisel. Plow steel of every kind is easier cut with this hammer than any other way. In cutting with the set hammer hold the steel so that your inner side of the set hammer will be over the outside edge of the anvil. Let the helper strike on the outside corner of the set hammer and it will cut easy. The steel to be cut should be just a little hot, not enough to be noticed. If the steel is red hot the set hammer cannot cut it. The heat must be what is called blue heat. I would not be without the set hammer for money, and still I often meet smiths who have never seen this use made of the set hammer. Plow points, corn shovels, and seeder shovels are quicker cut with this tool than any other way, with the exception of shears.

TWIST DRILLS

Twist drills are not easy to make by hand, as they should be turned to be true, but a twist drill can be made this way. Take a piece of tool steel round and the size of the chuck hole in your drill press. Flatten it down to the size wanted, heat, put the shank in the vise, take with the tongs over the end and give one turn to the whole length, turn to the left. When finished be sure that it is not thicker up than it is at point, and straight. Now harden, heat to a low cherry red, cool off in luke-warm water — salt water, if you have it — brighten it and hold over a hot bar of iron to draw temper, cool off when brown, the whole length of the twist should be tempered.

Another way to make a drill is to just flatten the steel and shape to a diamond point and bend the shares forward. This is a simple but good idea and such drills cut easy. In cooling for hardening turn the drill in the water so that the edge or shares are cooled in proportion to point, or the shares will be too soft and the point of such a drill too hard. Our trade journals, in giving receipts for hardening drills, often get watch-makers receipts. This is misleading: watch-makers heat their drills to a white heat. Now, remember, as I have already said, when your drill or tool of this kind is heated to this heat the best thing to do is to cut that part off. It is different with watch-makers, they do not look for strength, but hardness. They run their drills with a high speed, cut chips that cannot be discerned with the naked eye, and must have a drill that is hard like a diamond. For drilling iron or steel the drill does not need to be so very hard, but tough rather, because of the slow speed and thick chips. Few smiths have been able to master the simplest tempering, and they think if they could get a complicated receipt they would be all right. We are all more or less built that way. Anything we do not understand we admire. Simple soft water and the right heat is, in most cases, the only thing needed for hardening. I had occasion to consult a doctor once who was noted for his simple remedies. A lady got some medicine and she wanted to know what it was so she could get it when the doctor was not at home, but he refused to reveal it to her. When the lady had left the doctor told me the reason why. "This lady," said the doctor, "does not believe in simple remedies which she knows, but believes in those remedies she knows nothing about." I think it is better for us to try to understand things and not believe much in them before we understand them.

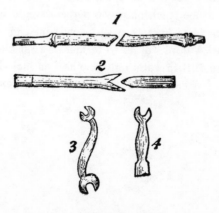

FIG. 6

S WRENCH

See Fig. 6, No. 3. This wrench is for ⅜ nut on one end and
½ on the other, just the kind for plow work. To make one, take a
piece of tool steel 1½ × ⅝, start as you see in No. 4, Fig. 6.
Set the jaws down with the fullers, punch a round hole as in end
No. 4, cut out from hole and finish the jaws to make the right
length, now bend it in S shape and finish. This makes the best
wrench. Do not heat over a red heat.

ROCK DRILLS

Few blacksmiths know how to make a rock drill. Take a piece
of round or octagon steel, the desired length and thickness,
shape it, but it must be remembered that if during the process
you ever get it over a red heat there is no use to proceed, but
just cut off that much and start again, no hardening will prevail
if it is burnt. The trouble begins when you put the steel into the
fire, and you must watch until you have it finished. When ready
to harden heat it to a cherry red heat, cool in water not too cold,
brighten and watch for temper. When it is yellow, cool it off, but
not entirely, take it out of the water before it is quite cold and
let it cool slowly, this will make the drill both hard and tough.
By this simple process I have been able to dress drills and get
such a good temper than only two percent would break. Another
way to harden is to heat to a very low heat and cool it off entirely at once. A third way is to temper as first stated and when
yellow set the drill in water only one half an inch deep and let it
cool. By this process a good percent will break just at the water
line.

CHAPTER II

WORKING METHODS AND EQUIPMENT

The smith should never turn the iron on the helper's blow, he should turn on his own blow, that is, never turn the iron so that the helper's blow will hit it first because he is not prepared for it and cannot strike with confidence, but the smith will not be bothered by turning the iron for himself as he knows when he turns and is prepared for it. The smith should strike the first blow in starting, or signal the helper where to strike, in case the smith cannot strike the first blow. The smith calls the helper by three blows on the anvil with his hammer, and when the smith wants the helper to cease striking he taps with the hammer twice on the anvil. The helper should strike the blow he has started when the smith signals him to stop. The helper should watch the time of the smith's hammer; if fast, keep time with it, if slow, keep time with it. The helper should strike where the smith strikes or over the center of the anvil. The helper should always lift the sledge high, in order to give the smith a chance to get in with the hammer.

THE FIRE

It is proper before we go any farther to say a few words about the fire.

An old foreman in the blacksmith department of a factory told me once in a conversation we had about the fire, that he had come to the conclusion that very few blacksmiths have learned how to make a good fire. It takes years of study and practice

FIG. 7 "CORRECT POSITION" AT THE ANVIL

before the eye is able to discern a good fire from a bad one. A good fire must be a clear fire, the flame must be concentrated and of a white color. Even the nose must serve to decide a bad fire from a good one. A strong sulphur smell indicates a poor fire for welding. In order to get a good fire there must be, first, good coal; second, plenty of it. It is no use to pile a lot of coal on an old fire, full of cinders and slag. The fire-pot must be clean. Many blacksmiths are too saving about the coal. They take a shovel of coal, drop it on the forge in the vicinity of the fire and sprinkle a handful of it in the fire once in a while. In such a case it is impossible to do good work and turn it out quick. Have a scoop shovel and put on one or two shovels at a time, the coal should be wet. Then pack it in the fire as hard together as you can. Sprinkle the fire with water when it begins to spread. In this way you get a hard fire. The flames are concentrated and give great heat. Saving coal is just like saving feed to a horse, or grub to your apprentice. Neither will give you a good day's work unless he has all he wants to eat. The fire, of course, should be in proportion to the work, but in every case should the fire be large enough to raise it up from the tuyer iron as much as possible. In a small fire the blast strikes directly on the iron and it begins to scale off; in a good fire these scales melt and make it sticky, while in a low and poor fire the scales blacken and fall off. This never happens if the fire is full of good coal and high up from the tuyer iron.

Good strong blast is also necessary for heavy work. There is an old whim about the fire that everybody, farmers and others, as well as blacksmiths, are infected with, and that is, if a piece of brass is put in the fire it renders the fire useless to weld with. Now, while it is a fact that brass is not conducive to welding it takes a good deal of it before the fire is made useless. One smith will not dare to heat a galvanized pipe in his fire, for fear it will spoil it, while another smith will weld a piece of iron or steel to such a pipe without difficulty. Don't swear and curse if the fire is not what you expect it to be, but simply make it right. Some smiths have the habit of continually poking in the fire, if they weld a piece of iron they never give it rest enough to get hot, but turn it over from one side to another and try to fish up all the cinders and dust to be found in the fire. This is a bad habit. Yellow colored fire is a sign of sulphur in the fire and makes a poor fire for welding. Dead coal makes a poor fire.

TUYER IRON

One of the chief reasons for a poor fire is a poor blast. No patent tuyer will give blast enough unless you run it by steam and have a fan blower. Ninety percent of the blast is lost in transmission through patent tuyers. The only way to get a good blast is to have a direct tuyer, and one with a water space in.

To make a direct tuyer take a pipe $1\frac{1}{4} \times 12$ inches long, weld around one end of this pipe an iron $3\frac{5}{8}$ to make it thick on the end that is in the fire, flare out the other end for the wind pipe to go in and place it horizontal in the fire and fill up around it with fireproof clay. This gives the best fire. The only objection to this tuyer is that where soft coal is used, as is mostly the case in country shops, it gets hot and clogs up, but with a strong blast and good hard coal it never gets hot, provided the fire is deep enough. From five to eight inches is the right distance from the tuyer to the face of the fire. In factories this kind of tuyer is used, and I have seen them used for ten years, and never found them to clog once. The tuyer was just as good after ten years use as it was when put in.

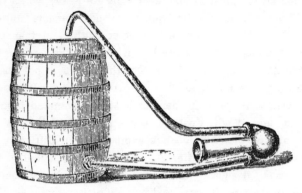

FIG. 8 WATER TUYER

To make a water tuyer take a pipe 1¼ × 12 inches, weld a flange on each end for water space, now weld another pipe over this, and bore holes for ¼ inch pipes in the end, where the blast goes in. One hole on the lower or bottom side should be for the cold water to go in through, and one hole on the upper side for the hot water to go out through. These pipes to connect with a little water tank for this purpose. The pipes should be watched so that they will not be allowed to freeze or clog, as an explosion might follow. These tuyers never clog. I now use one that I have made as above described. The dealers now have them to sell. Any smith can get them as they are hard to make by the average smith.

BLOWERS

I have tried many kinds of blowers and I shall give my brother smiths the advantage of my experience.

Portable forges run with fan blowers are fair blowers if you are strong enough to pump away at high speed, but it takes a horse to do that, and as soon as you drop the lever the blast ceases. Root's blower works easier, but the objection is the same, as soon as you drop the crank the blast stops. Besides this trouble, this blower is often in the way. I have never found anything to beat the bellows yet, if you only know how to use them.

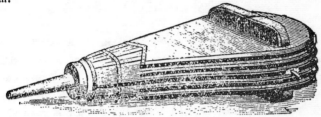

FIG. 9

Never take a set of bellows less than 48 extra long. Cut the snout off so that it will give a hole 1½, and with a water tuyer this blower cannot be beaten, except by a fan blower run by steam. The bellows should be hung over head to be out of the way. When these bellows are full of wind they will blow long enough after you have dropped the lever to do quite a good many things around the forge, and to handle the iron in the fire with both hands as is often necessary.

WELDING IRON

Welding iron is easy and no other welding compound is needed than sand, unless it is a case when the iron is liable to burn or scale off, borax will prevent this. There are three kinds of welds, butt, lap and split. The butt weld is most used in welding iron. The ends should be rounded off a little so that the center will weld first. Weld the ends this way either in the fire or on the anvil, butting the ends while you strike over and dress down the weld. In welding lap welds upset the ends and make them a good deal heavier than the size of the iron is; then lap the ends with a short lap. New beginners will always make a long lap. This is wrong, for if the lap is long it will reach beyond the upset part and the ends cannot then be welded down, without you make it weak. If soft steel is welded cut a short cut with the chisel in the center of the lap, as shown in Fig. 6, No. 1. This cut will hook and prevent the ends from slipping; if properly prepared this weld will not show at all when done.

SPLIT WELDS

Split weld is preferable when steel is to be welded, especially tool steel of a heavy nature, like drill bits for well drillers.

If the steel is welded to iron, split the iron and draw out the ends as thin as possible and make it the shape shown in Fig. 6, No. 2. Taper the steel to fill the split made in the iron, when it fits perfectly cut beard in it to catch in the lips of the iron when fitted in. See Fig. 6, No. 2. When finished heat the split end and cool off the tapered end. Place the tapered end snug up in the split and hammer it together with a heavy sledge. If there is any crack or opening at the end of the tapered end, plug it up with iron plugs, if this is not done, these holes will be almost as they are, because it is hard to weld a heavy shaft or drill, or rather, it is hard to hammer them together so the holes will close in. Now heat, but if you have tool steel go slow, or your steel will burn before the iron is hot enough. Weld the lips while the rod or drill is in the fire. For this purpose use a hammer with an iron handle in. When the lips are welded all around take it out and let two good helpers come down on it with all their might. When welded smooth it up with the hammer or flat hammer.

WELDING STEEL

Welding steel is quite a trick, especially tool or spring steel. The most important part to remember is, to have a good clean fire, and not to overheat the steel. To a good smith no other compound is needed than borax, but if this is not sufficient, take some borings from your drill, especially fine steel borings, and cover the weld with this and borax, and if a smith cannot weld with this compound there is no use for him to try. Most of the welding compounds are inferior to this, but some smiths would rather believe in something they don't know anything about; another will not believe in anything he can get for nothing.

BANDS OR HOOPS

When a round object is to be ironed or a hoop put on to anything round, measure, that is, take the diameter then multiply by three, add three times the thickness of the iron (not the width), add to this one time the thickness of the hoop for the weld and you have the exact length of the iron needed; in other words, three times the diameter, four times the thickness of the band. This is a simple rule, but I know a good many old smiths who never knew it.

SEEDER SHOVELS

To weld seeder shovels is no easy job. Prepare the shovel; shape almost to it proper shape, draw out the shanks, weld the points first, heat shovel and shank slow, then fit them together so that no cinders can get in between. Now remember, if your fire is not at least five inches up from the tuyer iron, and clear, it is no use to try. Hold your shovel in the fire, shank down. Heat slow, use borax freely and apply it on the face side of the shovel to prevent it from burning. When ready, weld it over the mandrill and the shovel will have the right shape. If soft center, harden like a plow lay.

DRILLING IRON

Every smith knows how to drill, sometimes it gives even an old smith trouble. The drill must be true, the center to be right, if one side of the drill is wider than the other or the drill not in proper shape the hole will not be true. For centuries oil has been used for drilling and millions of dollars have been spent in vain. It is a wonder how people will learn to use the wrong thing. I don't think that I have ever met a man yet who did not know that oil was used in drilling. In drilling hard steel, turpentine or kerosene is used as oil will then prevent cutting entirely. Nothing is better than water, but turpentine or kerosene is not as bad as oil; if you think water is too cheap use turpentine or kerosene. I had occasion once to do a little work for a man eighty years old, and when I drilled a hole, used water. The old man asked if water was as good as oil, and when informed that it was better, said: "I used to be quite a blacksmith myself, I am now eighty years old, too old to do anything, but I am not too old to learn." It ought to suggest itself to every smith that while oil is used in boxes to prevent cutting, it will also prevent cutting in drilling.

HOW TO DRILL CHILLED IRON

First prepare a drill which is thicker at the point than usual, and oval in form, then harden it as follows: heat to a low cherry red heat and cool in the following hardening compound: two quarts soft water, one-half ounce sal-ammoniac, salt, three ounces. Don't draw the temper, for if you have the right heat you will get the right temper. Now drill and use water, not oil. Feed carefully but so the drill will cut right along. If you have no chance to get the compound, harden in water but draw no temper, let it be as hard as it will.

If the iron is too hard to be drilled and you can heat the same do so, heat to a low red heat and place a piece of brimstone just where the hole is to be; this will soften the iron through, so the hole can be drilled. Let it cool slowly.

STANDING COULTERS

Standing coulters are made of different materials and of different shapes. Take a piece of iron $2\frac{1}{4} \times \frac{1}{2}$, twenty-eight inches long. Cut off the end after you have thinned it out about 5 inches from the end, cut diagonally. Now weld the cut-off piece to the main shank. The cut-off piece to be laid on the outside and welded, bend the iron as soon as it is welded so that it has the shape of the coulter, draw out a good point and sharpen the iron just the same as if it was a finished coulter. This done, cut off a piece of steel, an old plow lay that is not too much worn will do, cut the shape of the coulter you have now in the iron, and let the steel be half an inch wider than the iron, but on the point let it be as long as it will, because the point ought to be quite long, say about nine inches. Next draw the steel out thin on the upper end, heat the iron red hot, place it on the anvil outside up, put a pinch of borax on it at the heel, then a pinch of steel borings, place the steel on top of this and keep in position with a pair of tongs; now hold it on the fire heel down, and heat slow.

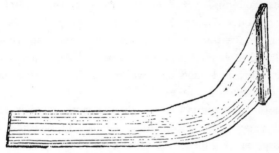

FIG. 10 STANDING COULTER

When it is hot let the helper strike a pressing blow or two on it and it will stick until you have taken the next weld. Put borings and borax between steel and iron for each weld. When finished, the angle should be that of the square; that is, when you place the coulter in the square the shank should follow one end of the square and the foot of the coulter the other. The edge of the outside side should follow the square from the point up. When it does it looks like a hummock in the coulter but it is not. Old breakers will be particular about this as it will cut a clean furrow if it is made in this way and it will work easier. If the edge stands under the square the coulter will wedge the plow out of land and make a poor furrow. Next finish the chisel point, soft or hard steel as you please; weld it to the coulter on the inside, that is, the side next to the furrow.

Last punch or drill the hole in the heel. The coulter should not be hardened except a little on and along the point. There is no need of a double chisel point, such a point will be too clumsy and run heavy. I have received a premium on a coulter made in this shape.

MILL PICKS

Mill picks are very easily dressed and hardened, the whole trick in this case, as in many others, lies in the right heat of the steel. Be careful not to heat to a higher than a red heat. Dress the pick and temper with a low heat, when the color is dark yellow the temper is right, if the steel is of the right kind. No other hardening compound is necessary than water. After a little experience any smith can do this work first class.

A smith once wanted to buy my receipt for tempering. He believed I had a wonderful prescription, or I could not succeed as I did. I told him I used only water, but he insisted that I was selfish and would not reveal it to him.

If tools and receipts would do the work there would be no need of experienced mechanics. Tools and receipts are both necessary, but it must be a skilled hand to apply them.

HARDEN FILES

The best way to harden files is to have a cast iron bucket filled with lead. Heat it until the lead is red hot, then plunge the file into this, handle up. This will give a uniform heat and the file will not warp so easy if the heat is right. In cooling the file off, use a box four or five feet long with salt water in, run the file back and forth endwise, not sideways, that will warp the file, take it out of the water while yet sizzling. Now, if warped, set it between a device so that you can bend it right. While in this position sprinkle water over where you straighten until cold and the file will be right.

HARDEN TAPS AND DIES

Heat the tap or die to a red cherry, cool off entirely in water, brighten with an emery paper. Now, hold over a hot iron until the tap or die has a dark straw color, then cool off. If a light tap, the temper can be drawn over a gaslight, using a blowpipe.

BUTCHER KNIFE

To make a butcher knife, one smith will simply take an old file, shape it into a knife, and harden. The best way to make a knife is to first draw out a piece of iron ¾ inch wide and $\frac{1}{16}$ of an inch thick, twice the length of the knife. Prepare the steel the same width as the iron, $\frac{1}{8}$ of an inch thick, weld this steel in between the iron. This will make a knife that will not break. When ready to harden heat to a low red heat, cool off entirely in water. Brighten and hold over a hot iron until brown, then cool off.

The steel should be good tool steel, a flat file will do, but the cuts must be ground or filed off entirely before you touch it with the hammer, for if the cuts are hammered in they will make cracks in the edge of the knife, and the same will break out.

HOW TO REPAIR CRACKED CIRCULAR SAWS

If a circular saw is cracked it can be repaired so that the crack will go no further, and if the crack is deep, it can be so remedied that there will be no danger in using it. Ascertain the end of the crack, then drill a $\frac{3}{16}$-inch hole so that the crack will end in that hole. Countersink on each side and put in a rivet. Don't let the rivet stick its head over the face of the saw.

If the crack is deep put another rivet about half an inch from the edge. If the saw is too hard to drill, heat two irons about 1 square or round, square up the ends and set the saw between the ends so that they will meet over the place where the hole is to be drilled. When the saw is dark blue, the temper is out. It might be a possibility that this will spring the saw in some cases, therefore, I advise you to try drilling the hole without any change in temper. Prepare a drill that is harder than usual, use no oil, but water.

HOW TO PREVENT A CIRCULAR SAW
FROM CRACKING

The reason why a circular saw cracks is, in most cases, incorrect filing. In filing a saw, never let a flat file with its square corners touch the bottom of the teeth you are filing; if you do, you will make a short cut that will start the crack. The best way is to gum the saw in a saw gummer or on an emery wheel, or use a round-edged file.

HOW TO SEW A BELT

Belts can be riveted, sewed, or hooked together. A new leather belt should not be riveted, because such a belt will stretch and have to be cut out and sewed over quite often at first. There are hooks made of steel for belt sewing, these are all right when the pulleys are not less than six inches in diameter and the speed is slow. In using the hooks be careful not to bend them too sharp or drive the bends together too hard; in so doing they will cut through the leather and pull out. Lacing is the best for all kinds of belts.

In sewing a belt with lacing, first punch with a punch made for this purpose, holes in proportion to the width. Don't punch them too close to the ends. Begin sewing in the center holes and start so that both ends of the lacing will come out on the outside of the belt. Now sew with one end to each side, and be careful not to cross the lacing on the side next to the pulleys. The lacing should be straight on that side. When the belt is sewed punch a small hole a little up in the belt to receive the last end of the lacing; the last end should come out on the outside of the belt. In this end cut a little notch about three-fourths through the lacing close to the belt, and then cut the lacing off a quarter of an inch outside of this notch. This notch will act as a prong and prevent the lacing from pulling out. Tap it lightly with a hammer above the seam to smooth it down.

POINTS ON BELTS

In placing shafts to be connected by belts, care should be taken to get the right working distance one from the other. For smaller belts 12 to 15 feet is about the right distance. For large belts, a greater distance is wanted. The reason for this is that when pulleys are too close together there is no sag in the belts and they must therefore be very tight in order to work.

Belts should not have too much sag, or they will, if the distance between the pulleys is too far apart, produce a great sag and a jerking motion which will be hard on the bearings. Never place one shaft directly over another, for then the belts must be very tight to do the work, and a tight belt will wear quicker and break more often in the lacing than a loose one; besides this the bearings will give out sooner.

If a belt slips use belt oil or resin, or both.

BOB SHOES

In repairing old bob sleds it is difficult to find shoes to suit. But in every case the shoe can be fitted to suit without touching the runner. The trick here as in many other cases in the blacksmith business, lies in the heating. Any shoe can be straightened or bent to fit the runner if only heated right. A low cherry-red heat and a piece of iron to reach from the crooked end of the shoe and far enough back to leave a space between where it wants to be straightened. Now put it in the vise and turn the screws slowly and the shoe will stand a great deal. If too straight, put the shoe in between a couple of beams so that you can bend it back to the right shape. Remember the heat.

I have put on hundreds and never knew of a shoe that broke when the heat was right. I must confess, however, that my two first shoes broke, but I think I learned it cheap when I consider my success after that. The shoe should fit the runner snug. Ironing bobs is a very simple and easy thing, every blacksmith, and even farmers sometimes, are able to iron their own sleds fairly well, and I don't think it will be of much interest for the readers of this book to treat that subject any further.

AXES AND HATCHETS

Dressing axes is quite a trick and few blacksmiths have mastered it. It is comparatively easy when one knows how. I have several times already warned against overheating and if this has been necessary before, it is more so now in this case. In heating an ax do not let the edge rest in the center of the fire, it will then be too hot at the edge before it is hot enough to hammer it out. Place the edge far enough in to let it over the hottest place in the fire. Go slow. When hot, draw it to the shape of a new axe, don't hammer on one side only. In so doing the ax will be flat on one side and curved up on the other. If uneven, trim it off; trim the sides also if too wide; don't heat it over the eye; be sure you have it straight. When ready to harden, heat to a low red heat and harden in lukewarm water. The heat should be only brown if it is a bright sunny day. Brighten and look for the temper. You will notice that the temper runs uneven; it goes out to the corners first, therefore dip them (the corners) deeper when cooling, and with a wet rag touch the place on the edge where the temper wants to run out. Some smiths, when hardening, will smear the ax with tallow instead of brightening it, and hold it over the fire until the tallow catches fire, then cool it off. This is guess work, and the ax is soft in one place and too hard in another. The best way is to brighten the ax and you can see the temper, then there is no guess work about it. When blue, cool it partly off, and then while the ax is still wet you will observe under the water or through the water a copper color. This color will turn blue as soon as the ax is dry, and it is the right color and temper. Cool it slowly, don't cool it off at once, but let it cool gradually, and it will be both hard and tough.

By this simple method I have been very successful, breaking only three percent, while no new ax of any make will ever do better than ten percent. Some will even break at the rate of twelve and thirteen percent.

The ax factories, with all their skill and hardening compounds, have to do better yet to compete with me and my simple method.

WELL DRILLS

Well drills are made of different sizes and kinds. Club bits and Z bits. How to dress: heat to a low red heat. If nicked or broken, cut out, otherwise draw it out to the size wanted. The caliper should touch the lips of the bit when measured diagonally so that the bit has the size on all corners. Heat to a low red heat and harden, the temper to be from dark straw color to blue according to the kind of drilling to be done. The trick, in two words, low heat.

GRANITE TOOLS

By granite tools is meant tools or chisels used by granite or marble workers for cutting inscriptions on tombstones.

When a man understands how these tools are used it is easier to prepare them. These are the kind of tools where an unusual hardness is required. The hammer used in cutting with this chisel is very small, and the blow would not hurt your nose, so light it is, therefore they will stand a high heat and temper. The chisels should be very thin for this work. When dressed and ready to harden, heat to a red heat and harden in the following solution: one gallon soft water, four ounces salt. Draw the temper to a straw color.

A blacksmith once paid a high price for a receipt for hardening granite tools. The receipt was, aqua, one gallon; chloride of sodium, four ounces. This receipt he kept as a secret and the prepared compound he bought at the drug store, thus paying 50 cents for one gallon of water and four ounces of salt. The real worth is less than a cent. It is said he succeeded remarkably well with his great compound, which he kept in a jug and only used when anything like granite tools were to be hardened. The reason why he succeeded so well was because of his ignorance concerning his compound, not because it was not good enough. I hold that it is one of the best compounds, in fact, the best he could get. People in general like to be humbugged. If they only get something new or something they don't know anything about, then they think it wonderful.

Salt and water should be called salt and water, and be just as much valued. Let us "call a spade a spade," the spade will not be more useful by another name, nor will it be less useful by calling it by its proper name.

CHAPTER III

WAGON WHEEL AND AXLE REPAIRING

When vehicles were first used is hard to tell, but we know that they have been used for thousands of years before the Christian era. It is easy to imagine how they looked at that time, when we know how half-civilized people now make wagons. The first vehicle was only a two-wheeled cart called chariot. Such chariots were used in war and that it was a case of "great cry and little wool" is certain.

The blacksmith used to be the wagon and carriage maker. Now it is only a rare case when a blacksmith makes a carriage, and when it happens most of the parts are bought. In 1565 the first coach was made in England.

Now there are hundreds of factories making wagons and carriages and parts of them for repair use by blacksmiths and wagon makers. It is no use for any blacksmith or wagon maker to compete with these factories. We have neither the means nor the facilities to do it, and have to be content with the repairs they need. The most important repairs are the setting of tire, welding, and setting axle stubs.

SETTING TIRE

Wagon tire is often set so that more harm than good is done to the wheel.

In setting tire the first thing to do is to mark the tire. Many blacksmiths set tires without marking the tire. This is poor work. In order to do a good job the tire should be set so that it is in the same place it had. There are generally some uneven places in the fellows and when the tire is set the first time, it is hot all around and will settle down in these low places. Now, if the tire is not marked and set back in its exact bed, it will soon work loose again, and it is liable to dish the wheel too much as it don't sink into its place, but is held up in some places. Another thing, when a tire is worn so that it becomes thin it will settle down on the outside, especially when the wheel is much dished. Now if you reverse the tire it will only touch the fellow on the inner edge of the wheel, and leave an open space between the fellow and the tire on the outside. When a wheel has bolts every smith knows that it will make trouble for him if he don't get the tire back where it was. In every case take a file or a chisel and cut a mark in the tire near to the fellow plates; cut also a light mark in the fellow. These marks are to be on the inside of the wheel: 1) because it will not be seen on that side, and 2) because in putting the tire on, the wheel should be placed with that side up. If there are nails in the tire cut them off with a thin chisel so that it will not mark the fellow, or drive them into the fellow with a punch. Next, measure the wheel with the gauge (the wheel is supposed to be right, not fellow bound nor any spokes loose in the tenon). This done, heat the tire and shrink it. If the wheel is straight give it half an inch draw, sometimes even five-eighths if the wheel is heavy and strong. But if the wheel is poor and dished, do not give it more than one-fourth-inch draw. One tire only with a little draw can be heated in the forge, but if there is more than one tire, heat them outside in a fire made for this purpose, or in a tire heater.

There are different ways of cooling the tire. Some smiths have a table in a tank; they place the wheel on the table and with a lever sink both wheel and tire in the water. There are many objections to this. 1) You will have to soak the whole wheel; 2) it is inconvenient to put the tire on; 3) in order to set the tire right, it is necessary to reach the tire from both sides with the hammer; and 4) when spokes have a tendency to creep out, or when the wheel is much dished, the wheel should be tapped with the hammer over the spokes. Now, to be able to perform all these moves, one must have, first, a table; this table to be about twelve inches high and wide enough to take any wheel, with a hole in the center to receive the hub. On one side you may make a hook that will fall over the wheel and hold the tire down while you get it on. Close to this table have a box 5½ feet long, 12 inches wide and 12 inches deep. On each side bolt a piece of two by six about three feet long. In these planks cut notches in which you place an iron rod, run through the hub. On this rod the wheel will hang. The notches can be made so that any sized wheel will just hang down enough to cover the tire in the water. In this concern you can give the wheel a whirl and it will turn so swift that there will be water all around the tire. It can be stopped at any time and the tire set right, or the spokes tapped. With these accommodations and four helpers I have set six hundred hay rake wheels in nine and one-half hours. This was in a factory where all the tires were welded and the wheels ready so that it was nothing but to heat the tires and put them on. I had three fires with twelve tires in each fire. An artesian well running through the water box kept the water cool.

If the fire is not hot enough to make it expand, a tire puller is needed. A tire puller can be made in many ways and of either wood or iron. Buggy tire is more particular than wagon tire and there are thousands of buggy wheels spoiled every year by poor or careless blacksmiths. In a buggy tire one-eighth of an inch draw is the most that it will stand, while most wheels will stand only one-sixteenth. If the wheel is badly dished don't give it any draw at all, the tire should then measure the same as the wheel, the heat in the tire is enough.

If the wheel is fellow-bound cut the fellows to let them down on the spokes.

If the spokes are loose on the tenon wedge them up tight.

BACK-DISHED WHEEL

For a back-dished wheel a screw should be used to set the wheel right. Place the wheel on the table front side up. Put wood blocks under the fellow to raise the wheel up from the table. Place a two by four over the hole under the table; have a bolt long enough to reach through the two by four and up through the hub, a piece of wood over the hub for the bolt to go through; screw it down with a tail nut. When the wheel is right, put the tire on. The tire for such a wheel should have more draw than for a wheel that is right.

If a buggy wheel has been dished it can be helped a little without taking the tire off. Place the wheel on the anvil so that the tire will rest against the anvil. Don't let the tire rest lengthwise on the anvil. If you do, the tire will be bent out of shape when you begin to hammer on it. Use the least surface possible of the anvil and hammer on the edge of the tire; the stroke of the hammer to be such that the blow will draw the tire out from the fellow. A tire too tight can be remedied this way.

When bolting a wheel the tire will be out of place unless the tire has been shrunk alike on both sides of the fellow plates. A smith used to setting tires will be able to get the holes almost to a perfect fit. If a tire is too short, don't stretch it with a sharp fuller that will cut down into the tire; when the tire is a little worn it will break in this cut. Draw it out with a wide fuller and smooth it down with the hammer. If it is much too short, weld in a piece. This is easily done. Take a piece of iron ¼-inch thick, the width of the tire and the length needed, say about three inches. Taper the ends and heat it to a red heat. Place it on the tire in the fire and weld. This will give material for stretching.

If the wheel has a strong back dish it cannot be set right to stay with the tire alone, as a bump against the fellow is apt to throw the dish back. It is therefore safer in all back-dished wheels to take the spokes out of the hole and set them right by wedges in the end of the spokes. These wedges should not be driven from outside in but be placed in the end of the spoke so that they will wedge into the spoke when the same is driven back into its place. Use glue.

HOW TO PUT ON NEW TIRE

When you have the bar of either steel or iron for the tire, first see if it is straight, if not sure to make it. Next place the tire on the floor and place the wheel on top of the tire. Begin in such a way that the end of the fellow will be even with the end of the tire Now roll the wheel over the tire. If a heavy tire, cut it three inches longer than the wheel; if a thin tire, two inches. Now bend the tire in the bender. Measure the wheel with the gauge, then measure the tire; if it is a heavy wagon tire and a straight wheel, cut the tire one-fourth of an inch shorter than the wheel. If it is a buggy tire, cut it the size of the wheel. In welding these tires they will shorten enough to be the size wanted.

HOW TO WELD TIRES

There are many different ideas practiced in welding tires. One smith will narrow both ends before welding; another will cut the edges off after it is welded. This is done to prevent it from spreading or getting too wide over the weld. I hold that both these ideas are wrong. The first one is wrong because when the ends are narrowed down it is impossible to make them stay to-gether until the weld is taken, especially if it is a narrow tire. The second idea is wrong because it cuts off the best part of the weld and weakens it. Some smiths will split the tires, others will rivet them together. This is done to hold the tire in place until it has been welded. There is no need of this trouble, but for a new beginner a rivet is all right.

I shall now give my experience in welding tire, and as this experience has been in a factory where thousands of wheels are made yearly, I suppose it will be worth something to the reader.

When the tire is ready to weld, draw down the ends and let them swell as much as they want to. Now let the helper take the end that is to lay on top and pull it towards the floor, the other end to rest on the anvil. This will give that end a tendency to press itself steadily against the lower end. Next, place this end on top of the other end. The ends must now be hot enough to allow them to be shaped. You will now notice that the top end is wider than the tire, so is the lower end. The tire is to be so placed that the swelled parts reach over and inside of each other a little. Now give a couple of blows right over the end of the under tire. Next tap the swelled sides down over the tire. This will hold the tire together so that it cannot slip to either side, and the swelled end of the under tire will prevent it from pulling out. If the top end has been so bent that it has a tendency to press down and out a little, the tire will now be in a good shape to weld.

Before you put the tire into the fire, let me remind you of what I have said before about the fire. Many blacksmiths are never able to weld a tire tight on the outside because of a poor, low, and unclean fire. If the fire is too old or too fresh it will not give a good heat for welding tire. If you have a good big fire high up from the tuyer, then you are all right. Place your tire in the fire and proceed as follows: No matter whether it is an iron or soft steel tire, sand is the best welding compound and nothing else should be used; but if you lose the first heat then borax might be used as it will prevent the tire from scaling and burning. When you have the right heat, place the tire on the anvil this way; let the tire rest against the inside edge of the anvil. If the lower end of the tire is allowed to come down on the anvil, it will cool off and can never be welded that way. Now hold the tire this way until you have the hammer ready to give the first blow. Then let the tire down and strike the first blows directly on top and over the end of the under end. This is important and if the first blows are not directed to this very place, the lower end will be too cool to weld when you get to it. Next weld down the upper end; this done turn the tire on edge and while it is in a welding heat come down on it heavy with hammer, if a buggy tire, and with a sledge and hammer if a heavy wagon tire. Hammer it down until it is considerably narrower over the weld as it will swell out when dressed down. This way the weld has all the material in the iron and the lapped lips will help hold the weld together. A very poor smith can weld tires to stay in this manner. The edges should be rounded off with the hammer and filed to make the tire look the same over the weld as in the iron. If there should be any trouble to weld a steel tire, place a little steel borings over the weld and use borax.

A blacksmith in Silver Lake, Minn., working for a wagon maker of that place, when welding a tire failed entirely after half a dozen attempts, and he got so angry that he threw the tire down on the floor with all his might. It happened to crush the wagon maker's big toe. This was more than the otherwise good-natured man could stand, and instantly the smith was seen hurled through an open window — the wagon maker attached. Result: separation and law suit. All this because the smith had not read my book.

When a light buggy tire is to be set mistakes are often made in measuring the tire. The tire is too light in itself to resist the pressure of the gauge. The smith tries to go it light and if there is not the same pressure in measuring the tire there was in measuring the wheel, it will not give the same results; and when the tire is put on it is either too tight or too loose. I worked for many years on a tool to hold the tire steady in order to overcome this trouble. The only device that I have ever seen for this purpose before is, the anvil close up to the forge, one side of the tire on the forge, the other on the anvil. This arrangement would crowd the smith, roast his back and expose him to ridicule, but it will not help to ruin the tire.

The tool I invented is a tire holder made of cast iron. It consists of a standard or frame with a shank in to fit in the square hole in the anvil; in the standard is a slot hole from the bottom up. On the back of the standard are cogs on both sides of the slot hole. Through this goes a clutch hub with cogs in to correspond with the cogs in the standard. On the outside of the standard is an eccentric lever. Through this lever is a tapered hole to fit over the clutch hub. This lever is tapered so that it will fit different thicknesses, while the cogs and eccentric lever will adjust it to different widths. This device is so cheap that any smith can afford to have it. See Fig. 11.

TIRE IN SECTIONS

Many of us remember the time when tires were made in sections and nailed on. At this time the wheels were more substantially made, because the tire could not be set as tight as it is now, and the wheel had to be made so that it would stand the

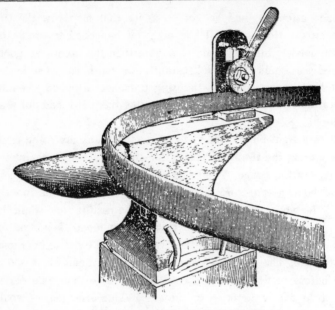

FIG. 11 HOLMSTROM TIRE HOLDER

usage almost independent of the tire. Our endless tire is a great
improvement over the tires made in sections. The wagon tires as
they are made now are, I think, as near right as they can be, in
regard to size of iron, in proportion to the wheel. But it is different with buggy tires. I hold that they are all made too light to
be of any protection to the fellows. I understand the reason why
they are made this way, but if a man wants a light rig, let that
be the exception and not the rule. Tire should not be less than
one-fourth of an inch thick for seven-eighths wide, and five-
sixteenths for an inch wide and over. See Fig. 12.

EXPANSION OF THE TIRE

A tire four feet in diameter will expand two inches and a
quarter, or three-sixteenths of an inch to the foot. Steel tire
expands less. This is the expansion of red heat. If heated less
it expands less, but it is no trouble to make the tire expand for
all the draw it needs.

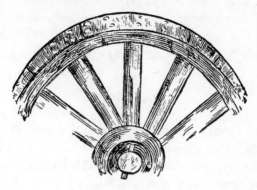

FIG. 12

A furnace for tire heating comes handy in cities where there is no chance for making a fire outside, but every smith that has room for a fire outside will do better to heat the tire that way. Don't build a tire-heating furnace in the shop if wood is to be used for fuel, because the heat and smoke will turn in your face as soon as the doors of the furnace are opened.

WELDING AXLES

When a worn buggy axle is to be stubbed, proceed as follows: First, measure the length of the old axle. For this purpose take a quarter inch rod of iron, bend a square bend about an inch long on one end. With this rod measure from the end of the bearing, that is, let the hook of your rod catch against the shoulder at the end where the thread begins, not against the collars, for they are worn, nor should you measure from the end of the axle, for the threaded part is not of the same length. Now place your stub on the end of the axle and mark it where you want to cut it off. Cut the axle one-fourth inch longer than it should be when finished. Next heat the ends to be welded and upset them so that they are considerably thicker over the weld; lap the ends like No. 1, Fig. 6, weld and use sand, but if the ends should not be welded very well, then use borax. These stubs are made of soft steel, and will stand a higher heat than tool steel, but remember it is steel. If the ends have been upset enough they will have stock enough to draw down on, and be of the right length. If this is rightly done one cannot tell where the weld is. Set the axle by the gauge, if you have one, if not, by the wheels.

AXLE GAUGE

A gauge to set axles can be made in this way: When you have set an axle by the wheels so that it is right, take a piece of iron 1¼ × ¼, six feet long, bend a foot on this about six inches long, with a leg on the other end. See No. 5, Fig. 13. The leg to be movable, set either with a wedge or a set screw to fit for wide and narrow track. The gauge to be set against the bottom side of the axle. The pitch to be given a set of buggy wheels should

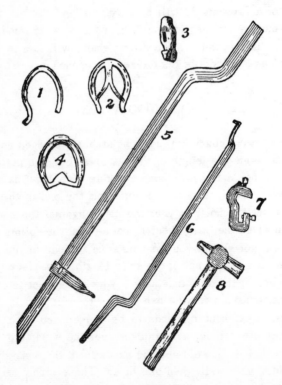

FIG. 13

be from one to one and one-half inches. I would recommend one and a half inches. This will be enough to insure a plumb spoke when the vehicle is loaded. It will also insure safety to the rider from mud slinging. By pitch I mean that the wheels are one and a half inches wider at the upper rim than they are down at the ground. Every smith ought to have a gauge of this kind. It is easy to make and it saves a lot of work, as there is no use of the wheels being put on and an endless measuring in order to get the axle set right.

GATHER GAUGE

By gather I mean that the wheels should be from one-fourth to one-half of an inch wider back than in front. Don't misunderstand me now. I don't mean that the hind wheels should be wider than the front wheels. I mean that a wheel should have a little gather in front, as they are inclined to spread and throw the bearing on the nut, while, if they have a little gather, they will run right, and have a tendency to throw the bearing on the collars of the axle. If they do they will run more steady, especially when the axle is a little worn.

A gauge for this purpose can be made like in Fig. 13, No. 6. This gauge is to be fitted to the front side of the axle when you make it. It can be made of 1 × ¼ about three feet long, the forked end to reach the center of the axle. With these two gauges axles can be set right without the wheels.

CHAPTER IV

HOW TO MAKE PLOWSHARES

There are two kinds of shares: lip shares and bar shares, and they must be treated differently. We will first treat of bar shares. The first thing to do when a plow is brought for a new lay is to look over the condition of the landside. By landside is meant the bar to which the share is welded. Now if this bar is worn down so that you think it too weak to stand for a new share, then make a new one.

HOW TO MAKE A LANDSIDE

For a 14-inch plow take $2\frac{1}{2} \times \frac{3}{8}$, or $2\frac{1}{2} \times \frac{7}{16}$. For a 16-inch plow, use $2\frac{1}{2} \times \frac{7}{16}$, or $3 \times \frac{7}{16}$ common iron. Cut the iron diagonally at the point. This will prepare a point on each side of the cut; that is, you had better cut out two landsides at a time. But if you do not want to do that, then cut the iron off square. Next take a piece of common iron $3 \times \frac{1}{4}$, 13 inches long for a shin; cut this diagonally, and it will make shins for two. Some plow factories use steel for shins, but that is not necessary, for it will not make the plowshare any better, but, on the other hand, will be quite a bother when you want to drill a hole for a fin-coulter if it is hardened. Place this shin on the land side of the landside, and weld. In preparing the shoulder of the shin for the plate use a ship upsetter. See Fig. 13, No. 3.

Not one out of 500 blacksmiths have this tool. Every smith should have one. You cannot do a good and quick job without it.

When you shape the point of the landside hold it vertical, that is, the edge straight up and down, or plumb. If you don't do this, there will be trouble in welding, especially if you have held it under. Then it will lean under the square when welded, and in such a case it is hard to get a good weld, and if you do, you will break it up when you attempt to set it to the square. Another thing, don't make much slant on the landside up at the joint, for, if you do, you can never weld the share good up there. Give more slant towards the point. Be sure to have the right curve. It is very important to have the landside right: 1) Because it is the foundation for the plow; 2) if the landside is right, the start is right, and then there is no trouble to get the share right. When finished place the old landside on top of the new, with the upper edges even; don't go by the bottom edges, as they are worn. Now mark the hole. You may leave the front hole for the foot of the beam this time. When holes are drilled, then put a bolt through the hole of the foot of beam and landside; now place the plow on the landside and measure 14 inches from the floor up to the beam. In this position mark the front hole of the foot of the beam. If the beam has been sprung up you will now have remedied that. So much about a new landside. On the other side, if the old landside is not too much worn to be used, then repair as follows: Take a piece of $\frac{3}{8}$-inch thick flat iron the width of the landside about ten inches long. Cut one end off diagonally, this end to be flattened down. Why should this end be cut diagonally? This piece of iron is to be placed on the inner side of the landside and as far back as to cover the hole that holds the plate. Now, if this iron is cut square off, and left a little too thick on that end, it will cut into the landside and weaken it; but if cut diagonally and drawn out thin it will not weaken, nor can it break when cut in this manner. To be sure of a good strong weld, upset over the weld. I hold that this is the most important thing in making a new lay. "No hoof, no horse" — no landside, no plow. There are only a few blacksmiths recognizing this fact. Most of the smiths will simply take a piece of iron about half an inch square and weld it on top of the point. This is the quickest way, but it is also the poorest way, but they cannot very well do it in any other way, for if you have no shin upsetter to dress and shape the shoulder for the plate, then it is quite a job to repair any other way. There are three reasons why a landside cannot be repaired with a patch on top of the point: 1) The shin or shoulder is an old landside is worn down sometimes to almost nothing, and the only way to get stock enough to make a good shoulder is to put a good-sized piece of iron on the inside, back and behind this shoulder. If a new plate is to be put on and this is not done, you will have to draw down the plate to the thickness of the old shoulder, and in such a case the plate will add no strength to the share. 2) The landside is, in many cases, worn down on the bottom to a thin, sharp edge, and by placing the piece on top the landside will be as it was on the bottom side, where it ought to be as thick as you can make it. 3) The weakest place in the landside is just at the shoulder of the shin, and by placing the piece on top it will not reach over this weak place, and with a new long point on, the strain will be heavier than before, and the landside will either bend or break. I have in my experience had thousands of plows that have been broken or bent on account of a poorly-repaired landside. Blacksmiths, with only a few exceptions, are all making this mistake.

The landside is to the plow what the foundation is to the house. No architect will ever think of building a substantial house without a solid foundation. No practical plowsmith will ever try to make a good plow without a solid landside.

For prairie or brush breakers, where no plate is used, it will be all right to repair the landside by placing a piece of iron on top of it, provided it is not much worn, and the patch reaches back far enough to strengthen the landside. But even in such cases it is better to lay it on the inner side.

LANDSIDE POINT FOR SLIPSHARE

We have now learned how to prepare the landside for a solid or long bar share. We shall now learn how to make a landside point for slipshares. There are smiths that will take the old worn-out stub of a slipshare point, weld a piece to it, and then weld the share on. This is very ridiculous and silly. There is nothing left in such a point to be of any use. Make a new one;

be sure to make it high enough — at least half an inch higher than the share is to be when finished. This will give you material to weld down on. If the landside is not high enough the share will be lower — that is, the joint of the lay will be lower than the joint of the mouldboard, and it should be the other way. On this point many an old smith and every beginner makes mistakes, and not only in this case, but in everything else. Whatever you have to make, be sure to have stock enough to work down on, and you will be all right. It is better to have too much than not enough.

FIG. 14 PLOW OF 200 YEARS AGO

In shaping the point remember to hold it perpendicular, and give very little slant up at the joint, but more towards the point. If too much slant up at the joint there will be difficulty in welding it. Remember this. Don't make the point straight like a wedge; if you do, the share will be above the frog. Give it the same circle it had, and the share will rest solid on the frog. This is another important point to remember: The lay will not have the full strength if it don't rest on the frog, and it will not be steady, and the plow will not run good, for in a few days the share flops up and down.

When a 14-inch share is finished the point, from the joint of the share to the extreme end of the point, should be 11 inches, not longer, and for a 16-inch lay, 12 inches, not longer. The point acts as a lever on the plow, and if it is too long, the plow will not work good, and it is liable to break. Shape the point so that when you hold it up against the plow it will be in line with the bottom of the landside, but about half an inch wider than the landside to weld on. If it is a plow where the point of the mouldboard rests on the landside point, and it is a double shin, then cut out in the landside point for the point of the mouldboard to rest in. See Fig. 15, No. 1. This will be a guide for you when

welding the share, and it will slip onto the plow easier when
you come to fit it to the same. I think enough has been said
about the landside to give the beginner a good idea of how to
make one. And if the landside is right, it comes easier to do the
rest. In making a plowshare there are many things to remember,
and one must be on the alert right along, for it will give lots of
trouble if any point is overlooked.

FIG. 15

We will now weld a share to a long bar landside. The landside having been finished and bolted to the beam of its foot,
or to a standard, the share is to be shaped to fit. Hold the share
up to the plow. First look if the angle for the point is right in
the share; if not, heat the share, and if under the angle wanted,
upset up at the joint; if over the angle wanted, drive it back at
the point. In doing this hold the edge of the share over a wooden
block instead of the anvil, so as not to batter the thin edge of
the share. If the share has been upset so that it has a narrow
rib along the point where it is to be welded, draw this down and
make it level. In most blank shares the point should be raised to
fit the landside point, so that when the same is placed on the
floor, the edge of the share will follow the floor or leveling
block (if you have it), from the heel right up to the point, then
it will be easy to make the edge come down to the square in
finishing it up. If this is not done the edge of the share from the
throat back will generally be too high.

In Fig. 15 two shares are represented, one with the landside point on ready for welding. In this share the point of the same has been raised so that the share comes down to the square in the throat. The other is a blank share, straight in the point between Nos. 4 and 5, resting on the extreme heel and point with gap between the edge of share and floor at No. 3. In most blank shares the point is too straight, and the point too much bent down at No. 4. Bend the share so that the whole length from heel to point will follow the floor. When the share is held in a position as shown in this cut, don't fit the share to the brace, for in most old plows the brace has been bent out of shape. Fit the share to the square, and then fit the brace to the share, and you are right. Many a blacksmith will never think of this, but it is important.

Next, joint the share; that is, if the joint does not fit the joint of the mouldboard, make it fit either by filing or grinding. This done, make the holes, and when you center-punch for same, draw the holes a trifle; that means, make the center-mark a little towards the inner side of the mark, especially for the hole next to the point. This is also an important point overlooked by most blacksmiths. The holes that hold the joints together should act as a wedge. If they don't, the joints will pull apart and leave a gap between, where dirt and straw will gather, and if a slipshare, the share will soon work loose and the plow will flop.

The holes having been punched and countersunk, the share should be bolted to the brace. Next put on the clamp. It is not necessary that the clamp should be put on while the share is on the plow. I never do that. I used to for many years, but there is no need of doing it, for if the share has the right angle it must come to its place when even with the point on the outside, and a cut should be made in the landside just at the place where the point of the mouldboard rests on same, this cut will also be a guide.

Now a few words concerning the clamp. Figure 13, No. 7 illustrates a clamp for this purpose. The set screw at the bottom serves to hold the landside from leaning over or under, while the setscrew at the upper end holds the share against the point.

If this clamp is rightly made it works splendid. The clamp should
be placed over the plowshare up at the joint, because the first
heat or weld should be on the point. Some smiths — well, for a
fact, most smiths — take the first weld up at the joint. This is
wrong. The point should be welded first. Then you have a chance
to set the share right and fit it snug to the point the whole way
up. You cannot make a good weld if the share does not fit snug
against the landside point, to prevent air and cinders from play-
ing between. Further, the share should be upset over the weld,
when this is not done in the blank share; the lower corner of the
share will protrude over the landside. This should be dressed
down smooth. The next weld should be taken up at the joint.
For welding compound use steel borings and scales from either
steel or iron.

After you have moistened the place where the weld is to be
taken with borax, then fill in between the share and point with
steel borings, and on top of this a little steel or iron scales.
Do not buy any welding compound of any kind, because if you
learn to know what you have in the shop you will find that there
never was a welding compound made to excel borax, steel
scales, steel or iron borings, and powdered glass. All these
you have without buying.

In heating go slow. If you put on too strong blast, the share
will burn before the iron is hot enough to weld. When ready to
weld let your helper take with a pair of tongs over the share and
landside to hold them tight together while you strike the first
blow. Use a large hammer and strike with a pressure on the
hammer the first blows, until you are sure it sticks; then come
down on it with force.

I have made it a practice, no matter how good this weld
seems to be, to always take a second weld. This weld to be a
light one. The share and landside are after the first weld settled,
so it takes very little to weld them then. On the other hand, the
first weld might look to all appearances solid, but it is not
always. With this precaution I never had a share that ripped
open in the weld, while it is a rare thing to find a share made
by a blacksmith that does not rip. Now then, weld down toward

the point. The point should not be allowed to have any twist, for if it does, it will turn the plow over on the side. Now set the edge right, beginning at the heel. If the share is made for hard fall plowing give more suction than for a share for soft spring plowing. Grind and polish before you harden, and after it is hardened touch it up lightly with the polish wheel. Much polishing or grinding after hardening will wear off the case hardening.

SLIPSHARE

We shall now weld a slipshare. When the point is finished, hold it to the plow with a pair of tongs while you fit the share. When the share is fitted take the point off from the plow and fasten it to the share with the clamp. As I have said before, there is no need of fastening the share to the landside point with the plow as a guide. If the landside and share are right there cannot be any mistake, and it comes easier to screw them together over the anvil. Now proceed as with a long bar share, and when the weld up at the joint has been taken, fit the share to the plow while hot. Some smiths in preparing the landside point for a slipshare will place the share so that the point is a little too short back where it rests against the end of the plate. This is a bad idea. It is claimed that, in welding, the landside point will swell enough to make it reach up against the plate. This is true, if the landside point is only high enough; but if it is low and you lose a heat in welding, as most smiths do, then your landside point will be both too low and too short. Thousands of shares are made every year that have this fault. Therefore, whatever you are doing, have stock enough. It is easy to cut off from the landside while yet hot, but it is difficult to repair if too short. No share will work steadily if the point does not rest right against the plate.

In blacksmithing, every beginner, and many an old smith, makes the mistake of providing less stock than is needed for the work to be done. It is essential to have material to dress down on; and if a heat is lost, or a weld, it will make the stock in the article weaker, and to meet these exigencies there must be material from the start, enough for all purposes. There is also a wide difference of opinion as to whether the share should be welded at the point or at the joint first. While I was yet a young man and employed in a plow factory, I had an opportunity to see the different ideas set to a test. In the factory the practice was to weld the point first. A plowman from another state was engaged, and he claimed that it would be better to weld the share

FIG. 16

first up at the joint. He was given a chance to prove his assertion, and the result was that 3 percent of his shares broke over the inner side of the landside at the joint in the hardening, and 10 percent ripped up in the weld at the same place. These are results that will always follow this method.

The first, because the share was not upset over the weld; the second, because a good weld cannot be taken unless the share is dressed down snug against the point when hot. As far as the number of shares welded per day was concerned, this man was not in it. Still, this man was a good plowman, and was doing better than I ever saw a man with this idea do before. For it is a fact, that out of one thousand plowshares welded by country blacksmiths, nine hundred and ninety will rip up. I have been in different states, and seen more than many have of this kind of work, but, to tell the truth, there is no profession or trade where there is so much poor work done as in blacksmithing, and especially in plow work. Blacksmiths often come to me, even from other states, to learn my ideas of making plowshares. On inquiring, I generally find that they weld a piece on the top of the old landside and proceed to weld without touching the share or trying to fit it at all.

CHAPTER V

PLOWSHARE HARDENING, POINTING, SHARPENING, AND SETTING

If the share is of soft center steel, harden as follows: First, heat the whole point to a very low red heat; then turn the share face down, with the heel over the fire, and the point in such a position that it is about two inches higher than the heel. This will draw the fire from the heel along towards the point, and the whole length of the share will be heated almost in one heat. Be sure to get an even heat, for it will warp or crack if the heat is uneven. When the share has a moderate red heat take it out, and you will notice that it is sprung up along the edge. This is the rule, but there are exceptions, and the share is then sprung down. In either case set it right; if sprung up set it down a little under the square; if sprung down set it a little over the square. You cannot with any success set it by a table or leveling block, because this will, first, cool off the edge, second, it must be either over or under the square a little. Therefore, you must use your eye and set the share with the hammer over the anvil. This done, hold the share over the fire until it has a low red heat, as stated before; then plunge it into a tub of hardening compound, such as is sold by the traveling man, or sprinkle the share with prussiate of potash and plunge it into a barrel of salt water.

You will notice that the share will warp or spring out of shape more in the heating than it does in the cooling, if the heat is right. Some smiths never look at the share when hot for hardening, but simply plunge it into the tub, and then they say it warped in hardening, while it was in the heating. If the share is too hot it will warp in cooling also.

HOW TO POINT A SHARE

Points are now sold by dealers in hardware, and every smith knows how they are shaped. There is, however, no need of buying these; every smith has old plowshares from which points can be cut, provided you don't use an old share too much worn. The points sold are cut with the intention that most of the point is to be placed on top of the plow point. This is all right in some instances, while it is wrong in others. When you cut a piece for a point make it the same shape at both ends. Now, when a plow needs the most of the point on top, bend the end to be on top longer than the end to go underneath, and vice versa, when the point wants to be heaviest on the bottom side. I hold that in ordinary cases the most of the point should be on the bottom side. If it is, it will wear better and keep in the ground longer, for as soon as the point is worn off underneath it comes out of the ground.

FIG. 17   JAPANESE PLOW

Don't monkey with old mower sections or anything like them for points, for, although the material is good, it is not the quality alone but also the quantity that goes to make up a good point. It takes only a few hours' plowing to wear off a section from the extreme point of the share, and then there is only the iron of the plow point left to wear against, and your time spent for such a point is lost. Another thing, it takes just as much time to put on such a point as it does to put on a good one for which you charge the regular price.

In putting on a point of thin material you must go unusually slow, or you will burn the steel before the plow point is hot.

Smiths, as a rule, draw out a round back point. They seem to be afraid of coming down on the point with the hammer for fear it will spring the point towards the land. This can be remedied by using a wooden block for anvil. Then you can set the point back without battering the edge of the share. The such of a point should be one-eighth of an inch. Don't split the steel of

FIG. 18 BENCH FOR HOLDING PLOWS WITHOUT BEAM

the point of a share open and wedge a point in. Make one long enough to reach around the point, say from 8 to 10 inches long, and you will have a good substantial job. There is too much experimenting in putting on points yet, but the method just described is the only good one.

HOW TO SHARPEN A PLOWSHARE

If the share to be sharpened is a hardened share, and it is the first time it is sharpened, then be careful not to heat it too far towards the joint, so as to leave the temper as much the same as possible. For my part, I never follow this rule. I heat it as much as is needed to draw it out good, and then harden it over again. But beginners can sharpen a new share once without hardening it over, if the temper is not entirely out of the share.

To sharpen a share without springing it some is an impossibility. No device will prevent this, and the only way to set it right is to heat it all over. In sharpening a share it is drawn out on one side, and it is natural that that side is made longer, and as a result the share must warp. In a circular saw it takes only a couple of blows on one side to get it out of shape; then what else can we expect in a plowshare, when all the hammering is done on one side?

Some smiths turn the bottom side of the share up and hammer on that side, but this is wrong; first, because in so doing you unshape the share; second, the scales on the anvil will mark the face of the share just as bad as the hammer, so nothing is gained by this. Place the share on the anvil, face up, and use a hammer with a big round face, and when you get used to this, the best result is obtained. Don't draw the edge out too thin. There is no need of a thin edge on a plow that has to cut gravel and snags, but for sod breaking a thin edge is wanted, and the smith has to use his best judgment even in such a case.

HOW TO PUT ON A HEEL

Cut a piece of steel about eight inches long, three inches wide on one end, and pointed down to a sharp point on the other. Draw out one side thin to nothing. Next, draw out the heel of the share. Now place the heel piece on the bottom side of the share, and hold it in place with a pair of tongs and tong rings. Take the first heat at the pointed end of the piece, next heat at the heel, share down, then turn the share over, heel down; go slow, use borax freely, and place a little steel borings between the heel piece and the share. After a little practice almost any smith ought to be able to put on a heel, while now it is only a few smiths that can do it. I never put on a heel yet but the owner of the plow would tell me that other smiths tell him it cannot be done. When welded good be sure to get the right shape in the share. Grind and polish carefully, as the dirt is inclined to stick to the share in this place more easily than in any other.

HOW TO REPAIR A FLOPPING PLOW

When a plow is flopping or going everywhere so that the owner don't know what is the matter, the fault should be looked for first in the beam. If the beam is loose the plow will not run steady, but the reason for this trouble, in most cases, is in the share. If the point has too little "suction," and the edge of the share is too much rolling, the plow generally acts this way. To remedy this, sharpen the share, set the point down, and the edge of the lay from the point all the way back to the heel, and the plow will work right.

HOW TO SET A PLOW RIGHT THAT TIPS ON ONE SIDE

If a plow is inclined to fall over on the right handle, the fault is in the share. The share in such a case has too much suction along the edge. Heat the whole share and roll the edge of it up, and the plow will work all right.

If a plow tips over on the left side handle, the share in such a case is too much rolled up. Heat it all over and set the edge down to give it more suction.

WHEN A PLOW RUNS TOO DEEP

There are two reasons for a plow running too deep: 1) If the beam is more than fourteen inches high from the floor up to the lower side of it, then the beam should be heated over a place as far back as possible, and the same set down to its proper place. 2) If the point of the share has too much suction the plow will also run too deep. The right suction to give a plowshare is from $\frac{1}{8}$ to $\frac{3}{16}$ of an inch. If a plow don't run deep enough with this much as a draw, there must be something else out of shape; or, if it goes too deep, the fault must be looked for in the beam or in the tugs with small-sized horses. The point of a share should never be bent upwards in order to prevent the plow from going too deep. Set the share right, and if the plow then goes out of its proper way the fault must be found somewhere else.

WHEN A PLOW TAKES TOO MUCH LAND

If a 14-inch plow takes too much land the fault is either in the point of the share or in the beam. The point of a share should stand one-eighth of an inch to land, and the beam should stand about three inches to the right. This will be right for a 14-inch plow and two horses. If for a 16-inch plow and three horses, the beam should be in line with the landside.

HOW TO FIX A GANG PLOW THAT RUNS ON ITS NOSE

When a gang or sulky plow runs on its nose and shoves itself through the dirt, the fault is with the share or in the beam. In most cases this fault is a set back beam, but it might also be the result of a badly-bent-down and out-of-shape landside point. If it is in the beam, take it out and heat it in the arch, then bend it forward until the plow has the right shape, and it will run right.

HOW TO HARDEN A MOULDBOARD

To harden a mouldboard is no easy job in a blacksmith's forge, and it is no use trying this in a portable forge, because there is no room enough for the fire required for this purpose. First, dig the firepot out clean, then make a charcoal fire of two bushels of this coal, have some dry basswood or wood like it, and when the charcoal begins to get red all over, then pile the wood on the outside corners of the fire. Heat the point of the mouldboard first, because this being shinned, it is thicker and must be heated first or it will not be hot enough; then hold the mouldboard on the fire and pile the wood and hot coal on top of it. Keep it only until red hot in the same place, then move it around, especially so that the edges get the force of the fire, or they will be yet cold while the center might be too hot.

HOW TO PATCH A MOULDBOARD

When the mouldboard is red hot all over, sprinkle with prussiate of potash, and plunge into a barrel of ice or salt water. A mouldboard will stand a good heat if the heat is even; otherwise it will warp or crack. Another way to heat a mouldboard: if you have a boiler, fill the fireplace with wood and heat your mouldboard there. This will give you a very good heat. If it is a shinned mouldboard, the point must be heated first in the forge, then place it under the boiler for heating. This must be done to insure a good heat on the point, which is thicker than the mouldboard and therefore would not be hot enough in the time the other parts get hot.

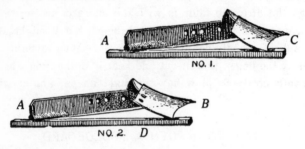

FIG. 19

When a mouldboard is worn out on the point a patch can be put on, if the mouldboard is not too much worn otherwise. Cut a piece of soft center steel to fit over the part to be repaired. Draw this piece out thin where it is to be welded to face of mouldboard. Hold this piece in position while taking the first weld, with a pair of tongs. Weld the point first, then the edges, last the center. The patch should be welded to face of mouldboard. When the last weld is taken, place the mouldboard face up, with some live coal over it, in the fire; use borax freely, and, when ready to weld, weld the patch while the mouldboard is in the fire, using a $\frac{3}{8}$ rod of round iron as a hammer with one end of it bent for this purpose. When the patch is thus welded in its thinnest place then take it out and weld on the anvil. In heating for the weld never place the patch down towards the tuyer, for there the blast will make it scale, and it will never weld this way. Remember this in all kinds of welding.

Figure 19 represents two shares. Number 1 represents a share set for spring plowing, when the ground is soft. Notice the heel of the share following the square for about one inch at *C*, while the heel in No. 2 rests with the extreme edge on the square, and is set for fall plowing, when the ground is hard. The line between *A* and *B* shows the suction at *D*, which is not more than an eighth of an inch. Breaking plows and large plows which are run shallow, should have a wide bearing at *C*. In breaking plows the heel will sometimes have to be rolled up a little at this place.

CHAPTER VI

BABBITTING AND STEEL WORKING

In filling a sickle bar there are two ways to remove the old sections. One way is to punch the rivets out, but in every case where the back of the section sticks out over the sickle bar they can be removed easier in this way: Just open the vise enough to receive the section, then strike with the hammer on the back of the section, and this blow will cut the rivets off. You can cut out ten to one by this method to any other.

Sometimes the sickle bar is bent out of shape in the fitting. To straighten it place the sickle on the anvil, sections down; now strike with the hammer so that it will touch the bar only on one half of its face, the blow to be on the inner side of the curve.

BABBITTING

When a box is to be babbitted, the first thing to do is to clean the box. If it can be placed over the fire the old babbitt will melt out easily. If the box cannot be held over the fire, then chisel the old babbitt out. At each end of the box there is a ridge to hold the babbitt in the box; that is, in cast iron boxes. On top of this ridge, place a strip of leather as thick as you want the babbitt to be. This done, place the shaft in the box. Pour the babbitt in level with the box. Be careful about having the box dry; if any dampness is in the box the babbitt will explode. Now place a thick paper on each side of the box and put on the top box, with the bolts in to hold it in place tight, then close up at the ends with putty. In some cases it is best to heat the box a little, for if the box is cold and there is little room for the babbitt, it will cool off before it can float around. In such a case the boxes should be warm and the babbitt heated to a red heat. Now pour the babbitt in through the oil hole.

In cases where there are wooden boxes, and the babbitt is to reach out against the collars, the shaft must be elevated or hung on pieces of boards on each side with notches in for the shaft to rest in. Use putty to fill up and make tight, so that the babbitt must stay where wanted. For slow motion babbitt with a less-cooling percentage (tin); for high speed, more-cooling (tin). Grooves may be cut in the bottom box for oil. When a shaft is to be babbitted all around in a solid box, the shaft is inclined to stick in the babbitt. To prevent this, smoke the shaft a little and have it warm. When cool, it will come out all right. Or wind thin paper around the shaft, the paper to be tied with strings to the shaft.

ANNEALING

By gradually heating and cooling, steel will be softened, brittleness reduced, and flexibility increased. In this state steel is tough and easiest drilled or filed. Tool steel is sometimes too hard to drill or file without first annealing it; and the best way to do this is to slowly heat to a red heat, then bury the steel in the cinders and let it cool slowly. To heat and let the steel cool exposed to the air will do no good, as it cools off too quick, and when cool the steel is as hard as ever. This is air temper.

HOW TO REPAIR BROKEN COGS

Cogs can be inserted in a cogwheel in different ways. If the rim of the wheel is thick enough a cog can be dovetailed in. That is, cut a slot in the rim from the root of the cog down, this slot to be wider at the bottom. Prepare a cog the exact size of the cogs, but just as much deeper as the slot. Before you drive this cog in, cut out a chip on each end of the slot, and when the cog is driven in, you can clinch the ends where you cut out. This will make a strong cog, and if properly made will never get loose.

Another way: If the rim is thin, then make a cog with a shank on, or a bolt cog. If the rim is wide, make two bolts. The cog can be either riveted or fastened with nuts. If only one shank is made, the same must be square up at the cog, or the cog will turn and cause a breakdown. But a shallow slot can be cut in the rim to receive and hold the cog, and then a bolt shank will hold it in place, whether the shank is round or square.

HOW TO RESTORE OVERHEATED STEEL

If steel has been burnt, the best thing to do is to throw it in the scraps; but if overheated, it can be improved. Heat to a low red heat, and hammer lightly and cool off in salt water, while yet hot enough to be of a brown color. Repeat this a half a dozen times, and the steel will be greatly bettered. Of course, this is only in cases when a tool or something like it has been overheated which cannot be thrown away without loss. By this simple method I have restored tools overheated by ignorant smiths, and in some cases the owner would declare that it was "better than ever."

HOW TO DRESS AND HARDEN STONE HAMMERS

Care must be taken in heating stone hammers not to overheat them. Dress the hammer so that the edges are a little higher than the center, thus making a slight curve. A hammer dressed this way will cut better and stay sharp longer than if the face is level. Dress both ends before hardening, then harden face end first. Heat to a red heat, and cool off in cold water about one inch up, let the temper return to half an inch from the face, that is, draw the temper as much as you can without changing the temper at the face. There it should be as hard as you can make it. When heating the peen end, keep a wet rag over the face to prevent it from becoming hot. This end should not be tempered quite as hard as the face.

HOW TO DRILL CHILLED CAST IRON

Chilled cast iron can be easily drilled if properly annealed, but it cannot be annealed simply by heating and slowly cooling. Heat the iron to a red heat and place it over the anvil in a level position; place a piece of brimstone just where the hole is to be drilled, and let it soak in. If it is a thick article, place a piece on each side over the hole, as it will better penetrate and soften the iron. Next, heat it again until red, then bury it in the cinders, and let it cool slowly. To heat and anneal chilled iron is of no avail unless it is allowed to remain hot for hours. Chilled iron will, if heated and allowed to cool quick, retain its hardness. The only way to anneal is to let it remain in the fire for hours. Brimstone will help considerably, but even with that it is best to let cool as slowly as your time will admit.

HOW TO DRILL HARD STEEL

First, make your drill of good steel, oval in form, and a little heavier than usual on point, and temper as hard as it will without drawing the temper, the heat to be a low red cherry. Diluted muriatic acid is a good thing to roughen the surface with where you want the hole. Use kerosene instead of oil, or turpentine. The pressure on the drill should be steady so that it will cut right along, as it is hard to start again if it stops cutting, but if it does, again use diluted muriatic acid. The hole should be cleaned after the use of the acid.

FACTS ABOUT STEEL

I have repeatedly warned against overheating steel. Don't heat too fast, for if it is a piece of a large dimension the outside corners will be burnt, while the bar is yet too cool inside to be worked. Don't let steel remain for any length of time in the fire at a high heat, for both steel and iron will then become brittle. This is supposed by some to be due to the formation of oxide disseminated through the mass of the metal, but many others believe that a more or less crystalline structure is set up under the influence of a softening heat, and is the sole cause of the diminution in strength and tenacity. The fiber of the steel is spoiled through overheating; this can, to some extent, be remedied by heavy forging if it is a heavy bar.

Steel is harder to weld than iron, because it contains less cinders and slag, which will produce a fusible fluid in iron that will make it weld without trouble. Steel contains from 2 to 25 percent carbon, and varies in quality according to the percent of carbon, and it is claimed that there are twenty different kinds of steel. To blacksmiths only a few kinds are known, and the sturdy smith discards both "physical tests and chemical analysis," and he thinks he knows just as much as do those who write volumes about these tests.

To weld tool steel, or steel of a high percent of carbon, borax must be used freely to prevent burning and promote fusing. Steel with less carbon, or what smiths call "soft steel," "sleigh steel," should be welded with sand only. This soft steel stands a higher heat than the harder kinds.

Good tool steel will break easy when cold if it is cut into a little with a cold chisel all around, and the bar then placed with the cut over the hole in the anvil, the helper striking directly over the hole. If it is good steel it will break easy, and the broken ends are fine grain, of a light color. If it shows glistening or glittering qualities, it is a bad sign.

Good steel will crumble under the hammer when white hot.

To test steel, draw out to a sharp point, heat to a red heat, cool in salt water; if it cuts glass it is a steel of high hardening quality.

For armor piercing, frogs, tiles, safes, and crushing machinery, alloy steel is used. This steel contains chromium, manganese or nickel, which renders it intensely hard. Tungsten is another alloy that is used in iron-cutting tools, because it does not lose its hardness by friction.

TO MEND A BAND SAW

If a band saw is broken, file the ends level, and lap one end over the other far enough to take up one tooth; place the saw in such a position that the saw will be straight when mended; use silver, copper, and brass; file into a fine powder; place this over the point and cover with borax. Now heat two irons one inch square, or a pair of heavy tongs, and place one on each side of the joint, and when the powdered metal is melted, have a pair of tongs ready to take hold over the joint with, while it cools. File off and smooth the sides, not leaving the blade any thicker than in other places.

CASE HARDENING

Iron and steel may be case hardened with either of the following compounds: Prussiate of potash, salt-ammoniac of equal parts. Heat the iron red hot and sprinkle it with this compound, then heat again and sprinkle, and plunge it while yet hot in a bath of salt water.

Another: Cyanide of potassium; grind it into a fine powder and sprinkle over the iron while red hot, and plunge into a bath of salt water. This powder will coagulate if it is held against the fire so it gets warm. Be careful with this powder, as it is a strong poison. It is the best thing that I have ever tried for case hardening iron. It will case-harden the softest iron so that it cannot be touched with any tool. It is also good for plows, especially where it is hard to make a plow scour. The only objection is the price, as it costs more than prussiate of potash or other hardening compounds.

HOW TO HARDEN SPRINGS

Heat to a heat that will be discerned in the dark as a low red heat. Plunge into a bath of lukewarm water. Such a heat cannot be noticed in a light sunny day, but it is just the heat required.

Another way: Heat to a low red heat and bury the spring in cold sand. Another: Heat to a low red heat in the dark, and cool in oil.

TO MAKE STEEL AND IRON AS WHITE
AS SILVER

Take one pound of ashes from white ash bark, dissolve in soft water. Heat your iron red, and cool in this solution, and the iron will turn white as silver.

TO MEND BROKEN SAWS

Silver, 15 parts; copper, 2 parts. These should be filed into powder and mixed. Now place your saw level with the broken ends tight up against each other; put a little of the mixture along the seam, and cover with powdered charcoal; with a spirit lamp and a blowpipe melt the mixture, then with the hammer set the joint smooth.

CHAPTER VII

BOILER REPAIRING AND HOISTING HOOKS

When the leak or weak place in the boiler is found, take a ripping chisel and cut out all of the weak, thin, and cracked parts. This done, make the patch. The patch must be large, not less than an inch lap on all sides, but if double rows of rivets are wanted, the lap should be two inches on all sides. Bevel or scrape the patch on all edges to allow calking. The bolt holes should be about two inches apart and countersunk for patch bolts, if patch bolts are used. Next, drill two holes in the boiler shell, one on each side of the patch, and put in the bolts. These bolts should be put in to stay and hold the patch in position while the rest of the holes are drilled and bolted. When the bolts are all in, take your wrench and tighten the bolts one after the other, harder and harder, striking at the same time on the patch around its edges. At last, strike light on the bolt heads when you tighten and draw the bolt until its head breaks off. These bolts are made for this purpose and in such a shape that the head will break at a high strain. This done, use the calking iron all around the patch.

The patch should be put on the inside of the boiler, especially if on the bottom of a horizontal boiler. If the patch is put on the outside in this place the sediment or solid matter which the water contains will quickly fill up over the patch and there is danger of overheating the boiler and an explosion may follow.

HOW TO PUT IN FLUES

The tools necessary to retube an old boiler are, first, a good expander of the proper size; a roller expander preferred; a crow foot or calking iron, made from good tool steel. A cutting-off

tool can be made to do very good service, in the following man-
ner: Take a piece of steel, say ½ × 1¼, about ten inches long.
Draw one end out to a sharp point and bend to a right angle of a
length just enough to let it pass inside of the flue to be cut.
A gas pipe can be used for a handle. In cutting the flues set this
tool just inside the flue sheet and press down on the handle.
If this tool is properly made, it cuts the old flues out with ease.
After both ends have been cut, the flues will come out.

FIG. 20   TUBE TO BE WELDED

Next, cut the tubes about ⅜ of an inch longer than the flue
sheet. After the tubes are cut the proper length, and placed in
the boiler, expand the same in both ends with a flue expander.
After the flues are expanded until they fit the holes solid, turn
them over with the peen of a hammer to make them bell-shaped.

FIG. 21   TUBE EXPANDER

Now take a crowsfoot, or calking tool, and turn the ends in a
uniform head and tight all around. If the flues should leak, and
there is water on the boiler, take a boiler expander and tighten
them up. But never attempt to tighten a flue with the hammer if
there is water on the boiler.

HOW TO WELD FLUES

In welding flues or putting new tips on old flues, you must
find out how far the old tubes are damaged, and cut that part off.
Next clean the scales off in a tumbling box; if you have none,
with an old rasp.

Now take a piece of tubing the size of the old, and scarf the
ends down thin, the new tube to go over the old, and drive them

together. In welding a rest can be made in the forge to push the tube against while welding, to prevent the pieces from pulling apart. A three-eighths rod, with thread on one end and a head on the other, run through the flue, will be found handy for holding the pipes or flues together. In welding these together, don't take them out of the fire and strike with a hammer, but take a rod $\frac{3}{8}$-inch round, and bend one end to serve as a hammer. Strike with this hammer lightly over the lap, at the same time turning the flue around in the fire. Use borax to prevent the flue from scaling and burning.

FOAMING IN BOILERS

There are many reasons for foaming in boilers, but the chief reason is dirty water. In some cases it is imperfect construction of boiler, such as insufficient room for the steam and a too small steam pipe or dome. When a boiler is large enough for the steam and clean water is used there is no danger of foaming. When more water is evaporated than there is steam room or heating surface for, then the boiler will foam. When a boiler is overworked, more steam than its capacity will admit is required, and the engine is run at a high speed, the steam will carry with it more water than usual.

When a boiler foams, shut the throttle partly to check the outflow of steam and lessen the suction of water, because the water is sucked up and follows the sides of the dome up.

If the steam pipe in the dome sticks through the flange a few inches the water will not escape so easy. A boiler that is inclined to foam should not be filled too full with dirty water; if it is, it is best to blow off a little. Foul water can be cleaned by different methods before it enters the boiler, so as to prevent foaming and scaling.

BLOWING OUT THE BOILER

A boiler should not be blowed out under a high steam pressure, because the change is so sudden that it has a tendency to contract the iron, and if repeated often the boiler will leak. If it is done when there is brickwork around the boiler and the same is hot, it will in a short time ruin the boiler. In such a case the boiler should not be blowed out for hours after you have ceased firing.

DESIGN AND TREATMENT OF HOISTING HOOKS

The construction and treatment of a hook intended for a crane or hoist involves a problem deserving of careful consideration. This fact has impressed itself upon the writer from his experience in lawsuits arising from damages caused by the failure of a defective hook.

To make a hook safe for the purpose for which it is intended two important requisites must be fulfilled:

1. Correct design.
2. Proper treatment.

The design is guided to a large extent by the service which the hook is to perform; that is, whether the hook will be subjected to high or low, frequent or rare stresses, and whether the hook is likely to be loaded above its normal capacity.

Hooks on small cranes and hoists, of about 2 to 3 tons' capacity, may be loaded to full capacity several times every day; while hooks on cranes of 50 tons' capacity may carry full load at remote intervals only. Due to the repeated stresses on small hooks occurring possibly under extreme temperatures, the hook may become fatigued and liable to break. It is, therefore, advisable to keep the stresses low in comparatively small hooks to provide a factor of safety.

This precaution can readily be observed with hooks for small loads, as the size would scarcely render them unwieldy. But as the size of the hook increases it becomes necessary to increase the stress; that is, the load per square inch or cross section, in order to avoid the construction of a clumsy hook. A high stress is permissible with high loads because they are applied to the hook less frequently than in the case of small hooks and light loads. We may consider a stress of 15,000 lbs. per sq. in. as safe for a 50-ton hook as a stress of 10,000 lbs. per sq. in. on a 10-ton hook.

The material for a hook may be ordinary steel, cast steel or wrought iron depending on the load the hook is to carry. For small loads where a hook of ample size, yet not bulky, can be constructed, cast steel may be used. But for heavy loads a ductile material, having practically the same elastic limit for compression and tension, should be selected.

Mr. F.A. Waldron, for many years connected with the manufacturing of hooks in the works of the Yale & Towne Mfg. Co.,

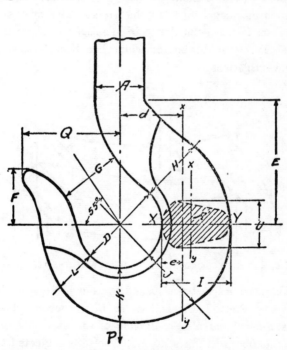

FIG. 22 THE CORRECTLY PROPORTIONED HOOK IS BASED UPON
DEFINITE FORMULAE

made careful observations with different materials, and his conclusion is, that the only reliable material for hooks is a high grade puddled iron. A steel hook may carry a load from 25 to 50% greater than the wrought iron hook, but it is not reliable. This fact will be borne out more clearly by the results of tests made by the writer and given further in this section.

The design of a hook should be based on formulae deduced from practice with successful hooks, rather than to depend on theoretical computations. In the latter method, conditions are assumed which are hardly ever realized in actual practice. It is, therefore, absurd to aim at mathematical precision at the expense of reliability.

The exact analysis of the stresses in a hook is based on the theory of curved beams. In the theory of straight beams it is assumed that any cross section which is a plane section before flexure will remain a plane section after flexure, and that the deformation is proportional to the stress. The analysis of a curved beam is based on the same assumption. There is, however, one important distinction which has been brought out by recent investigations.

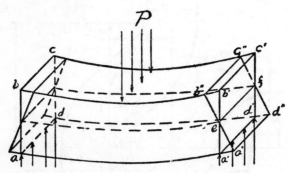

FIG. 23   THE HOOK CONSIDERED A BEAM WITH THE LOAD AT P

Consider a straight beam loaded transversely with a load P, as shown by Fig. 23. Originally, the fibers between the cross sections a-b-c-d and a'-b'-c'-d' were of the same length. When loaded, the fibers in the strip b-c, b'-c' are subjected to compression; and the fibers in the strip a-d, a'-d' are under tension; consequently, the upper fibers will shorten and the lower fibers will lengthen. Somewhere between b-c, b'-c' and a-d, a'-d', there must exist a layer of fibers which have neither shortened nor elongated. The intersection of this layer with the section a''-b''-c''-d'' (the position of a'-b'-c'-d' when the beam is loaded) is a straight line (e, f) called the "neutral axis," which for straight beams coincides with the gravity axis of the cross section.

In a curved beam the neutral axis, x-y, Fig. 22, does not coincide with the gravity axis, x'-y', Fig. 22, but falls somewhere between the gravity axis and the tension side of the hook. This is due to the fact that the fibers on the convex side of the hook are longer than those on the concave side, and therefore require less stress than the shorter fibers for the same amount of deformation.

The application of the theory of curved beams is somewhat complicated for practical purposes, and a simpler form can be used; provided that care is taken in assigning the limits of stress. Referring to Fig. 22, assume the beam with a load P. The most dangerous section is, evidently, along X-Y; it is acted upon by a direct tension stress ($f' = P/A'$) and a flexure stress (f'') due to the bending moment ($P \times a$); the combined stress is the sum of f' and f''. Let f represent the combined stress; then

$$f = \frac{P}{A'} + \frac{Pde}{I}$$

in which A' is the area of the cross section, e the distance of the neutral axis from the tension side, and I the moment of inertia of the section about the neutral axis.

If the material has, practically, the same elastic limit for compression and tension, the neutral axis needs not be far from the gravity axis; otherwise, it is advisable to distribute the metal more toward the tension side. The most reliable data on the construction of hooks, resulting from extensive experimental and mathematical investigations, is that given by Mr. Henry R. Towne in his treatise on cranes.

The following formulae for determining the dimensions of the various portions will give the greatest resistance to spreading and rupture that the original bar will permit. Referring again to Fig. 22:

$$D = 0.5 \Delta + 1.25$$
$$H = 1.08 A$$
$$L = 1.05 A$$

$$U = 0.886 \, A$$
$$G = 0.75 \, D$$
$$F = 0.33 \, \Delta + 0.85$$
$$I = 1.33 \, A$$
$$J = 1.20 \, A$$
$$K = 1.13 \, A$$
$$E = 0.64 \, \Delta + 1.6$$
$$Q = 0.64 \, \Delta + 1.6$$

In the above formulae the dimensions are in inches, Δ is the load in tons of 2,000 lbs.

Having discussed, to some extent, the design of the hook, we may now consider the care which should attend the making of a hook. As already mentioned, the writer on several occasions gave expert testimony on lawsuits before the court arising from injuries incurred and damages caused by the failure of defective hooks.

To investigate the subject thoroughly, a series of careful experiments were made to determine how a hook should be made to insure reasonable safety and facilitate the location of responsibility in case of failure.

Hooks may become hardened in course of time when exposed to extreme temperatures. Repeated stresses combined with extreme temperatures will change the molecular structure and, to some extent, the physical properties of the metal.

The fact that chain links and hooks break more often in cold weather, suggests the advisability of annealing chains and hooks at suitable intervals, to refine the grain which may have crystallized. A crystallized grain is always a weak grain and is especially objectionable where a sudden or "shock" load is likely to be applied.

In conclusion it may be remarked that the courts do not consider the correct size of the stock as the determining factor when locating the responsibility in case of accident. If it can be shown that the hook was too hard, overheated or too high in carbon, or there was a flaw in workmanship, there is undisputed evidence of negligence which constitutes sufficient ground for suit to recover damages.

There is a simple method for avoiding accidents by failure of hooks. If you buy or make your hooks, see to it that they contain the proper amount of carbon, and anneal before using; continue annealing, at least once a year, if the hooks are subjected to varying and extreme temperatures.

CHAPTER VIII

HORSESHOEING

The horse in a wild state needs no shoes, the wear and tear that the feet are subjected to while the horse is hunting for his food in a wild country on soft meadows, is just right to keep the hoofs down in a normal condition. But when the horse is in bondage and must serve as a burden-carrying animal, traveling

Cross Section.

FIG. 24 TOE AND SIDE WEIGHT AND PLAIN RACING PLATES, AS MANUFACTURED BY BRYDEN HORSE SHOE CO.

on hard roads or paved streets, the horse must be shod to prevent a foot wear which nature cannot recuperate. Horseshoes were first made of iron in 480 A.D. Before that time, and even after, horseshoes have been made of leather and other materials.

74

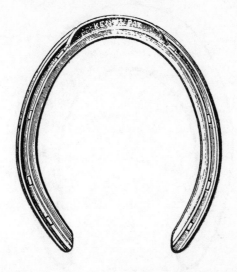

FIG. 25 TOE AND SIDE WEIGHT AND PLAIN RACING PLATES, AS MANUFACTURED BY BRYDEN HORSE SHOE CO.

ANATOMY

It is necessary in order to be a successful horse-shoer to know something about the anatomical construction of the feet and legs of the horse. Of course, any little boy can learn the names of the bones and tendons in a horse's foot in an hour, but this does not make a horse-shoer out of him. No board of examiners should allow any horse-shoer to pass an examination merely because he can answer the questions put to him in regard to the anatomy of the horse, for as I have said before, these names are easily learned, but practical horse-shoeing is not learned in hours; it takes years of study and practice.

It is not my intention to treat on this subject. I could not; first, because there is no room for such a discourse, second, there are numerous books on the subject better than I could write, available to every horse-shoer. I shall only give a few names of such parts of the anatomy as is essential to know. What the horse-shoer wants to know is the parts of the foot connected with the hoof, as his work is confined solely to the foot.

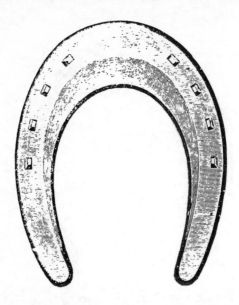

FIG. 26 TOE AND SIDE WEIGHT AND PLAIN RACING PLATES, AS
MANUFACTURED BY BRYDEN HORSE SHOE CO.

THE WALL

The wall or crust is the horny sheath incasing the end of the foot, in the front and on the sides from the coronet to the ground. It is through this crust the nail is driven, and it is upon this crust the shoe rests. In front it is deepest, towards the quarter and heel it becomes thinner. It is of equal thickness from the upper end to the ground (from top to bottom). The white colored wall is the poorest, while the iron colored wall is the toughest. The growth of the wall is different at different ages. It grows more in a young horse and colt than in an old horse; in a healthy foot and soft, than in a diseased foot and hard. In a young horse the hoof will grow about three inches in a year and even more, while it grows less in an old horse. The wall is fibrous, the fibers going parallel to each other from the coronet to the ground.

THE SOLE

The horny sole is the bottom of the foot. This sole is fibrous like the wall. The sole is thickest at the border, where it connects

FIG. 27 TOE AND SIDE WEIGHT AND PLAIN RACING PLATES, AS
MANUFACTURED BY BRYDEN HORSE SHOE CO.

with the wall, and thinnest at the center. The sole, when in a
healthy condition, scales off in flakes. This scale is a guide to
the farrier whereby he can tell how much to pare off. There are
different opinions in regard to the paring of the sole, but that is
unnecessary, for nature will tell how much to cut off in a healthy
foot. In a diseased foot it is different; then the horse-shoer must
use his own good judgment. It is, however, in very few cases
that the shoer needs to do more than just clean the sole. Nature
does the scaling off, or paring business, better than any farrier.

THE FROG

The frog is situated at the heel and back part of the hoof,
within the bars; the point extending towards the center of the
sole, its base filling up the space left between the inflection of
the wall. This body is also fibrous. The frog is very elastic and
is evidently designed for contact with the ground, and for the
prevention of jars injurious to the limbs.

CORONET

Coronet is the name of the upper margin of the foot, the place
where the hair ceases and the horny hoof begins.

THE QUARTER

The quarter means a place at the bottom of the wall, say, about one-third the length from the heel towards the toe.

THE BARS

By the bars we mean the horny walls on each side of the frog, commencing at the heel of the wall and extending towards the point of the frog.

Any blacksmith or horse-shoer desiring to study more thoroughly the anatomy of the horse should procure a book treating on this subject.

HOW TO MAKE THE SHOE

It is only in exceptional cases that the shoer turns or makes a shoe. The shoes are now already shaped, creased and partly punched, so all that is needed is to weld on the toe calk and shape the heel calks.

Heat the shoe at the toe first, and when hot, bend the heels together a little. This is done because the shoes will spread when the toe calk is welded on, and the shoe should not be too wide on the toe, as is mostly the case. If the shoe is narrow at the toe it is easier to fit the same to the foot and get the shoe to fill out on the toe. Many smiths cut too much off from the toe. Before the toe calk is driven onto the shoe, bend it a little so as to give it the same curve the shoe has, and the corners of the calk will not stick out over the edge of the shoe. Now place the shoe in the fire, calk up. Heat to a good low welding heat, and use sand for welding compound. Don't take the shoe out of the fire to dip it in the sand, as most shoers do, for you will then cool it off by digging in the cold sand, of which you will get too much on the inner side of the calk. The same will, if allowed to stay, make the calk look rough. You will also have to make a new place for the shoe in the fire, which will take up a good deal of time, as the new place is not at once so hot as the place from which the shoe was taken; besides this,

you might tear the calk off and lose it. When hot give a couple
of good blows on the calk and then draw it out. Don't hold the
heels of the shoe too close to the anvil when you draw out the
calk, for if you do, the calk will stand under, and it should be
at a right angle with the shoe. Do not draw it out too long, as is
mostly done. Punch the hole from the upper side first. Many first-
class horse-shoers punch only from that side, while most shoers
punch from both sides.

There is no need of heating the shoe for punching the holes.
Punch the holes next to the heel first, for if you punch the holes
next to the toe when the shoe is hot, the punch will be hot,
upset, and bent. If it is a large shoe, punch only two holes on
each side for the toe calk heat. These holes to be the holes
next to the toe when the shoe is hot, and then punch the other
two when you draw out the heel calks, and the shoe is hot at the
heel. The heel calks should be as short as you can make them;
and so should the toe calks. I know but a few horse-shoers that
are able to weld on a toe calk good. The reason for their inability is lack of experience in general blacksmithing. Most
shoers know how to make a fire to weld in. They are too stingy
about the coal; try to weld in dirt and cinders, with a low fire,
the shoe almost touching the tuyer iron. I advise all horse-
shoers to read my article about the fire.

I have made a hammer specially for horse-shoeing with a peen
different from other hammers. With this hammer the beginner will
have no trouble in drawing out the calks. See Fig. 13, No. 8.
The hammers as now used by most smiths are short and clumsy;
they interfere too much with the air, and give a bump instead of
a sharp cutting blow that will stick to the calk.

The shoe should be so shaped at the heel as to give plenty
of room for the frog; the heels to be spread out as wide as possible. This is important, for if the shoe is wide between the
heels, the horse will stand more firm, and it will be to him a
comfortable shoe. The shoe should not be wider between the
calks at the expense of same, as is done by some shoers, for
this is only a half calk, and the heel is no wider. The shoe
should not be fitted to the foot when hot, as it will injure the
hoof if it is burned to the foot.

HOW TO PREPARE THE FOOT FOR THE SHOE

The foot should be level, no matter what the fault is with the horse. The hoof should not be cut down more than the loose scales will allow. In a healthy condition this scale is a guide. When the foot is diseased, it is different, and the shoer must use his own judgment.

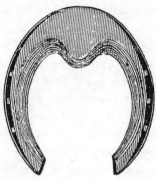

FIG. 28

The frog never grows too large. It should never be trimmed more than just to remove any loose scales.

The frog in its functions is very important to the well-being of the foot. In the unshod foot it projects beyond the level of the sole, always in contact with the ground; it obviates concussion; supports the tendons; prevents falls and contraction. The bars are also of importance, bracing the hoof, and should never be cut down as has been the practice for centuries by ignorant horseshoers.

FORGING

Forging or overreaching is a bad habit, and a horse with this fault is now very valuable. This habit can be overcome by shoeing; but it will not be done by making the shoes short on the heel in front and short in the toe behind. Never try this foolish method.

To overcome forging, the shoer should know what forging is. It is this: The horse breaks over with his hind feet quicker than he breaks over with the front feet; in other words, he has more action behind than in front, and the result is that the hind feet strike the front feet before they can get out of the way, often cutting the quarters badly, giving rise to quarter cracks and horny patches over the heel.

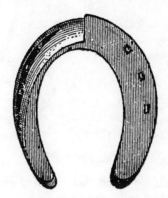

FIG. 29

Some writers make a difference between forging and over-reaching, but the cause of the trouble is the same — too much action behind in proportion to the front; and the remedy is the same — retard the action behind, increase it in front. There are different ideas about the remedy for this fault.

One method is to shoe heavy forward and light behind, but this is in my judgment a poor idea, although it might help in some cases. Another way is to shoe with side weight on the outer side behind, but it is not safe, because it is difficult to get a horse to throw the foot out to one side enough so as to pass by the front foot, except in a high trot.

The best way to shoe a forger or overreaching horse is to make a shoe for front of medium heft, not longer than just what is needed. The toe calk should be at the inner web of the shoe, or no toe calk at all, or, toe weight, to make the horse reach farther.

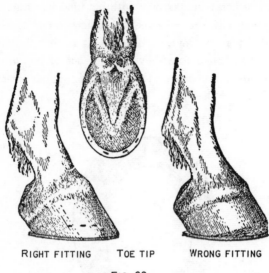

RIGHT FITTING   TOE TIP   WRONG FITTING

FIG. 30

It will sometimes be found that the hind foot is shorter than the front foot. To find this out, measure from the coronet to the end of the toe. The shorter the foot the quicker it breaks over. If it is found that the hind foot is shorter than the front foot, then the shoe should be made so that it will make up for this. Let the shoe stick out on the toe enough to make the foot of equal length with the front foot. It is well in any case of forging to make the hind shoe longer on the toe. If the hind shoe is back on the foot, as is often done, it will only make the horse forge all the more, for it will increase action behind, the horse breaks over quicker, and strikes the front foot before it is out of the way. Set the shoe forward as far as possible, and make long heels. The longer the shoe is behind, the longer it takes to raise the foot and break over.

Clack forging is meant by the habit of clacking the hind and fore shoes together. This kind of forging is not serious or harmful; it will only tend to wear off the toe of the hind foot and annoy the driver, possibly a little fatiguing to the horse.

The position of the feet at the time of the clack is different from that it is supposed to be. The toe of the hind feet is generally worn off, while no mark is made on the front feet. From this you will understand that the hind feet never touch the heel of the front feet, but the shoe. Just at the moment the fore foot is raised up enough on the heel to give room for the hind foot to

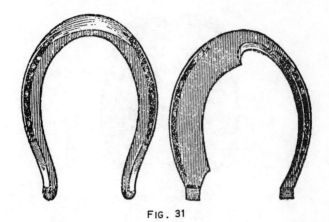

FIG. 31

wedge in under it, the hind foot comes flying under the fore foot, and the toe of the hind foot strikes the web of the toe on the front foot. This is the reason no mark is seen on the front foot, while the hind foot is badly worn off.

INTERFERING

Interfering is a bad fault in a horse. It is the effect of a variety of causes. In interfering the horse brushes the foot going forward against the other foot. Some horses strike the knee, others above it, the shin or coronet, but in most cases the fetlock.

Colts seldom interfere before they are shod, but then they sometimes interfere because the shoes are too heavy. This trouble disappears as soon as the colt is accustomed to carrying the shoes. Weakness is the most common cause. Malformation of the fetlock is another cause. The turning in or out of the toes, giving a swinging motion to the feet, is also conducive to interfering.

The first thing to do is to apply a boot to the place that is brushed. Next, proceed to remove the cause by shoeing, or by feeding and rest in cases of weakness. Nothing is better than flesh to spread the legs with. Some old horse-shoers in shoeing

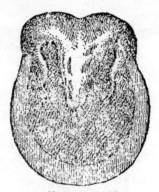

NATURAL FOOT

FIG. 32

for interfering will turn the feet so as to turn the fetlock out. This is done by paring down the outside and leaving the inside strong. This is a bad way of shoeing for interfering, as it might ruin the horse. The foot should be leveled as level as it is possible. The inner side of the hoof should be scant; instead of being curved it should be almost straight, as the horse generally strikes with the side of the hoof or quarter. This is done to make a side-weight shoe, the side weight not to reach over the center of the shoe, but to be only on one side. Pyt the shoe on with the weight on the outer side. If the horse still interferes, give more side weight to the shoe, and make the heel on the outer side about one and one-quarter inch longer than the inside heel; give it an outward turn. This heel will prevent the horse from turning the heel in the way of the other foot when it goes by, so as not to strike the fetlock.

Properly made and applied, side weight will stop interfering almost every time. If the side weight is heavy enough it will throw the foot out, and the trouble is overcome.

There are only a few horse-shoers that have any practical experience in making side-weight shoes, which we understand from the articles in our trade journals.

Some horse-shoers in shoeing to stop interfering will make common shoes shorter than they ought to be and set them far in under the foot, so that the hoof on the inner side will stick out over the shoe a quarter of an inch. These they don't rasp off, and everybody knows that the hoof adheres to and rubs harder against the leg than the hard smooth shoe. But, foolish as it is, such shoers stick to their foolish ideas. I call all such fads faith cures.

The rule is to have the side weight on the outer side, while the exception is to have the side weight on the inner side of the foot. For old and poor horses, ground feed and rest is better than any kind of shoes. It will give more strength and more flesh to spread the legs.

CHAPTER IX

HORSESHOEING TO CORRECT HOOF
IRREGULARITIES

Kneesprung is the result of disease that sometimes is brought about by bad shoeing. In a healthy leg the center of gravity is down through the center of the leg and out at the heels. This is changed in a case of kneesprung legs, giving the legs a bowed appearance. This trouble always comes on gradually; in some cases it will stop and never get worse, while in others it will keep on until it renders the horse useless. A horse with straight legs will sleep standing, but a knuckler cannot; he will fall as soon as he goes to sleep, on account of the center of gravity being thrown on a line forward of the suspensory ligaments. The cause of this trouble is sprain or injury to the back tendons of the legs, soreness of the feet, shins or joints. In old cases nothing can be done but just to relieve the strain a little by shoeing with a long shoe and high heel calks, with no toe calk. In cases not more than three months old, clip the hair off the back tendons when there is any soreness, and shower them with cold water several times a day for a week or two, and then turn the horse out for a long run in the pasture.

CONTRACTION

Contraction is in itself no original disease, except in a few cases. It is mostly the effect of some disease. Contraction follows sprains of the tendons, corns, founder, and navicular disease. When contraction is the result of a long-standing

FOOT PREPARED FOR CHARTIER TIP   FOOT SHOD WITH CHARTIER TIP

FIG. 33

disease of the foot or leg, it will be in only one of the feet, because the horse will rest the affected leg and stand most of the time on the healthy leg; thus the healthy foot receives more pressure than the diseased, and is spread out more; the foot becomes much uneven — they don't look like mates. This kind of contraction is generally the result of some chronic disease, but in most cases contraction is the result of shoeing and artificial living. Before the colt is shod, his hoofs are large and open-heeled, the quarters are spread out wide, and the foot on the under side is shaped like a saucer. The reason of the colt's foot being so large is that he has been running on the green and moist turf without shoes, and the feet have in walking in mud and dampness gathered so much moisture that they are growing and spreading at every step. This is changed when the colt is shod and put on hard roads, or taken from the pasture and put on hard floors where the feet become hard and dried up. A strong high heeled foot is predisposed to contraction, while a low heeled flat foot is seldom afflicted with this trouble.

When contraction comes from bad shoeing or from standing on hard floors, pull the shoes off, pare down the foot as much as you can, leaving the frog as large as it is. Rub in some hoof ointment once a day at the coronet and quarters, and turn the horse out in a wet pasture. But if the horse must be used on the

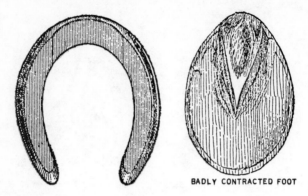

BADLY CONTRACTED FOOT

FIG. 34

road, proceed to shoe as follows: First, ascertain if the frog is hard or soft. If soft, put on a bar shoe with open bar. I have invented a shoe for this purpose. See Fig. 34, No. 1. The idea of shoeing with an endless bar shoe is wrong. In most cases contraction is brought on by letting the shoes stay on too long, whereby the hoof has been compelled to grow down with the

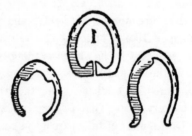

FIG. 35

shape of the shoe. If an open shoe has helped to bring on contraction, much more so will a bar shoe, which will tie the hoof to the shoe with no chance of spreading, no matter what frog pressure is put on. Make the shoe as light as you can, with very low or no calks; let the bar rest against the frog; keep the hoofs moist with hoof ointment; use an open bar shoe.

Make a low box and fill it with wet manure, mud or clay, and let the horse stand in it when convenient, to soften the hoofs. Spread the shoe a little every week to help the hoofs out, or the shoes will prevent what the frog pressure aims to do, but this spreading must be done with care. If the frog is dried up and hard, don't put on a bar shoe, as it will do more harm than good. In such a case make a common shoe with low or no calks; make holes in it as far back as you can nail; spread them with care a little every week. Let the horse stand in a box with mud or manure, even warm water, for a few hours at a time, and keep the hoofs moist with hoof ointment. In either case do not let the shoe stay on longer than four weeks at a time. In addition to the above, pack the feet with some wet packing, or a sponge can be applied to the feet and held in position by some of the many inventions for this purpose.

No man can comprehend how much a horse suffers from contraction when his feet are hoof-bound and pressed together as if they were in a vise. The pain from a pair of hard and tight boots on a man are nothing compared to the agony endured by this noble and silent sufferer. It must be remembered that there is no such a thing as shoeing for contraction. Contraction is brought on by artificial living and shoeing. A bar shoe for contraction is the most foolish thing to imagine. The pressure intended on the frog is a dead pressure, and in a few days it will settle itself so that there is no pressure at all. If a bar shoe is to be used it must be an open bar shoe like the one referred to. This shoe will give a live pressure, and if made of steel will spring up against the frog at every step and it can be spread. I will say, however, that I don't recommend spreading, for it will part if not done with care. It is better to drive the shoe on with only four or five nails, and set them over often. Contraction never affects the hind feet because of the moisture they receive. This should suggest to every shoer that moisture is better than shoes.

CORNS

Corns are very common to horses' feet, a majority of all cases of lameness is due to this trouble.

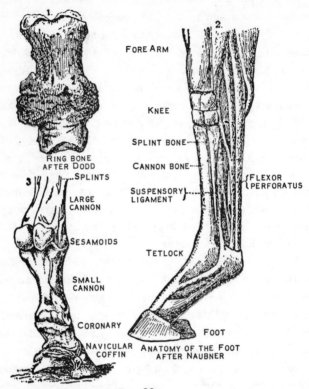

RING BONE
AFTER DODD

SPLINTS

LARGE
CANNON

SESAMOIDS

SMALL
CANNON

CORONARY

NAVICULAR
COFFIN

FORE ARM

KNEE

SPLINT BONE

CANNON BONE

SUSPENSORY
LIGAMENT

TETLOCK

FLEXOR
PERFORATUS

FOOT

ANATOMY OF THE FOOT
AFTER NAUBNER

FIG. 36

Corns are the result of shoes being allowed to stay on too long. The shoe, in such a case grows under the foot and presses on the sole and corns are formed. Even pressure of the shoe and sometimes too heavy bearing on the heel causes corns. Gravel wedging in under the shoe or between the bar and the wall is sometimes the cause of corns. Leaving the heel and quarters too high, whereby they will bend under and press against the sole, is another cause of corns.

The seat of corns is generally in the sole of the foot at the quarter or heels between the bar and the wall, at the angle made by the wall and bar.

Anything that will bruise the underlying and sensitive membrane of the sole will produce corn. This bruise gives rise to soreness, the sole becomes blood colored and reddish; if bad, it might break out, either at the bottom or the junction of the hoof and hair or coronet, forming a quittor.

Cut out the corn or red sole clear down. If the corn is the result of contraction, pare down the hoof and sole, put the foot into linseed poultice that is warm, for twenty-four hours, then renew it. If the corn is deep, be sure to cut down enough to let the matter out. It is a good thing to pour into the hole hot pine tar. In shoeing the bearing should be taken off the quarter or from the wall over the corn by rasping it down so that it will not touch the shoe. A bar shoe is a good thing as it will not spring

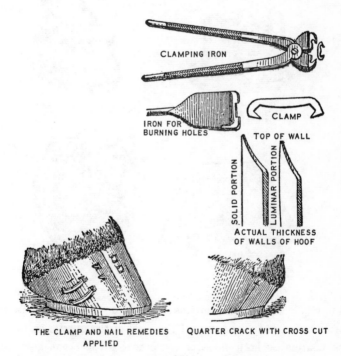

CLAMPING IRON

IRON FOR
BURNING HOLES

CLAMP

TOP OF WALL

SOLID PORTION

LUMINAR PORTION

ACTUAL THICKNESS
OF WALLS OF HOOF

THE CLAMP AND NAIL REMEDIES
APPLIED

QUARTER CRACK WITH CROSS CUT

FIG. 37

as much as to come in contact with the hoof over the corn. Give very little frog pressure. An open shoe can be used and in such a case there should be no calk at the heel. A calk should be welded on directly over the corn and the shoe will not spring up against the wall.

QUARTER AND SAND CRACKS

Quarter and sand cracks are cracks in the hoof, usually running lengthwise of the fibers, but sometimes they will be running across the fiber for an inch or more. Quarter cracks are cracks mostly on the inside of the foot, because that side is thinner and weaker than the outside. The cause of it is a hard and brittle hoof with no elasticity, brought on by poor assimilation and a want of good nutrition to the hoof. Hot, sandy or hard roads are

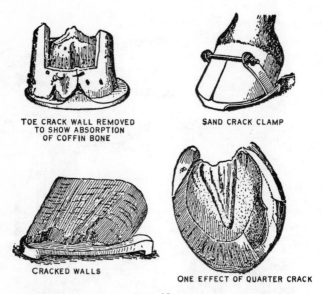

TOE CRACK WALL REMOVED
TO SHOW ABSORPTION
OF COFFIN BONE

SAND CRACK CLAMP

CRACKED WALLS

ONE EFFECT OF QUARTER CRACK

FIG. 38

also conducive to these cracks. What to do: If the horse is shod remove the shoes, and cut off the wall of the quarter to take off the bearing on both sides of the crack. If the crack goes up to the coronet and is deep, cut off both sides of the crack the whole length. About one inch below the coronet, cut a deep cut clear through, either with a knife or hot sharp iron, across the crack. This will help to start a new hoof.

If the flesh sticks up between the cracks, let a veterinarian burn it off. In shoeing for this trouble, it is best to use a bar shoe (endless) and shoe the horse often.

SEEDY TOE

When shoes with a clip or a cap on the toe are used, it sometimes happens that the toe is bruised and it starts a dry rot extending up between the wall and the laminæ. Remove the shoe, pare away the hoof at the toe so as to take away the bearing from the toe. Any white or meaty substance should be picked out. Apply hot pine tar into the hole, and dip a little wad of tow in the hole to fill up. Replace the shoe, but don't let the clip touch the wall.

PRICKING

Pricking often happens in shoeing from a nail running into the quick, but the horse if often pricked by stepping on a nail or anything that will penetrate the sole and run into the quick. If the horse is pricked by shoeing, pull off the shoes and examine each nail, the nail which has gone into the quick is wet and of a blue color.

If it is a bad case, the sole or wall must be cut down to let the matter out and the foot put into a boot of linseed poultice. In milder cases a little pine tar put into the hole will be enough.

STIFLED

Mistakes are often made by inexperienced men and horse-shoers when a case of this kind is to be treated, and I would advise every horse-shoer to call in a veterinarian when he gets a case of this kind. Cramps of the muscles of the thighs are sometimes taken for stifle.

When stifle appears in an old horse, three ounces of lead through his brain is the best, but for a young horse a cruel method of shoeing might be tried. Make a shoe with heels three inches high, or a shoe with cross bands as shown in illustration, Fig. 31, No. 2, for stifle shoe. This shoe must be placed on the well foot. The idea is to have the horse stand on the stifled leg until the muscles and cords are relaxed.

STRING HALT

String halt or spring halt is a kind of affection of the hind legs, occasioning a sudden jerk of the legs upward towards the belly. Sometimes only one leg is affected.

In some cases it is milder, in others more severe. In some cases it is difficult to start the horse. He will jerk up on one leg and then on the other, but when started will go along all right.

For this fault there is no cure because it is a nervous affection. If there is any local disorder it is best to treat this, as it might alleviate the jerk. For the jerk itself bathe the hind quarters once a day with cold water. If this don't help, try warm water, once a day for two weeks. Rub the quarters dry after bathing.

HOW TO SHOE A KICKING HORSE

Many devices are now gotten up for shoeing kicking horses. It is no use for a man to wrestle with a horse, and every horse-shoer should try to find out the best way to handle vicious horses.

One simple way, which will answer in most cases, is to put a twist on one of the horse's lips or on one ear. To make a twist, take a piece of broom handle two feet long, bore a half-inch hole in one end and put a piece of a clothesline through so as to make a loop six inches in diameter.

Another way: Make a leather strap with a ring in, put this strap around the foot of the horse; in the ring of the strap tie a rope. Now braid or tie a ring in the horse's tail and run the rope through this ring and back through the ring in the strap, then pull the foot up. See Fig. 40. The front foot can be held up by this device also, by simply buckling the strap to the foot and throwing the strap up over the neck of the horse.

Shoeing stalls are also used, but they are yet too expensive for small shops.

FIG. 39 EASY POSITION FOR FINISHING

No horse-shoer should lose his temper in handling a nervous horse and abuse the animal; for, in nine cases out of ten, will hard treatment make the horse worse, and many horse owners would rather be hit themselves than to have anybody hit their horse.

Don't curse. Be cool, use a little patience, and you will, in most cases, succeed. To a nervous horse you should talk gently, as you would to a scared child. The horse is the noblest and most useful animal to man, but is often maltreated and abused. Amongst our dumb friends, the horse is the best, but few recognize this fact.

HOW TO SHOE A TROTTER

In shoeing a trotter it is no use to follow a certain rule for the angle, because the angle must vary a little in proportion to the different shape of the horse's foot.

FIG. 40

Every owner of a trotter will test the speed by having shoes in different shapes and sizes, as well as having the feet trimmed at different angles, and when the angle is found, that will give the best results; the owner will keep a record of the same and give the horse-shoer directions and points in each case.

The average weight of a horse-shoe should be eight ounces. Remember this is for a trotter. Make the shoe fit to the edges of the wall so that there will be no rasping done on the outside. In farm and draft horses this is impossible, as there is hardly a foot of such a uniform shape but what some has to be rasped off.

Use No. 4 nails, or No. 5.

Don't rasp under the clinches of the nails.

Make the shoes the shape of No. 1, Fig. 31.

HOW TO SHOE A HORSE WITH POOR OR
BRITTLE HOOFS

Sometimes it is difficult to shoe so as to make the shoe stay on on account of poor and brittle hoofs. In such a case the shoe should be fitted snug. Make a shoe with a toe clip.

HOW TO SHOE A WEAK-HEELED HORSE

In weak heels the hoof is found to be low and thin from the quarters back. The balls are soft and tender. The shoes should not touch the hoof from the quarters back to the heels. An endless bar shoe is often the best thing for this trouble, giving some frog pressure to help relieve the pressure against the heels.

FOUNDER

Founder is a disease manifested by fever in the feet in different degrees from a simple congestion to a severe inflammation. It is mostly exhibited in the fore feet, being uncommon in the hind feet. The reason for this is the harder pressure, a much greater amount of weight coming on the front feet, the strain and pressure on the soft tissues heavier. The disease is either acute or chronic, in one foot or both. When both feet are diseased the horse will put both feet forward and rest upon the heels so as to relieve the pressure of the foot. If only one foot is affected that foot is put forward and sometimes kept in continual motion, indicating severe pain. The foot is hot, especially around the coronary band. The disease, if not checked, will render the horse useless. When such a horse is brought to you for shoeing it would be best to send him to a veterinarian.

How to shoe: Let the horse stand in a warm mud puddle for six hours, then put on rubber pads or common shoes with feet between the web of the shoe and the hoof, with sharp calks to take up the jar. It would be best not to shoe at all, but let the horse loose in a wet pasture for a good while.

CHAPTER X

COMMON HORSE DISEASES AND THEIR TREATMENT

In this chapter the author desires to give some hints about the treatment for diseases most common to horses.

COLIC

There are two kinds of colic, spasmodic and flatulent.

Spasmodic colic is known by the pains and cramps being spasmodic, in which there are moments of relief and the horse is quiet.

Flatulent colic is known by bloating symptoms and the pain is continual, the horse kicks, paws, tries to roll and lie on his back.

For spasmodic colic give ½ ounce laudanum, ½ pint whisky, ½ pint water; mix well and give in one dose. If this does not help, repeat the dose in half an hour.

For flatulent colic give ½ ounce laudanum, ½ ounce turpentine, ½ pint raw linseed oil, ¼ ounce chloroform, ½ pint water. Mix well and give in one dose. Repeat in one hour if the pain is not relieved.

BOTS

Sometimes there is no other symptom than the bots seen in the dung, and in most cases no other treatment is needed than some purgative.

MANGE

Mange is a disease of the skin due to a class of insects that burrow in the skin, producing a terrible itch and scab, the hair falling off in patches, and the horse rubs against everything. After the affected parts have been washed in soap-water quite warm, dry and rub in the following: 4 ounces oil of tar, 6 ounces sulphur, 1 pint linseed oil.

LICE

Make a strong tea of tobacco and wash the horse with it.

WORMS

There are many kinds of worms. Three kinds of tape worms and seven kinds of other worms have been found in the horse. The tape worms are very seldom found in a horse and the other kinds are easily treated by the following: One dram of calomel, 1 dram of tartar emetic, 1 dram of sulphate of iron, 3 drams of linseed meal. Mix and give in one dose for a few days; then give a purgative. Repeat in three weeks to get rid of the young worms left in the bowels in the form of eggs, but which have since hatched out.

DISTEMPER

Distemper is a disease of the blood. The symptoms are: Swelling under the jaws; inability to swallow; a mucous discharge from the nose.

Give the horse a dry and warm place and nourishing food. Apply hot linseed poultice to the swellings under the jaws and give small doses of cleansing powder for a few days.

HYDROPHOBIA

As soon as a case is satisfactorily recognized, kill the horse, as there is no remedy yet discovered that will cure this terrible disease.

SPAVIN

There are four kinds of spavin and it is difficult for anyone but a veterinarian to tell one kind from another. In all cases of spavin (except blood spavin) the horse will start lame, but after he gets warmed up the lameness disappears and he goes all right until stopped and cooled off; when he starts again, the lameness is worse than before.

There are many so-called spavin cures on the market, some of them good, others worse than nothing. If you don't want to call a veterinarian, I would advise you to use "Kendall's Spavin Cure." This cure is one of the best ever gotten up for this disease, and no bad results will follow the use of it if it does not cure. It is for sale by most druggists.

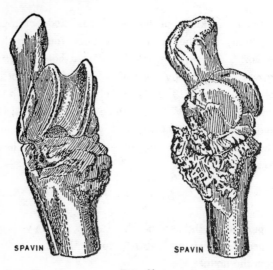

FIG. 41

In nearly all cases of lameness in the hind leg the seat of the disease will be found to be in the hock-joint, although many persons (not having had experience) locate the difficulty in the hip, simply because they cannot detect any swelling of the hock-joint; but in many of the worst cases there is not seen any swelling or enlargement for a long time, and perhaps never.

BONE SPAVIN

Bone spavin is a growth of irregular bony matter from the bones of the joint, and situated on the inside and in front of the joint.

Cause. — The causes of spavins are quite numerous, but usually they are sprains, blows, hard work, and, in fact, any cause exciting inflammation of this part of the joint. Hereditary predisposition in horses is a frequent cause.

Symptoms. — The symptoms vary in different cases. In some horses the lameness comes on very gradually, while in others it comes on more rapidly. It is usually five to eight weeks before any enlargement appears. There is marked lameness when the horse starts out, but he usually gets over it after driving a short distance, and, if allowed to stand for awhile, will start lame again.

There is sometimes a reflected action, causing a little difference in the appearance over the hip joint, and if no enlargement has made its appearance, a person not having had experience is very liable to be deceived in regard to the true location of the difficulty. The horse will stand on either leg in resting in the stable, but when he is resting the lame leg, he stands on the toe.

If the joint becomes consolidated, the horse will be stiff in the leg, but may not have much pain.

Treatment. — That it may not be misunderstood in regard to what is meant by a cure, would say that to stop the lameness, and in most cases to remove the bunch on such cases as are not past any reasonable hopes of a cure.

But I do not mean to be understood that in a case of anchylosis (stiff joint), I can again restore the joint to its original condition; for this is an impossibility, owing to the union of the two bones, making them as one. Neither do I mean that, in any ordinary case of bone spavin which has become completely ossified (that is, the bunch become solid bone), that, in such a case, the enlargement will be removed.

In any bony growths, like spavin or ringbone, it will be exceedingly difficult to determine just when there is a sufficient deposit of phosphate of lime so that it is completely ossified,

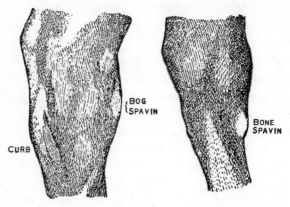

FIG. 42

for the reason that in some cases the lime is deposited faster than in others, and therefore one case may be completely ossified in a few months, while in another it will be as many years.

The cases which are not completely ossified are those that I claim to remove. One of this class which I have seen removed, was a large bone spavin of four or five years standing, and I think that a large percent of cases are not fully ossified for several months or years.

I am well aware that many good horsemen say that it is impossible to cure spavins, and, in fact, this has been the experience of horsemen until the discovery of Kendall's Spavin Cure. It is now known that the treatment which we recommend here will cure nearly every case of bone spavin which is not past any reasonable hopes of a cure, if the directions are followed, and the horse if properly used.

OCCULT SPAVIN

This is similar to bone spavin in its nature, the difference being that the location is within the joint, so that no enlargement is seen, which makes it more difficult to come to a definite conclusion as to its location, and consequently the horse is oftentimes blistered and tormented in nearly all parts of the leg but in the right place.

The causes and effects are the same as in bone spavin, and it should be treated in the same way.

These cases are often mistaken for hip disease, because no enlargement can be seen.

BOG SPAVIN

The location of this kind of a spavin is more in front of the hock-joint than that of bone spavin, and it is a soft and yet firm swelling. It does not generally cause lameness.

BLOOD SPAVIN

This is similar to bog spavin but more extended, and generally involves the front, inside, and outside of the joint, giving it a rounded appearance. The swelling is soft and fluctuating.

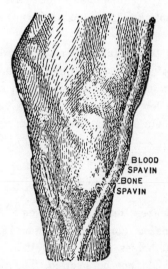

FIG. 43

Young horses and colts, especially if driven or worked hard, are more liable to have this form of spavin than older horses.

SPLINT

This is a small bony enlargement, and generally situated on the inside of the foreleg about three or four inches below the knee point, and occurs frequently in young horses when they are worked too hard.

SPRAIN

By this is meant the sudden shifting of a joint farther than is natural, but not so as to produce dislocation. Every joint is liable to sprain by the horse's falling, slipping, or being over-worked. These cases cause a great deal of trouble, oftentimes producing lameness, pain, swelling, tenderness, and an unusual amount of heat in the part.

Treatment. – Entire rest should be given the horse, and if the part is found hot, as is usually the case, apply cold water cloths, changing frequently, for from one to three days until the heat has subsided, then apply Kendall's Spavin Cure, twice or three times a day, rubbing well with the hand.

If the fever is considerable, it might be well to give fifteen drops of tincture of aconite root, three times a day for one or two days, while the cold water cloths are being applied. Allow the horse a rest of a few weeks, especially in bad cases, as it is very difficult to cure some of these cases, unless the horse is allowed to rest.

STAGGERS

A disease of horses, resulting from some lesion of the brain, which causes a loss of control of voluntary motion. As it gener-ally occurs in fat horses which are well fed, those subject to these attacks should not be overfed. The cause is an undue amount of blood flowing to the brain.

Treatment. – The aim of the treatment should be to remove the cause. In ordinary cases give half a pound of epsom salts, and repeat if necessary to have it physic, and be careful about overfeeding.

In mad staggers, it would be well to bleed from the neck in addition to giving the epsom salts.

RINGWORM

Ringworm is a contagious disease and attacks all kinds of animals, but it often arises from poverty and filth. It first appears in a round bald spot, the scurf coming off in scales.

Cure. – Wash with soap water and dry, then apply the following once a day. Mix 25 grains of corrosive sublimate in half a pint of water and wash once a day till cured.

BALKING

Balking is the result of abuse. If a horse is overloaded and then whipped unmercifully to make the victim perform impossibilities, he will resent the abuse by balking.

There are many cruel methods for curing balking horses, but kindness is the best. Don't hitch him to a load he cannot easily pull. Let the man that is used to handling him drive him. Try to divert his mind from himself. Talk to him; pat him; give him a handful of oats or salt. But if there is no time to wait pass a chain or rope around his neck and pull him along with another horse. This done once, all there is needed in most cases, is to pass the rope around and the horse will start. It is no use trying to whip a balking horse, because balking horses are generally horses of more than common spirit and determination, and they will resent abuse every time. Kindness, patience, and perseverance are the best remedies.

RATTLE-SNAKE BITE

When a horse has been bitten by a rattlesnake, copperhead, or other venomous serpent, give the following: One-half teaspoonful of hartshorn, 1 pint whisky, ½ pint of warm water. Mix well and give one dose. Repeat in one hour if not relieved. Burn the wound at once with a hot iron, and keep a sponge soaked in ammonia over the wound for a couple of hours.

HOOF OINTMENT

Rosin, 4 ounces; bees wax, 4 ounces; pine tar, 4 ounces; fish oil, 4 ounces; mutton tallow, 4 ounces. Mix and apply once a day.

PURGATIVE

Aloes, 3 drams; gamboge, 2 drams; ginger, 1 dram; gentian, 1 dram; molasses, enough to combine the above. Give in one dose, prepared in the form of a ball.

HINTS TO BLACKSMITHS AND HORSE-SHOERS

Don't burn the shoe on.

Don't rasp under the clinchers.

Don't rasp on the outer side of the wall more than is absolutely necessary.

Don't rasp or file the clinch heads.

Don't make the shoes too short. Don't make high calks. Don't pare the frog.

Don't cut down the bars. Don't load the horse down with iron.

ADVICE TO HORSE OWNERS

Every horse-raiser should begin while the colt is only a few days old to drill him for the shoeing. The feet should be taken, one after the other, and held in the same position as a horse-shoer does, a light hammer or even the fist will do, to tap on the foot with, and the feet should be handled and manipulated in the same manner the horse-shoer does when shoeing. This practice should be kept up and repeated at least once a week and the colt when brought to the shop for shoeing will suffer no inconvenience.

WEIGHT OF ONE FOOT IN LENGTH OF
SQUARE AND ROUND BAR IRON

SIZE	SQUARE	ROUND	SIZE	SQUARE	ROUND
1/4	.209	.164	2 1/8	15.000	11.840
5/16	.326	.256	2 1/4	16.900	13.280
3/8	.469	.368	2 3/8	18.835	14.792
7/16	.638	.504	2 1/2	20.871	16.392
1/2	.833	.654	2 5/8	23.112	18.142
9/16	1.057	.831	2 3/4	25.250	19.840
5/8	1.305	1.025	2 7/8	27.600	21.681
11/16	1.579	1.241	3	30.065	23.650
3/4	1.875	1.473	3 1/8	32.610	25.615
13/16	2.201	1.728	3 1/4	35.270	27.702
7/8	2.552	2.004	3 3/8	38.040	29.875
15/16	2.930	2.301	3 1/2	40.900	32.160
1	3.340	2.625	3 5/8	43.860	34.470
1 1/8	4.222	3.320	3 3/4	46.960	36.890
1 1/4	5.215	4.098	3 7/8	50.150	39.390
1 3/8	6.310	4.960	4	53.435	41.980
1 1/2	7.508	5.900	4 1/4	60.320	47.380
1 5/8	8.810	6.920	4 1/2	67.635	53.130
1 3/4	10.200	8.040	4 3/4	75.350	59.185
1 7/8	11.740	9.222	5	83.505	65.585
2	13.300	10.490	6	120.240	94.608

WEIGHTS OF ONE LINEAL FOOT OF FLAT
BAR IRON

THICK-NESS	WIDTH 1	WIDTH 1 1/4	WIDTH 1 1/2	WIDTH 1 3/4
1/8	.416	.521	.624	.728
3/16	.625	.780	.938	1.090
1/4	.833	1.040	1.250	1.461
5/16	1.041	1.301	1.560	1.821
3/8	1.252	1.562	1.881	2.190
7/16	1.462	1.822	2.191	2.550
1/2	1.675	2.085	2.505	2.925
9/16	1.884	2.345	2.815	3.285
5/8	2.085	2.605	3.132	3.655
11/16	2.295	2.860	3.442	4.010
3/4	2.502	3.131	3.752	4.381
7/8	2.921	3.650	4.382	5.100
1	3.331	4.170	5.005	5.832
1 1/8	3.750	4.694	5.630	6.560
1 1/4	4.175	5.210	6.251	7.290
1 3/8	4.580	5.728	6.879	8.022
1 1/2	5.005	6.248	7.502	8.750
1 5/8	5.425	6.769	8.130	9.480
1 3/4	5.832	7.289	8.749	10.208
1 7/8	6.248	7.800	9.380	10.938
2	6.675	8.332	10.005	11.675

WEIGHTS OF ONE LINEAL FOOT OF FLAT
BAR IRON (Continued)

THICK-NESS	WIDTH 2	WIDTH 2 $\frac{1}{4}$	WIDTH 2 $\frac{1}{2}$	WIDTH 2 $\frac{3}{4}$
$\frac{1}{8}$	.832	.937	1.040	1.151
$\frac{3}{16}$	1.251	1.410	1.562	1.720
$\frac{1}{4}$	1.675	1.878	2.080	2.290
$\frac{5}{16}$	2.081	2.342	2.000	2.862
$\frac{3}{8}$	2.502	2.811	3.135	3.445
$\frac{7}{16}$	2.920	3.278	3.650	4.010
$\frac{1}{2}$	3.335	3.748	4.175	4.580
$\frac{9}{16}$	3.748	4.220	4.089	5.160
$\frac{5}{8}$	4.168	4.690	5.211	5.730
$\frac{11}{16}$	4.578	5.160	5.735	6.150
$\frac{3}{4}$	5.005	5.630	6.255	6.880
$\frac{7}{8}$	5.830	6.558	7.395	8.025
1	6.668	7.500	8.332	9.170
1 $\frac{1}{8}$	7.498	8.441	9.382	10.310
1 $\frac{1}{4}$	8.333	9.382	10.421	11.460
1 $\frac{3}{8}$	9.775	10.310	11.460	12.605
1 $\frac{1}{2}$	10.000	11.255	12.505	13.750
1 $\frac{5}{8}$	10.835	12.190	13.545	14.905
1 $\frac{3}{4}$	11.675	13.135	14.585	16.045
1 $\frac{7}{8}$	12.505	14.065	15.635	17.195
2	13.335	15.000	16.675	18.335

WEIGHTS OF ONE LINEAL FOOT OF FLAT
BAR IRON (Continued)

THICK-NESS	WIDTH 3	WIDTH 3 1/4	WIDTH 3 1/2	WIDTH 3 3/4
1/8	1.250	1.350	1.465	1.658
3/16	1.879	2.035	2.195	2.345
1/4	2.505	2.710	2.925	3.135
5/16	3.135	3.391	3.650	3.901
3/8	3.750	4.060	4.380	4.695
7/16	4.385	4.740	5.105	5.470
1/2	5.000	5.425	5.832	6.250
9/16	5.635	6.090	6.565	7.030
5/8	6.255	6.775	7.290	7.805
11/16	6.885	7.455	8.020	8.590
3/4	7.500	8.135	8.750	9.380
7/8	8.750	9.480	10.210	10.940
1	10.000	10.835	11.675	12.500
1 1/8	11.255	12.190	13.135	14.065
1 1/4	12.505	13.540	14.585	15.635
1 3/8	13.750	14.905	16.045	17.195
1 1/2	15.000	16.250	17.500	18.750
1 5/8	16.255	17.605	18.960	20.310
1 3/4	17.505	18.965	20.425	21.880
1 7/8	18.750	20.305	21.885	23.445
2	20.000	21.670	23.335	25.000

WEIGHTS OF ONE LINEAL FOOT OF FLAT
BAR IRON (Continued)

THICK-NESS	WIDTH 4	WIDTH 4¼	WIDTH 4½	WIDTH 4¾
⅛	1.670	1.774	1.887	1.989
³⁄₁₆	2.500	2.658	2.811	2.971
¼	3.331	3.538	3.750	3.960
⁵⁄₁₆	4.168	4.430	4.689	4.950
⅜	5.000	5.311	5.630	5.940
⁷⁄₁₆	5.831	6.200	6.560	6.930
½	6.670	7.082	7.502	7.925
⁹⁄₁₆	7.500	7.965	8.435	8.910
⅝	8.330	8.855	9.380	9.900
¹¹⁄₁₆	9.165	9.740	10.310	10.890
¾	10.000	10.630	11.250	11.880
⅞	11.670	12.400	13.140	13.845
1	13.340	14.165	15.000	15.830
1⅛	15.000	15.940	16.880	17.815
1¼	16.660	17.710	18.755	19.179
1⅜	18.335	19.480	20.650	21.770
1½	20.000	21.255	22.505	23.750
1⅝	21.675	23.025	24.380	25.730
1¾	23.335	24.790	26.240	27.710
1⅞	25.000	26.560	28.140	29.000
2	26.670	28.335	30.000	31.670

INDEX

SOLDERING AND WELDING

B.M. ALLEN
SENIOR WORKS CHEMIST
MULTICORE SOLDERS LIMITED

drake publishers, inc.
new york · london

Published in 1975 by
Drake Publishers Inc.
381 Park Avenue South
New York, N.Y. 10016

ISBN: 0-8473-1120-1

Printed in The United States Of America

CONTENTS

PREFACE

Soldering is the joining of metal parts by melting another, more easily melted, metal between them. It is a very ancient craft, which continues to be used very widely in present-day industrial processes because it is inexpensive, versatile and reliable. The essential requirements have always been quite simple. The parts to be joined must be clean; enough heat must be applied; good quality solder of the correct grade must be used; and a flux is needed to keep the surfaces clean during soldering.

This, together with considerable manual skill and some acquaintance with a few simple solders and fluxes, constituted the traditional craft of fifty years ago. Since then, the rise of the electronic industry in particular has greatly stimulated the development of soldering techniques. To this period belongs the development of the electric soldering iron, multi-cored solder wire, printed wiring, a large range of solder alloys, and of active but non-corrosive fluxes. At the same time, mechanization of the soldering process has reduced (but by no means eliminated) the need for manual skill.

Part 1 of this book, for operators, describes how to use the more common of the methods and material now available; it is hoped that it will be useful both for the industrial solderer and for the amateur. It is also intended to supply some of the basic knowledge required when writing industrial training programs. Part 2, for the designer and engineer, discusses how to choose the right methods and materials to solve particular soldering problems. To help in making this choice, Part 3 gives a number of tables of properties of materials, and of specifications. The emphasis throughout is on practical knowledge rather than theoretical understanding. No previous knowledge of soldering is assumed.

PART 1

MAKING A JOINT

1.1 JOINING METALS

Metals can be joined by — bolts, screws or rivets;
                  — adhesives;
                  — welding, brazing, or hard-soldering;
                  — soft-soldering.

This book deals with soft-soldering. This is usually called simply 'soldering', and is done by melting solder into the gap between the metal parts (the 'workpieces') to be joined.

The joint will not be good unless the solder adheres firmly to both workpieces and completely fills the gap between them. To do this it is essential to clean the workpieces thoroughly, and to apply a flux to the joint. A flux is a substance which melts easily and helps the molten solder to flow on the workpiece surface.

> METAL PARTS CAN BE JOINED BY RUNNING MOLTEN
>   SOLDER BETWEEN THEM
>
> THE SOLDER MUST BE COMPLETELY MOLTEN
>
> THE WORKPIECES MUST BE CLEAN
>
> THE SOLDER WILL NOT FLOW WITHOUT FLUX

1.2 WHEN TO SOLDER

Solder can be used to join practically any metals or alloys except those containing large amounts of chromium or aluminium; these have to be welded or hard-soldered.

Soft solders are so called because they are composed of the rather soft metals tin and lead. They are not so strong as other metals, so the joint should be shaped to give extra strength. This can be done by shaping the workpieces so that they hook together, or by making the joint area large.

1

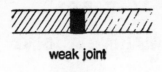

weak joint

strong joints

Fig. 1

Solder melts at much lower temperatures than most other metals, so making and repairing soldered joints is not difficult; but soldered joints must not be made on parts which become very hot in use, as the joints might become weak even before the solder is quite molten.

> DO NOT USE SOLDER ON CHROMIUM OR ALUMINIUM ALLOYS
>
> DO NOT EXPECT SOLDER TO SUPPLY ALL THE STRENGTH OF THE JOINT
>
> DO NOT USE SOLDER ON PARTS WHICH GET VERY HOT IN USE

1.3 TOOLS

1.3.1 SOLDERING IRON

When soldering small pieces, the best tool for heating the work is the electric soldering iron, the most commonly used. Heavy duty irons may be obtained to 750 watts. Irons are available with heating elements ranging from about 25 to 150 watts, and, on a 240 volt single phase supply, should be protected by a 3 ampere fuse. A 25 watt iron with a 5/32 inch diameter tip is satisfactory for electronic work and for small metalware. For large terminals (as on some transformers) and for medium-sized metalware, an 80 watt iron with a 3/8 inch diameter tip should be used. (In America, the word 'tip' is commonly used instead of 'bit').

2

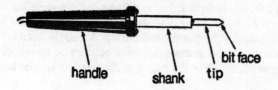

bit face

handle   shank   tip

(figure by courtesy of Weller Electric Limited

Fig. 2

The heating element is in the handle or the shank. The purpose of the **tip** is to carry heat from the shank down to the work, so it is usually made of copper, which conducts heat very easily. It must be big enough to contain reserve heat for keeping the work hot while the solder flows.

To help conduct heat from the tip into the work, it is coated ('tinned') with a layer of tin or solder. While working, this layer may get covered with a layer of oxide scale and charred flux. The scale and charred flux will not conduct heat properly; they must be removed frequently by wiping the tip with a wet sponge. If the tinning burns away completely, it must be renewed by melting a cored solder, such as ARAX, tip, afterwards wiping the re-tinned bit on the wet sponge.

The tip, being made of copper, will slowly get worn away by the solder. It becomes pitted quite quickly, and must then be re-shaped with a file. This wear is very much reduced by using a solder alloy, such as Savbit. Some bits are coated with tinned iron, which greatly reduces the rate of wear. Such bits must never be filed, as once the iron coating has gone, the tip wears out very quickly and must be replaced.

(photograph by courtesy of Weller Electric Limited

Fig. 3

3

Soldering iron bits are not as hot as a flame, but are quite hot enough to produce a serious burn. Soldering irons should therefore not be left lying on a bench, but put in a stand with a guard round the tip. A suitable stand is illustrated in Figure 3. Whatever stand is used, care must be taken to ensure that the bit is not touching anything while the iron is in the stand, otherwise heat will be wasted.

> USE A SOLDERING IRON FOR SMALL OR MEDIUM-SIZED WORK
>
> KEEP THE BIT CLEAN AND WELL-TINNED
>
> REPLACE OR FILE UP THE TIP WHEN IT IS WORN (BUT DO NOT FILE IRON-PLATED TIPS)
>
> KEEP THE IRON ON A GUARD STAND WHEN NOT IN USE

1.3.2 SOLDERING TORCH

(photograph by courtesy of Ronson Products Limited

Fig. 4

4

The soldering torch or blowlamp is used to heat workpieces which are too large to heat with a soldering iron. The work may be heated directly by the flame, or the flame may be used to heat a large copper tip. When used with the tip, the method of use and the care of the tip are exactly the same as for the soldering iron.

The torch, with or without the tip, should not be used on electrical or electronic equipment, partly because misdirection of the flame can cause instant damage and also because water vapor from the flame can condense on colder metal parts near the joint, causing corrosion and affecting insulation.

In some types of torch the temperature can be adjusted by controlling the air and gas flow, but in all types the amount of heat applied can be varied by using different parts of the flame. The tip of the blue part of the flame is the hottest.

A hook should be provided for hanging up blowpipes fed by hoses from natural gas or large cylinders. Torches running on alcohol (methylated spirit) are usually designed to stand on their own, without risk of being knocked over. The new small torches running on small gas bottles in the handle are very convenient but must be provided with a stand or hook so that they cannot fall over when put down. The flame is not easy to see, particularly when working in bright light, so care is required when using them.

> USE A TORCH FOR LARGE WORK
>
> DO NOT USE A TORCH ON ELECTRICAL OR ELECTRONIC WORK
>
> USE THE RIGHT PART OF THE FLAME
>
> BE CAREFUL – TORCHES CAN QUICKLY START FIRES

1.3.3 SOLDER BATH

With some joints the space to be filled is very deep and it is difficult to be sure that solder has penetrated right into the gap. In these cases it is best to coat each workpiece separately with solder before assembling the joint. This is called 'pre-tinning'. It is done by coating the workpiece with liquid flux, allowing the flux to dry, and then dipping it in a bath of molten solder for a few seconds. Parts pre-tinned in this way can often be soldered together simply by heating, if there is enough flux left on them after dipping. This method of soldering is called 'sweating'.

Solder baths are also widely used for making large numbers of joints simultaneously on a large assembly. This is known as 'mass-soldering'. For this purpose large rectangular baths up to several feet long may be used; but much smaller baths, down to crucibles only one inch in diameter, are available for small pre-tinning work. They are usually electrically heated. Solder baths frequently form part of automatic soldering machines more fully described in Section 2.7.

Before dipping any article, the surface of the molten solder in the bath must be scraped or skimmed free of dross (oxide), using a sheet of aluminium or stainless steel as a scraper. If aluminium is used, or if the scraper is small, a wooden handle should be fitted to it, as it quickly becomes too hot to hold. Alternatively, the formation of dross can be prevented by covering the surface with an oil or resin, such as MULTICORE PC 41 Anti-oxidant Solder Cover.

Molten solder splashes very easily and it splashes a long way. Nothing should be dropped or thrown into the bath, and it is particularly important that nothing wet gets into it; the sudden boiling of water or flux solvent can splash the solder out violently. Goggles should always be worn to protect the eyes when using a solder bath. Never use a mercury thermometer in a solder bath, as if it breaks the mercury may boil violently and throw molten solder out of the bath. Use a thermocouple thermometer instead.

USE A SOLDER BATH FOR PRE-TINNING AND MASS-
    SOLDERING

SKIM THE BATH SURFACE IMMEDIATELY BEFORE DIPPING

WEAR GOGGLES

NEVER PUT ANYTHING WET INTO THE BATH

1.3.4 OTHER TOOLS

When workpieces are being soldered together and particularly while the joint is cooling, they must not be allowed to move, because the soldered joint does not develop its full strength until a few minutes after it has cooled right down to room temperature. Some sort of vise or clamp is therefore necessary to hold the workpieces firm, when the hands are fully occupied with the solder and soldering iron. If many joints of the same type are to be made, it may be worthwhile to make a special clamp for that sort of joint only; such a clamp is called a jig.

6

Care must be taken that the clamp is not attached to the workpieces too near the parts of them which are to be soldered, or it will drain heat away from the joint faster than the soldering iron can put it in; the joint will never get hot enough for the solder to flow. If the clamp must be attached close the joint, soft asbestos board should be placed between the jaws and the work in order to cut down heat loss. The common wooden clothes peg makes a good insulated clamp for small work; plastic clothes pegs are unsuitable as the plastic may melt.

If there is a part of the workpiece which must be protected from the heat of soldering, attach a large clamp, without insulator on the jaws, close to that part; the clamp then acts as a 'heat-sink' and stops heat flowing to parts where it is not wanted.

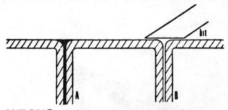

WRONG : Joint A may melt with the heat used when making B

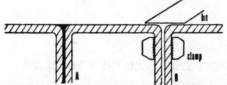

WRONG : Clamp prevents joint B from getting hot enough

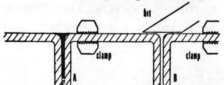

RIGHT : Parts are firmly clamped, but A is prevented from overheating

Fig. 5

7

Large pliers may be used for holding work which is to be dip-soldered. Electricians' narrow-nosed pliers, apart from their use in electronic assembly when putting wires into position before soldering, can also be used as a heat-sink to protect delicate components like transistors while these are being soldered.

For preparing insulated wires before soldering, the range of 'Bib' wire strippers and cutters is very useful. The Model 6 is illustrated (Figure 6). The wire is cut to length with the shears. The setting screw is adjusted with a screwdriver so that, when the tool is closed, the V slots leave a space big enough for the bare wire to pass through. The insulation can then be stripped off by closing the V slots firmly over the wire and pulling it through. Another model of this tool has a selector wheel so that the slot adjustment can be done without a screwdriver.

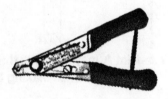

(12046-E

Fig. 6

WHEREVER POSSIBLE, JIG THE WORKPIECES

USE THE JIG AS A HEAT-SINK IF REQUIRED

BUT DO NOT LET THE JIG COOL THE JOINT ITSELF

USE PLIERS TO HOLD THE WORK WHEN DIP-SOLDERING

USE 'BIB' WIRE STRIPPERS FOR WIRE PREPARATION

1.4 MATERIALS

1.4.1 SOLDER

For industrial work, designers have a wide variety of solders to choose from, but for most purposes a choice of three solders is enough. These are: 40/60 tin/lead – This solder melts at a fairly high temperature and is rather soft. It is used for making and repairing metalware of copper, brass, steel or tinplate.

8

60/40 tin/lead – This alloy is more expensive, but melts at a lower temperature and is stronger. It is best suited for dip-soldering and is much used for electronic work. If it is used regularly for electronic circuit soldering with a copper soldering bit, it dissolves the copper rather quickly. It is satisfactory with iron-plated soldering bits.

Savbit 1 – This solder needs a little more heat than does 60/40 to melt it, but it is a little cheaper and just as strong. It contains a small percentage of copper, which prevents copper soldering bits being attacked by the solder. For this reason it is preferred for electronic work when plain copper bits are used.

USE 40/60 FOR METALWARE

60/40 FOR DIP-SOLDERING AND WITH IRON-PLATED SOLDERING BITS

SAVBIT 1 FOR ELECTRONIC WORK WITH PLAIN COPPER SOLDERING BITS

1.4.2 FLUX

Solders containing tin will adhere very firmly to most metals if the metal surface is clean. Solder will not adhere to a rusty or tarnished metal surface. This is because solder adheres by forming an alloy with the metal of the workpiece, and this alloy cannot form if there is a film of oxide, rust or tarnish in the way.

Fluxes are slightly acid materials which melt when heated. When molten they dissolve the rust or tarnish on the workpiece, leaving a perfectly clean surface to which the solder can adhere firmly.

Fluxes must not be too strong or they would attack the metal itself; so they cannot be expected to remove a very thick layer of dirt. Dirt and thick rust, scale or tarnish must therefore be removed first, with a file or wire wheel. Grease or oil should be removed with white spirit or dry-cleaning fluid. The flux will remove thin tarnish layers and prevent more from forming during soldering.

There are two basic types of flux in common use. These are:

SALT FLUXES – for metalware. These are rather corrosive and the residues must be removed, either by washing after the joint has cooled or by burning off while the joint is hot. The best-known of these fluxes is killed spirit (zinc chloride solution, which cannot be burnt off), but the least corrosive salt type is ARAX flux. This is strong enough for soldering most stainless steels. With enough heat, the residues of this flux can be completely burned away; they can also be washed away with hot water.

ROSIN FLUXES – for all electrical and electronic work. Plain rosin was formerly used, but it is not very fast-acting and will only solder tinplate and completely clean copper. For better results an 'activator' must be added. A good activated rosin flux must be non-corrosive, but active enough to allow soldering of copper, brass and other metals used for making electrical connections. ERSIN is a very active but non-corrosive flux of the rosin type. The residues are soluble in methylated spirit, proprietary solvent cleaners or in dry-cleaning fluids.

SOLDER JOINS WORKPIECES BY ALLOYING WITH THEM

SOLDER CANNOT ALLOY WITH METALS COATED WITH DIRT, GREASE OR OXIDE

DIRTY WORKPIECES MUST BE THOROUGHLY CLEANED BEFORE SOLDERING

FLUX DOES THE FINAL CLEANING AND PROTECTS THE SURFACES DURING SOLDERING

USE A SALT TYPE FLUX (such as ARAX) FOR METAL-WARE

USE A ROSIN TYPE FLUX (such as ERSIN) FOR ELEC-TRICAL AND ELECTRONIC WORK

1.4.3 CORED SOLDER AND LIQUID FLUXES

It is not usually convenient to apply the flux and solder separately. To avoid having to do this, fluxes are usually combined with the solder as flux-cored solder wire. This is solder wire with several cores of flux inside it, running the whole length of the wire. This multi-core construction ensures that there is always the right proportion of flux with every piece of solder, and permits rapid flow of flux on to the work when the wire is melted.

40/60 solder wire with four cores of ARAX flux is available for soldering metalware of copper, brass, steel, tinplate and stainless steel. Either Savbit 1 or 60/40 solder wire with five cores of ERSIN flux is used for electrical and electronic work, where the metals to be soldered are usually copper or brass, plain or with a plating of tin, solder or nickel.

The diameter of solder wire to be used depends on the size of the joint. In Great Britain, wire diameters are usually given in S.W.G. (Standard Wire Gauge), of which the higher numbers denote a thinner wire. For metalware, use 14 swg (0.080 inches, 2.0 mm) or 16 swg (0.064 inches, 1.6 mm) for bigger and smaller joints respectively. For ordinary electronic work, use 18 swg (0.048 inches, 1.2 mm) and for printed circuits, use 22 swg (0.028 inches, 0.7 mm).

For dip-soldering, cored solder cannot be used. The articles to be soldered are dipped in a liquid flux, removed, and dried. Not until the flux is nearly dry can the articles be safely dipped in the solder bath, unless there are shields available to protect the operator from solder splatter. For this reason it is best to avoid using water-based liquid fluxes for dipping as they take too long to dry. Instead, a solution of a rosin flux in alcohol (such as ERSIN Liquid Flux) should be used.

The alcohol solvent evaporates easily so the can of ERSIN liquid flux should be kept closed when not in use. The alcohol is also flammable and the flux should therefore be kept away from heat, sparks and flames. The vapour is non-toxic but very slightly soporific, like the thinners in an oil paint, so one should not work with it in a confined space for long periods without good ventilation.

USE FLUX-CORED SOLDER WIRE RATHER THAN APPLY
    THE FLUX SEPARATELY

USE 40/60 4-CORE ARAX, 14 OR 16 SWG, FOR METALWARE

USE SAVBIT 1 OR 60/40 5-CORE ERSIN, 18 OR 22 SWG, FOR
    ELECTRONICS

USE ERSIN LIQUID FLUX FOR DIP-SOLDERING

1.5 METHODS

NOTE: THIS SECTION IS PARTICULARLY IMPORTANT. IT SHOULD BE CAREFULLY READ SEVERAL TIMES BEFORE ATTEMPTING PRACTICAL SOLDERING, AND READ AGAIN AFTERWARDS. THE RULES GIVEN ARE NOT HARD AND FAST; BEGINNERS SHOULD FOLLOW THEM CAREFULLY BUT EXPERIENCED WORKERS MAY WISH TO VARY THEM TO SUIT SPECIAL CIRCUMSTANCES.

1.5.1 SOLDERING WITH AN IRON

It is important to use an iron big enough for the job. Ideally the tip face should be big enough to cover the whole joint. If the job is too large for this, use a torch. For long narrow joints like seams in cans, the bit face should at least equal the width of the seam.

Most electric irons take several minutes to heat up. The iron should therefore be switched on first. The parts to be joined are then cleaned where necessary. Electronic component terminations should not need more cleaning than a wipe to remove dust or grease; but sometimes (on small transformers for instance) there is a film of varnish on the tags, which does not burn off unless the soldering iron is very hot, and which should therefore be scraped off before soldering. Sometimes the nickel or tin coating on brass tags is very difficult to solder and may need cleaning up with a small flat file — this is better than emery, which cannot be completely wiped off. Emery particles easily become embedded in the metal surface, where they prevent solder flow and so weaken the joint.

The parts are then assembled ready for soldering, making sure that there are no large gaps for the solder to fill. In small metalware, the correct 'joint clearance' (the gap which the solder has to fill) is one which will just accept a thin piece of paper. The top of the joint surface should be level so that the solder does not run off, but a long seam may be tilted slightly so that excess solder can be drained away.

Cored solder, of the correct type for the job, is then applied to the bit of the soldering iron. It should melt immediately. If it does not, either the iron is not hot enough, or else the bit is too dirty, and the layer of dirt and charred flux prevents the heat getting through and melting the solder. If this is so the bit should be wiped clean on a wet sponge. If this is not enough, the tip should be cleaned with a file, and cored solder applied immediately afterwards to renew the tinning. (Remember that iron-plated tip should never be cleaned with a file).

12

Applying the iron directly to the work to heat it is very inefficient, and merely oxidises the workpiece surfaces, making them more difficult to solder. It is much better to apply cored solder to the work, and then melt the solder with the iron. This is the most efficient way of heating the work, by letting the solder and the flux carry the heat from the soldering tip to the workpiece surface.

Right   Wrong

Fig. 7

Rubbing the work with the iron should not normally be necessary, particularly on electronic joints, but on small metalware rubbing may help to spread the heat if the iron is not quite big enough to cover the whole joint.

While the work is heating up, the solder will remain of a muddy consistency. Then quite suddenly the solder becomes bright and fluid, flowing out and wetting the workpieces. In this condition, if enough solder has been applied, it will completely penetrate the joint gap. This should happen only a few seconds after starting to heat.

If it takes longer, the flux and even the solder will become burned. More cored solder wire must then be pushed in under the iron; when good wetting has been obtained, the excess solder must be drained off on to the bit, tilting the joint assembly if necessary. Such a joint will never look as good as one made right first time.

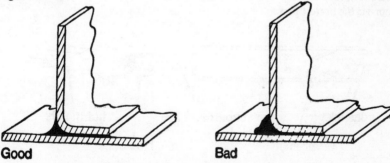

Good   Bad

Fig. 8

13

When the joint looks satisfactory, remove the iron and allow the joint to cool on its own, without disturbing it until it is quite cold. It is not usually good practice to cool a joint in water, because if the parts cool and shrink at different rates the joint may be weakened. The hot iron should be hung up or put in a guard stand when not in use.

USE THE RIGHT SIZE IRON

GIVE IT TIME TO HEAT UP

CLEAN AND CLAMP THE JOINT PARTS

CLEAN AND TIN THE SOLDERING IRON TIP

MELT THE SOLDER ON THE JOINT

WATCH IT FLOW, KEEPING THE JOINT HOT

LET THE JOINT COOL BEFORE REMOVING IT FROM
    THE CLAMP

1.5.2 TORCH SOLDERING

A flame is very much hotter than a soldering iron tip, so torch soldering should not be used on anything with parts which could melt or burn. Rosin-cored solder is not very satisfactory for use with a torch because the rosin burns off too quickly, and in any case a salt flux is needed to cope with the film of oxide rapidly formed on the hot metal.

The torch flame consists of an invisible cold inner zone of unburned gas, an intensely hot blue cone of burning gas, and an almost invisible outer 'mantle' of very hot burnt gas. Even the blue cone is not easy to see in bright sunlight, so care is needed to make sure that the flame is not misdirected. The tip of the blue cone is the hottest part.

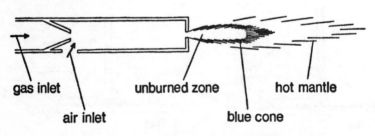

gas inlet   unburned zone   hot mantle

air inlet   blue cone

Fig..9

14

The workpieces should be cleaned thoroughly with a wire brush or file to remove all visible rust, scale and dirt, and washed if necessary in white spirit to remove grease. Paint can be burnt off with the torch, and the area then wire-brushed. The work should then be set up in a clamp or vise, allowing a paper-thin gap at the joint itself for the solder to penetrate. Make sure that the clamp is not so placed as to drain heat from the joint.

The torch should then be lit, after taking careful note of the maker's instructions for its operation.

The joint area should be heated first with the outer mantle of the flame because if the whole area is very warm it is easier to keep the joint itself very hot. Then the flame is moved in towards the joint and brought closer, so that the immediate neighbourhood of the joint is made very hot by the tip of the blue cone. Next the flame is moved right in so that the actual joint is just inside the blue tip, which spreads around it. This helps to de-oxidise the joint. Finally the flame is removed completely and cored solder quickly applied. This should melt and spread immediately; if it does not the joint is not hot enough. The right technique is quickly developed after a few trials; it is advisable to make some practice joints first on scrap metal to get used to it. The time taken to make a joint depends on its size, but is usually less than a minute from start of heating. (see Fig. 10, p.16).

When making a long seam, the flame is moved slowly down the seam with the solder wire following, so that all stages are proceeding simultaneously at different parts of the seam. The seam is clamped slightly sloping, so that any excess solder drains down towards the flame; but if solder wire is pushed in at the right rate there will not be much excess. The solder should not be heated directly by the blue cone of the flame.

The joint should not be removed from the clamp until quite cold. It should then be removed and scrubbed with hot water to remove the ARAX flux residue, which might otherwise corrode the joint in a damp atmosphere.

After use the torch should be put in a stand or hung up, and the flame extinguished unless it is to be used again soon afterwards. It should never be left burning unattended.

USE ARAX-CORED WIRE, NOT A ROSIN-CORED TYPE

CLEAN THE WORKPIECES THOROUGHLY AND CLAMP
THEM IN POSITION

15

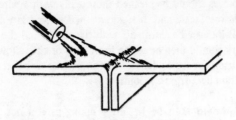

Stage 1 : General heating

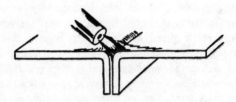

Stage 2 : Strong local heating

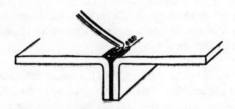

Stage 3 : Soldering

Fig. 10

16

LIGHT THE TORCH AND HEAT THE JOINT AREA

STRONGLY HEAT THE JOINT ITSELF

REMOVE THE FLAME AND APPLY ARAX CORED
SOLDER WIRE

WATCH THE SOLDER WETTING AND FILLING THE
JOINT

TURN OUT THE FLAME AND LET THE JOINT COOL

WASH THE JOINT

1.5.3 DIP-SOLDERING

This is used for pre-tinning parts which are later to be sweated together with an iron or flame, and for soldering pre-assembled work such as components on printed circuit boards.

The bath may need to be switched on anything from thirty minutes to three hours before use, depending on its size. It should be filled with good-quality 60/40 solder, such as MULTICORE EXTRUSOL.

The parts to be tinned should be thoroughly cleaned, and then dipped in a ERSIN Liquid Flux, such as Ersin. Excess flux is drained off and the solvent allowed to evaporate until the residue is sticky. This will take about five minutes at ordinary temperatures but can be speeded up by a warm air blast. The solvent must be dried off before dipping, partly to lessen the danger of solder being splashed out of the bath, and partly to ensure that bubbles of solvent vapour do not get trapped and prevent the solder from flowing to all parts of the area to be tinned. Presence of solvent would also cool the solder and so lengthen the time needed to make the joint.

The temperature of the bath should be tested with a thermocouple, not with a mercury thermometer. It should be 230 – 250°C (450 – 480°F) for printed circuits, and about 300°C (570°F) for dip-tinning larger pieces of metalwork. If a thermocouple is not available, a very rough indication of temperature is given by floating a small piece of white newspaper on the bath. At 240°C, it becomes light straw in colour after ½ minute, but at 300°C and over it becomes brown within five seconds. The bath surface should be scraped clean and bright before doing this test.

The bath surface should also be scraped mirror-bright immediately before dipping the workpiece, unless an anti-oxidant is used as a protective cover to prevent oxidation. The dipping should be done slowly, to allow time for flux to rise to the surface and not get trapped, and the workpiece held immersed for long enough to be sufficiently heated. This time varies from two or three seconds for printed circuits to about thirty seconds for very large workpieces. The work should then be withdrawn slowly enough for excess solder to run off it; this will prevent the formation of solder icicles, so long as the work has got sufficiently hot. The flux residues need not be removed, but if desired may be washed off with methylated spirit or dry-cleaning fluid. Flux should only be removed from printed circuit boards in special degreasing equipment with solvents which do not damage component identification paints.

SWITCH THE BATH ON WELL BEFORE IT IS NEEDED

CLEAN THE PARTS, DIP THEM IN LIQUID FLUX (such as ERSIN) AND SET TO DRY

SCRAPE THE BATH SURFACE AND CHECK THE TEMPERATURE

DIP THE PARTS SLOWLY

LEAVE THEM LONG ENOUGH TO HEAT THROUGH

REMOVE THEM SLOWLY

1.6 JOINTS

1.6.1 METALWARE

Fig. 11 The Butt

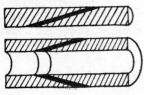

The butt joint is weak and should not be used for rod or pipe. In sheet metal work it is only used for lead roofing, guttering, and flashing (lead sheet used to prevent leakage at joints of roofing).

Fig. 12 The Scarf

The scarf joint may be used for rod or pipe in any metal, but is not usually used for sheet. It is most commonly used for lead pipe in domestic plumbing.

18

Fig. 13 The Lap

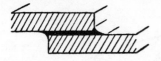

This is the simplest joint to use for sheet metal work. The strength of the joint may be increased by increasing the extent of the overlap; but if the overlap is very wide, it may be necessary to pre-tin the parts and sweat them together.

Fig. 14 The Double Lap or Lockseam

This joint is usually used for making the side seam of tinplate cans. It is very strong, but it is not easily formed without special equipment, which is needed to make it neatly and with the correct clearance.

Fig. 15 The Strap

The strap joint has similar applications as the lap joint, but is especially useful when one side of the joint must be smooth.

Fig. 16 The Sleeve

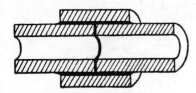

This is the application of the strap joint to rod or pipe; it is used in copper plumbing.

Fig. 17 The Double Strap

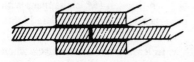

This has the same applications as the lap or strap, but has greater resistance to bending. It should be made by pre-tinning and sweating.

1.6.2 ELECTRONIC CIRCUIT ASSEMBLY

All wires should be cut to length before assembly, as it is difficult to trim them neatly afterwards, and the strains of cutting may seriously weaken the joint. If wires must be cut after soldering, cutters with a shearing action like the

Bib stripper (Figure 18b) should be used. 'Side-cutters' with a pinching action (Figure 18a) should never be used on wires already soldered or on termination

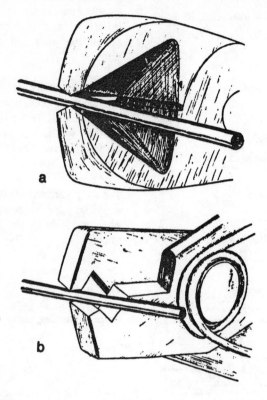

a

b

Fig. 18

wires of components, as the shock of the final pinch-through (which happens with a sharp click) may seriously damage the component or weaken a soldered joint.

Wires should be cut to such a length as to leave them a little slack when assembled, and should not be straightened by pulling. Such pulling tempers the wire, and if by either springiness or shortness or both, the wire is made taut, it and the soldered joints at each end of it are made more liable to damage by vibration.

Generally, soldered joints should not be made on component terminations closer than 1/16 inch (1.6 mm) to the body of the component, or it may be damaged by the heat of soldering. For some components the distance may be greater, and the component manufacturers' recommendations should be followed.

When soldering components into a circuit, if the joint cannot be made in two or three seconds it should be dismantled and the parts carefully cleaned by degreasing and scraping before trying again. The parts should then solder quickly. If attempts are made to improve the joint merely by continuing heating and applying more flux and solder, the component or the wire insulation will be damaged by the heat and the joint will have too much solder on it. This excess solder may hide the signs of a bad quality joint. Continued heating can also cause brittleness in soldered copper wires, especially if these are thin, because of the tendency of the copper to dissolve in the solder. This is particularly true of wires consisting of a bunch of strands, each strand being quite thin.

Soldered copper wires are weakest at the point where they emerge from the solder, and should not be bent at this point after soldering. It is sometimes useful, where space permits, to put a small S-bend or loop at this point of the wire before soldering, so that any shock or strain in the wire will be taken up by the spring in the loop and not transmitted to the joint.

Most electronic circuit joints are between a wire and a tag or between a wire and a printed circuit board. These should always be made by threading the wire through the hole in the tag or board and then bending it 90° (for a tag) or 45° (for a board), before soldering. Bends should not be made with any tool which might cut or nick the wire. The joint is then easy to inspect for proper

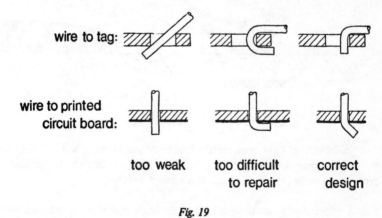

Fig. 19

wetting, can be easily unmade if the component has to be replaced, and yet is mechanically strong enough.

CUT WIRES TO LENGTH BEFORE SOLDERING

USE SHEARS, NOT NIPPERS, TO CUT SOLDERED
WIRES

LEAVE WIRES A LITTLE SLACK

DO NOT SOLDER TOO CLOSE TO THE COMPONENT
BODY

DO NOT HEAT FOR TOO LONG

DO NOT BEND WIRES AT THE JOINT AFTER SOLDERING

WIRES SHOULD NOT BE *FULLY* HOOKED ON TO TAGS
OR BOARDS

1.7 JOINT QUALITY

Solder adheres to a workpiece because the metals in the solder react with the metals of the workpiece to form a thin layer of alloy.

When the molten solder has alloyed with the workpiece, the solder surface forms a shallow angle with the workpiece surface, (Figure 20) and is said to have 'wetted' it.

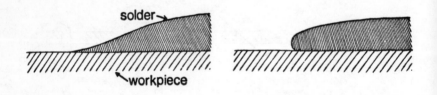

solder

workpiece

Fig. 20   *Fig. 21*

Solder will only wet clean metals. It will not wet oxide, rust, tarnish, grease, dirt, or any other non-metallic material. On a dirty surface the solder surface forms a deep angle (Figure 21) because it cannot wet the dirt.

A soldered joint is only good when the angle is shallow round ALL edges of the solder. The joint should be remade if there is a steep angle at ANY point of the edge.

22

When solder sets it shrinks. The centre of a mass of solder is the part which cools last and the part where most of the shrinkage takes place. A small dimple forms at the centre of the solder surface. This is normal and is not a defect.

When 60/40 solder freezes, the surface is usually mirror-bright all over, but when Savbit 1 or 40/60 freezes, the surface at the dimple becomes slightly frosty or crystalline. This is also quite normal.

The Figures 22 to 28 illustrate cross-sections of a good joint and six common faults. The important features for identifying the faults are the shape of the solder surface, the angle it makes with the workpiece surface, and the extent of penetration into the gap.

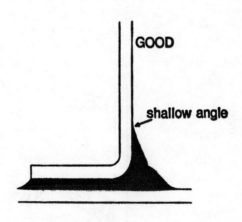

Fig. 22

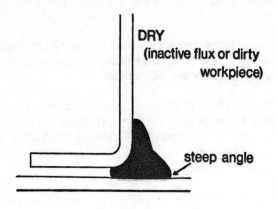

Fig. 23

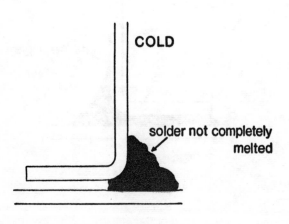

Fig. 24

24

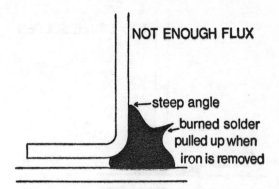

NOT ENOUGH FLUX

← steep angle

← burned solder
pulled up when
iron is removed

Fig. 25

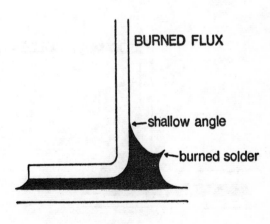

BURNED FLUX

←shallow angle

←burned solder

Fig. 26

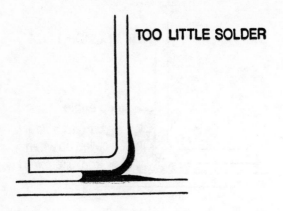

TOO LITTLE SOLDER

Fig. 27

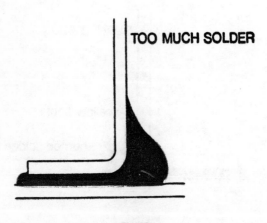

TOO MUCH SOLDER

Fig. 28

26

SOLDER ADHERES BY ALLOYING WITH THE
WORKPIECE

WETTING IS THE VISIBLE SIGN OF ALLOYING

WETTING CANNOT TAKE PLACE IF THE WORKPIECES
ARE DIRTY OR ARE NOT HOT ENOUGH

PART 2

CHOOSING METHODS AND MATERIALS

2.1 INTRODUCTION

In Part 1 the subject of soldering was discussed in terms of the technique used by the operator to make the joint. To avoid complication, attention was concentrated on the skill required and only a few essential solders and fluxes were described. However, the range of soldering materials now available to the designer is quite wide. The application of these materials is discussed in the sections which follow. The information supplements rather than repeats that given in Part 1. Of necessity, the approach has to be rather more technical; but technicalities have not been introduced for their own sake. They have only been included where they are needed to understand how to make a choice between alternatives.

Soldered joints are joints made between two metal surfaces by melting a third metal, the solder, between them. A distinction is made between hard-soldering, in which the operating temperature exceeds 450°C, and soft-soldering, where the operating temperature is less than 450°C. This choice of temperature is somewhat arbitrary but nevertheless convenient. Hard-soldering, as the name implies, is done with solders or brazing alloys very much harder than the tin-lead alloys used for soft-soldering, and the flux used is usually (though not always) based on borax. This, and other salts containing oxygen, are not satisfactory for soft-soldering. The boundary temperature of 450°C lies above the highest temperature at which rosin-based fluxes can be used, and below the lowest temperature at which the borax-based fluxes can be expected to operate.

The soldering of aluminium, which is done with the rather hard tin-zinc alloys, is really more akin to a hard-soldering process in spite of the low melting temperature (about 300°C) of the solders used; it is only briefly referred to (p. 42). The use of the soft-soldering process in joining lead pipe is not treated here as it is already fully described in texts on plumbing . Similarly, lead-burning (the low-temperature welding of lead sheet or pipe without the use of flux) is also excluded.

29

2.2 THE USES OF THE SOLDERED JOINT

The technique of soft-soldering is used for one or more of the following purposes:

filling: building up a surface with solder to give the surface some special shape.

bonding: increasing the mechanical strength of the joint.

caulking: sealing a joint against leakage of fluids.

electrical: providing a permanent electrical path.

thermal: providing good thermal contact.

Each of these types of joint demands good adhesion of the solder to the surface. To obtain good adhesion, the solder must react with and alloy with the workpiece surface. Unless this reaction takes place over the entire joint face of each workpiece, the joint is liable to fail. Fortunately, this reaction and formation of the alloy film is spontaneous and self-maintaining when certain conditions have been met. The designer has to ensure, by his design, that these conditions can always be secured, not merely on the prototype but also on the production line. He can do this by correctly specifying the joint form; the solder; the flux; the workpiece material; and the heating method.

2.3 JOINT FORM

2.3.1 JOINT STRENGTH

The tensile, creep and shear strength of solders is low compared with most other metals. In some small joints which are only very lightly loaded in service, it is permissible to rely entirely on the strength of the solder − in attaching a badge to a brooch or spoon for example. In all other cases, as much additional strength as possible must be derived from the shape of the joint. This can be done in several ways, which are illustrated in Figures 29 to 31.

Increasing the area of joint face, as in Figure 29, increases the strength in direct proportion. In Figure 30 an example is shown of an inherently weak joint, on which the stresses have been reduced by surrounding it with an array of similar joints. In this way, though each individual joint is weak, the complete framework is stiff.

a

b

Fig. 29

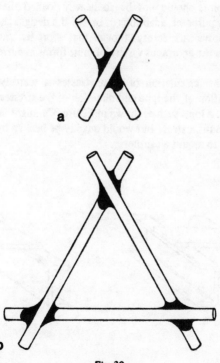

a

b

Fig. 30

A third method of increasing the strength of the joint is to interlock the joint members. The solder then serves only to make the joint rigid and so prevent it working loose. The lock-seam joint between two sheets is typical (Figure 31).

Fig. 31

It is rarely necessary to make detailed calculations of joint form or strength, since soldered joints should not be so heavily loaded that their strength is critical. For many purposes, adaptions of one of the designs shown in Section 3.1 (p. 87) should prove satisfactory, though that short list cannot claim to be a complete guide to the enormous variety of joint forms in current use.

Though exact calculation of joint stresses is scarcely ever necessary, a general consideration of the type and direction of the stresses is important when choosing a design. A joint such as shown in Figure 32a might be quite satisfactory when used to mount a strut, but would quickly be broken by vibration if used, as in Figure 32b, to mount a cantilever.

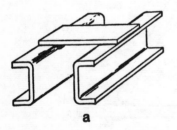

a

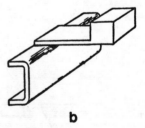

b

Fig. 32(a)   Fig. 32(b)

32

In the butt joint in pipe shown in Figure 33a, tension along or pressure within the pipe is thrown entirely on to the solder, whereas in the scarf joint of Figure 33b, pressure within the pipe is taken by the pipe; tension formerly concentrated into the small cross-section of the butt is now largely transformed into shear, reduced by being spread over a large area. The sleeve joint of Figure 33c converts the tension entirely into shear over as large an area as is required; it is also easier to produce a smooth bore in this type of joint.

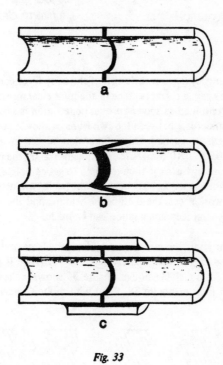

Fig. 33

2.3.2 JOINT CLEARANCE

As previously mentioned, solder adheres to each workpiece by the formation of a thin film of alloy. Adhesion will be bad if this film does not form properly; on the other hand, if alloying proceeds too far, the two films grow, at the expense of the solder, until they become one, and the joint though very hard is then brittle. Calculation of the growth rate is not practicable as the rate depends on the exact temperature and on the crystal structure of the workpiece metals.

There are two types of joint gap, as illustrated in **Figure 34**.

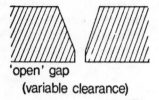
'open' gap
(variable clearance)

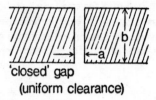
'closed' gap
(uniform clearance)

Fig. 34

In the open gap, there is little risk of the alloy layer completely filling the joint. In the closed gap, a correct choice of the joint clearance 'a' will ensure that, if heating is discontinued as soon as proper penetration has been achieved, there is still a layer of solder left between the two films of alloy. Experience shows that maximum strength is reached when dimension 'a' lies in the range 0.002 to 0.004 inches (0.05 to 0.10 mm). Clearly, dimension 'b', the joint depth, should not be too large, otherwise in the time required to get complete penetration, alloy formation will proceed too far. The upper limit for 'b' will depend very much on the size of the workpieces, the method of heating, and the type of solder and flux used – no general recommendation can be made.

In the open joint, the clearance may be quite large over most of the joint, but there must alway be some part where the clearance is small enough for liquid solder to form a stable bridge. Figure 35 shows, enlarged, the narrowest part of the open joint in Figure 34, filled with molten solder. In Figure 35a, a

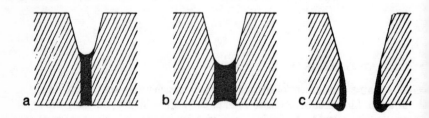

Fig. 35

34

stable film of liquid solder fills the gap. In Figure 35b, the gap is bigger and the film becomes less stable. In Figure 35c, the gap is too big and the film breaks. It can only be re-formed by using a very large excess of solder, added at a temperature just over its melting point; and such a joint will be very weak. This rule is very important: though the finished joint consists of *solid* solder, the joint form must be such that it is possible for a *liquid* to reach the desired position and remain in it.

Flow of molten solder in the joint gap is impeded by convexity of the surface over which it must flow, and is assisted by concavity. In Figure 36a, flow of solder over the sharp (highly convex) edge cannot occur. Flow is made easier if the angle is reduced (Figure 36b) or the edge is radiused (Figure 36c). Very

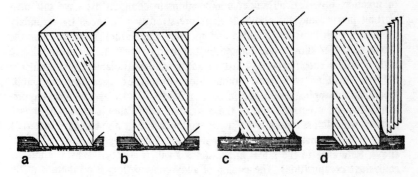

a   b   c   d

Fig. 36

concave shapes such as grooves (Figure 36d) take solder very readily. The extreme case of this effect occurs when the sides are parallel; if not too far apart, they will suck up molten solder very readily. This effect is usually termed 'capillarity'. It may be used to direct the solder flow where required. Conversely, sharp edges may be placed to stop solder flowing into places where it is not required; in Figure 37 for example, flow of solder down the bore (while soldering the end face) may be retarded be ensuring that the edge where the bore intersects the end face is sharp.

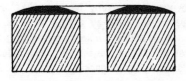

Fig. 37

An example of the use of capillarity is the removal of excess solder from the joint by dipping a fluxed multi-strand wire into the molten solder; the excess solder is sucked into the wire by capillary action. This practice is known as 'wicking', by analogy with the wick of an oil lamp. A joint so treated is sometimes described as a wicked joint, a somewhat ambiguous description.

2.4 SOLDER

2.4.1 GENERAL

Since adhesion of the joint members depends on their being wetted by the solder, the wetting power of the solder is the property of primary importance. In practice, however, all solder compositions in common use have sufficient wetting power, and the choice is therefore strongly influenced by secondary properties such as strength, price and melting temperature. In many cases, the choice of solder alloy is also limited by the need to use materials in compliance with a public specification. A list of solder alloys available from Multicore Solders, together with their composition, properties, uses and the public specifications applicable is given in Section 3.2 (p. 93) Unless technical requirements demand otherwise, one of these standard alloys should always be chosen as they will almost certainly be more economical than non-standard materials. There is unfortunately no international standard covering the range of solder alloys. Reference to the tables in Section 3.3 will, it is hoped, assist in choosing equivalent compositions. The coding of alloy compositions used there is made possible because, though the exact composition limits differ slightly between different specifications, the differences are not very significant in practice.

Soldering products suffer very little, if any, deterioration on storage under normal conditions, but some points are worth mentioning. Solders, particularly those containing a high proportion of lead, may eventually develop a fairly thick film of oxide on their surface. (This is most noticeable on the outer layer of wire on reels kept on workshop benches; it occurs only very slowly, if at all, on reels stored in the fibreboard cases in which they are supplied). When the solder is melted, the flux has to remove this oxide as well as the tarnish on the workpiece, and its efficiency may thereby be somewhat reduced. The oxide can easily be removed before soldering by wiping the wire with a cloth or tissue paper. The reduction of soldering efficiency by oxide is much more noticeable with solder baths (see p. 67) and it is therefore advisable to use only solder bars protected from oxidation by shrink-packing in polythene film.

2.4.2 TIN-LEAD SOLDERS

Almost all soft solders are tin alloys. The function of the tin is to react with and alloy with the workpiece metal. With most of the metals from which workpieces are made, tin reacts to form intermetallic compounds which, though strong, are rather brittle. It is therefore necessary to moderate the action of the tin by first alloying it with another metal, usually lead. This procedure also reduces the melting temperature and increases the strength. Figure 38 shows how the melting temperature of the tin-lead alloys varies with the tin content. Note that only the two pure metals and the eutectic melt at single temperatures.

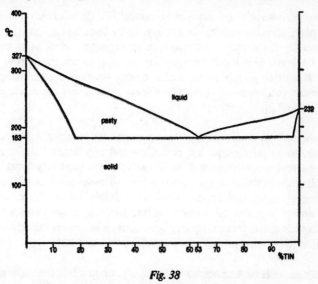

Fig. 38

All the other compositions melt over a temperature range, the upper limit of which is called the liquidus and the lower end the solidus. In between these two temperatures, the solder is of a more or less pasty consistency. There is a minimum melting temperature and maximum strength at 63% tin, 37% lead, the eutectic mixture. There is no advantage in using tin-lead solders with tin contents higher than 63% because the price and melting temperature increase while the strength decreases. Going to the other extreme, plain tin-lead solders containing less than 10% of tin are weak and brittle, and have poor wetting power. Interest therefore centres on solders containing between 10 and 60% of tin. The choice between various solders in this range depends on a balance between the price advantage of reducing the tin content (tin costs roughly fourteen times as much as lead) and the technical advantages of higher strength, lower soldering temperature and better wetting power. Now the wetting power of solders increases with increasing

37

soldering temperature. Where it is possible to use a high soldering temperature, one can use a solder with lower tin content. For repairing damage to automobile body-work, in making automobile radiators, in mechanical joints of many sorts, and in brass-capped electric lamps, solders containing 10 to 35% of tin are used. For smaller mechanical joints, in plumbing, and in motors and transformers, it is more usual to use 40% tin; while in electrical and electronic circuits, where there are heat-sensitive components, it is necessary to use 60% tin.

2.4.3 ANTIMONY IN SOLDERS

In small quantities, antimony behaves much like tin in its wetting behaviour, but on plain brass, its affinity for the zinc in the brass is much greater than that of the tin for the copper component; in consequence, when using antimonial solders on brass, it is much too easy for the joint to become brittle. For this reason, it is often prohibited for solders to contain more than 0.2% antimony, in particular for electrical work, where brass components are much used (see BS 441, table 3.3.1).

However, tin itself is subject to a recrystallisation when it gets very cold; it is then no longer metallic but crystalline and very brittle. The change also causes the solder containing the tin to swell and the joint may break up. This recrystallization of tin can be completely prevented by the presence of 0.2 to 0.5% of antimony in the solder (see QQ-S-571d, table 3.3.1). Such solders are recommended if prolonged exposure of the joint to temperatures well below 0°C is expected, but presumably any brass parts to be soldered should be nickel-plated first to prevent reaction of the antimony with the zinc.

Solders with larger amounts of antimony, up to 5% of the tin content, are much used on automobile body work. These must never be used on brass, galvanized surfaces or other zinc-bearing metals. The solders have a slightly higher strength than the simple tin-lead alloys.

2.4.4 IMPURITIES IN SOLDERS

The metals used in the manufacture of Multicore Solder are usually at least 99.95% pure. Most of the remaining 0.05% is antimony, with which tin is usually associated in the ore. In ordinary 'antimony-free' solders, the antimony content is usually between 0.03 to 0.09%. The copper content of a good tin-lead solder is somewhat lower, usually around 0.02 to 0.04%. Neither of these impurities are deleterious in themselves even at much higher concentrations, and may even be deliberately added to produce special qualities, but if they

38

are both present in large *undeclared* quantities, it implies that the solder has been made from scrap metal. Such solder must be viewed with suspicion, not because of the effects of copper or antimony themselves but because other more harmful impurities may also be present.

The quantity of impurity which may be permitted in solder for mass-soldering of printed circuits is subject to certain restrictions, which are dealt with in Section 2.7.3.8 (p. 76). In cored solder wire, rather larger quantities of impurity may be tolerated. The harmful impurities may be divided into three classes depending on their effect on solder flow, on brittleness, and on maximum service temperature. Some impurities belong to more than one of these classes.

Effect on solder flow:

The most harmful class, the oxidizers, include zinc and aluminium. These metals, in quantities above 0.005%, produce a skin of zinc or aluminium oxide on the solder surface which is not easily dissolved by flux; this skin is very strong and prevents the solder from flowing properly.

Effect on brittleness:

The second class of impurity includes metals which react with tin to produce a hard, crystalline alloy. The dangers of this class (which includes iron, copper and antimony) are somewhat overrated in the solder standards. It is true that they may make the solder a little more brittle if they are present in very large quantities, but since most workpieces are composed of such metals, they must also be present in appreciable quantities in any soldered joint, no matter how pure the solder was initially. The limits usually quoted for iron and arsenic are 0.02 and 0.05% respectively. Copper is usually limited to 0.3% of the tin content, though it can be as high as 3.0% of the tin content without in any way impairing the properties of the solder. The addition of copper in fact gives the solder certain additional properties which are discussed in more detail in the next section, 2.4.5. Silver and gold also belong to this class of crystal-forming metals. Silver, like copper, can with advantage be added to solder to produce alloys with special properties (see Section 2.4.5). It does not occur as an impurity in solders except in extremely small quantities, derived from the lead. Gold is not present in solder itself but, when soldering electronic parts plated with gold, the gold may dissolve in the solder and produce brittleness in the joint. This is discussed more fully in Section 2.6.3.

39

Effect on maximum service temperature:

The third class of impurities are those metals such as zinc, cadmium, bismuth and indium, which may affect the melting characteristics. Mixtures of these metals with tin and lead melt at very much lower temperatures than ordinary solders. Normally these metals are only present in very minute proportions. It is possible, though as yet unproved, that very minute amounts of these impurities account for the 'hot-shortness' of solders. Hot-shortness is the term used to describe the complete loss of mechanical strength a few degrees below the melting temperature. It occurs with all solders, even those having a very high degree of purity. Quite apart from hot-shortness, there is in any case a decline in strength as solder is heated above room temperature; a temperature of 40°C below the solidus should be regarded as the maximum safe service temperature for any solder alloy.

2.4.5 OTHER SOLDER ALLOYS

Tin-lead alloys containing 50 to 60% of tin wet the workpiece metal very rapidly; if the workpiece surface is of copper or silver, the attack may be too rapid in spite of the presence of 40 to 50% of lead. Solder alloys are available containing small quantities of added copper or silver, as appropriate, to suppress this attack at normal soldering temperatures while retaining adequate wetting power.

Alloys containing copper equal to 3% of the tin content are available from Multicore Solders under the name 'SAVBIT'. These alloys are particularly suitable for reducing the rate of attack on copper soldering iron tips and for soldering fine copper wire. The relative rates of attack on copper are shown in Figure 39. In Figure 39a is shown a copper soldering iron tip after it has made 10,000 joints with Savbit 1 alloy. Figure 39b shows an identical tip which has made only 7,500 joints with 60/40 alloy. Of course part of the loss is due to re-surfacing made necessary by the deep pitting of the tip which occurs when using plain tin-lead − the erosion is never uniform. By using Savbit alloys, the cost of tip maintenance and replacement is very much reduced.

This saving can only be made if the tip is run at temperatures up to about 320°C. Above this temperature, the rate of tip wear may increase rather rapidly. Multicore alloy Savbit 1 is approved for use in lieu of 60/40 under Mintech Approval No. DTD.900/4535.

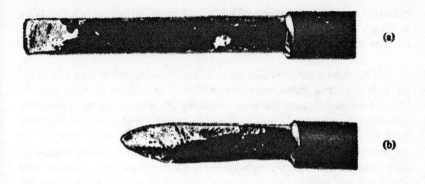

(a)

(b)

Fig. 39

Absorption of copper by tin-lead solder can cause serious weakening of thin copper workpieces such as fine wire or the conductive pattern of printed circuits. The use of Savbit solder prevents this attack.

The Multicore alloy LMP, containing silver, suppresses absorption of silver from the workpiece in just the same way as Savbit suppresses absorption of copper from the tip or from fine wire. It is used for soldering connections to the silvered surfaces of ceramic capacitors.

60/40 tin-lead alloy, commonly used in electronics, melts in the range 183 to 188°C and so requires a minimum soldering temperature of 230 to 250°C depending on the method of heating used. This temperature could damage certain components. It is necessary in these cases to use Multicore TLC alloy melting at 145°C and requiring a soldering temperature of only 210°C.

Though most solders are tin-lead alloys, there are several other alloys of tin available for special purposes. Pure tin itself is useful for certain purposes, in particular for the manufacture of transistor cases and in the making of jewellery and pewter ware. Tin with 5% of antimony is also used for soldering pewter ware; pewter itself is nowadays usually composed of tin with 5 to 10% of antimony. 95/5 tin-antimony melts in the range 236 to 242°C and is useful for joints which must withstand temperatures above 180°C. Another useful alloy for high temperature work is 96/4 tin-silver, which melts at 221°C. It is strong, does

41

not easily tarnish, has relatively high electrical conductivity, and being lead-free is completely non-toxic. It is therefore of value for high-quality electrical instruments, food-handling machinery and surgical implants.

It has been mentioned that tin-lead alloys containing less than 10% of tin are both weak and brittle, especially in the as-cast (unworked) state usual in soldered joints. However, the alloy containing 5% of tin is greatly improved in both strength and wetting power by the addition of 1.5% of silver. This Multicore HMP alloy melts in the range 296 to 301°C and is the highest-melting of the commonly-used solders. It is used on automobile radiators and on nickel-iron lamp caps, and wherever very high temperature service is required. It also remains plastic and non-brittle to much colder temperatures than the high-tin alloys, and is therefore recommended for service in extremely cold conditions.

With good control of soldering temperature it is possible, using successively HMP, 95/5 tin-antimony, 60/40 tin-lead and finally TLC, to make four joints close together on a workpiece, in such a way that the earlier joints are not re-melted while the later ones are being made. This can be of advantage on occasions when it is difficult to jig the work. The joints or seams in the work are first spot-soldered in their correct positions with a high-melting solder such as HMP, and then completed with a lower-melting alloy such as 60/40.

For completeness, one should mention here the soldering of aluminium. As mentioned in Section 2.1, the soldering of aluminium is really a type of brazing, requiring the use of corrosive fluxes and a rather hard solder alloy, tin-zinc. As might be expected, solders for aluminium do not have very good wetting power, and when wetting has been achieved there is always the danger of electrolytic corrosion. This danger is apparently least with the tin-zinc alloys, the composition commonly used being 70 tin 30 zinc. To prevent corrosion, the joint must be totally enclosed in pitch or plastics to keep moisture out. Such joints are successfully used for cable-jointing, the joint being made in a way not unlike the method used for making wiped joints in lead pipe.

2.5 FLUXES

2.5.1 HEAT TRANSFER

Fluxes for soft-soldering purposes are non-metallic solids melting at temperatures well below the melting temperature of the solder. One of their important functions is to transfer heat from the soldering iron to the solder and workpiece.

Solid surfaces are never perfectly smooth, and this is as true of soldering iron tips and workpiece surfaces as it is of any other surfaces. When the soldering iron is placed on the workpiece, the actual area of contact is small because of surface roughness (Figure 40).

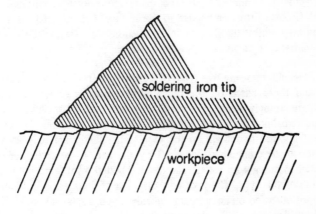

Fig. 40

The air trapped in the spaces acts as an insulator, so that the workpiece is only heated slowly. If now the spaces are filled with molten flux, which wets both surfaces, the workpiece is heated much more quickly.

It might be thought that molten solder on the iron would be equally effective; but this is not so, because at first the molten solder does not wet the workpiece, and will not do so until the workpiece has been cleaned by the flux.

If a piece of flux-cored solder wire is placed between the iron and the workpiece, the solder wire is quickly warmed to the fairly low temperature needed to make the flux run out, especially if the iron is pressed firmly on to the solder wire. As soon as the flux runs out, it wets the iron, the solder and the work. Both solder and work then heat up rapidly.

2.5.2 TARNISH REMOVAL

Tarnish is the film of oxides, sulphides or other corrosion products which cover all metal surfaces except those of gold or platinum. This film must be quickly dissolved by the flux, so that the joint can be completed without the

43

workpiece becoming overheated. To do this the flux must contain sufficient acid to dissolve the tarnish at soldering temperatures, but not enough to attack the workpiece at room temperature. This balance is delicate and can only be achieved if the tarnish film is initially quite thin. Thick films of tarnish must be removed by abrasion or strong acid treatment before soldering, and all traces of abrasive or acid removed. Incidentally, the complete removal of all particles of abrasive (which become firmly embedded in the surface) is quite difficult. If allowed to remain they inhibit the flow of solder. It is better therefore to use a file or wire brush rather than an abrasive powder or paper.

Basically there are two types of flux composition, those based on inorganic salts and those based on the much weaker organic acids. The inorganic salt fluxes are strongly acidic and can dissolve quite thick tarnish films, but the flux residue remaining after soldering is still rather acid and may corrode the workpiece if allowed to remain on the joint. Such fluxes are only used where the residue can be completely burnt off by the heat of soldering, or removed by thorough washing with water. The familiar 'killed spirit'(zinc chloride solution) is a flux of this type. The least corrosive flux of this class is Multicore ARAX, a composition based on ammonium chloride. Though relatively mild, this flux will readily solder plain 18/8 stainless steels.

The organic acid flux of most importance for soft-soldering is rosin (colophony). Unfortunately it is not strong enough to remove tarnish films easily and it is therefore necessary to add an activator. This is usually a basic organic chloride. Activated fluxes to BS 441 consist of rosin, with sufficient activator to give 0.5% chloride. Such fluxes will dissolve tarnish only when soldering temperature is reached and should not attack metals at all. Below this temperature, even in conditions of high humidity, there is no chemical action. In consequence the flux residues may safely be left on the joint. These fluxes are suitable for all electrical and electronic work. Typical fluxes of this class are ERSIN Multicore types 362, 362P, and 370.

Figure 41 illustrates the speed of action of these fluxes in comparison with pure unactivated rosin, compared by melting a 2-inch length of 18 swg flux-cored solder wire on a cleaned mild steel strip under standard conditions. When the solder melts, it rapidly flows together to form a nearly spherical droplet, unless the flux acts so quickly that adhesion to the steel can take place first.

The second strip shows the very limited wetting which can be obtained with pure rosin. Even though wetting can be achieved, the alloy film (between solder and steel) is very thin and the bond strength poor. The third strip shows

44

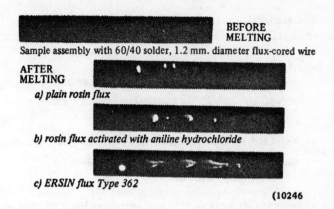

BEFORE MELTING

Sample assembly with 60/40 solder, 1.2 mm. diameter flux-cored wire

AFTER MELTING

a) plain rosin flux

b) rosin flux activated with aniline hydrochloride

c) ERSIN flux Type 362

(10246

Fig. 41

the action of rosin activated with aniline hydrochloride, a material sometimes used for this purpose. Good wetting is achieved, but only slowly. The fourth strip shows the extremely quick action of ERSIN Multicore 362 flux. This flux consists of rosin combined with a specially formulated activator which ensures exceedingly rapid cleaning of the steel. Spontaneous alloying of the solder with the steel then takes place the instant the solder has melted.

2.5.3 CHOICE OF FLUX

The main factor affecting the choice of flux is the nature of the metals to be joined, with other factors such as the size, shape and purpose of the joint having a secondary influence. In general, pure rosin can be used on workpieces of gold, platinum, tin, lead and pewter, or on platings of these metals. It can be used on copper, brass and silver but the speed of action is poor. It will not work at all on more easily oxidized metals such as iron, steel or nickel. For these metals, and to improve soldering speeds on the other metals already mentioned, one must use an activated rosin.

Where the work is of such a nature that the relevant specification requires a non-activated or only very mildly activated flux to be used, ERSIN Multicore fluxes R3 (non-activated) or 380 (mildly activated) are appropriate. These fluxes are used on very small or thin parts of good solderability, where the use of a standard activated flux might cause the solder to spread too far or too quickly. They are generally used in conjunction with 60/40 solder. These fluxes contain not more than 0.05% chloride.

45

For electrical, electronic and small metal work, the standard activated fluxes such as ERSIN Multicore 370, 362 and 362P are used. Typical applications are:

with Savbit 1 or 60/40, for all electronic assembly;

with 40/60 or 30/70, for transformers and motors;

with TLC, for heat-sensitive components;

with LMP, for the manufacture of silvered-ceramic capacitors;

with HMP, 95/5 tin-antimony or 96/4 tin-silver, for high-temperature use.

More highly activated rosin fluxes, containing about 2% chloride, are available for use when the soldering is done in a fairly open position, where the flux vapours will not condense on nearby parts. A typical application, in conjunction with 20/80 tin-lead, is in the soldering of brass lamp-caps. Though the flux vapours can be slightly corrosive on steel, the solid flux residues are inactive.

For large workpieces which are slow to heat, the more rapid (but more corrosive) inorganic salt fluxes such as Multicore ARAX may be used with advantage, and must in any case be used for more difficult alloys such as plain stainless steels. ARAX must always be used when soldering oxygen equipment, as the use of rosin fluxes is forbidden for this purpose. Typical uses of ARAX are:

with pure tin solder, in jewelry and transistor bodies;

with 40/60, in general metalwork, plumbing, and auto-radiator repair;

with 20/80, for car body repair and filling, and radiator manufacture;

with 96/4 tin-silver, in food-handling equipment;

with HMP, for car radiators and headlamps.

Such metals as chromium, titanium, and stainless steels containing hardening additions cannot be soldered at all. The soldering of aluminium usually requires the use of highly corrosive fluxes whose residues must be carefully removed or completely sealed from air and moisture.

A soldering application requiring a special flux is the manufacture of capacitors impregnated with tetrachlordiphenyl resin. The power factor of such capacitors would be adversely affected if ordinary fluxes were used; ERSIN Multicore 447 flux should be used for their assembly.

2.5.4 METHODS OF APPLYING FLUX

Solid fluxes are supplied already incorporated in the correct proportion as cores in solder wires of suitable composition. For almost all soldering applications, this is far more convenient than the traditional method of using separate paste or liquid fluxes in conjunction with stick solder. In Multicore solder wire, the flux is distributed in several cores instead of the usual single core. This has two great advantages. First, there is much less chance than there is with single-core wire, that any section of wire should be devoid of flux. Thus there is very little chance of producing dry joints. Second, the cores are nearer the wire surface, so giving more rapid release of flux from the wire on to the work.

ERSIN Multicore rosin-based fluxes are supplied in wires containing three or five cores of flux. Multicore ARAX flux is supplied in two- or four-core wire. The core construction is easily examined by pulling the wire apart over a small flame; the wire snaps cleanly and the cores can be clearly seen (Figure 42).

Fig. 42

There are two points to bear in mind when first using 'Multicore' solder wire. If one has previously been using stick solder and external flux, or a relatively slow-acting single-core solder, it is quite likely that one has become accustomed to using a very hot soldering iron. Unless slight modifications in technique are made (for instance using a rather cooler iron, and needing rather less solder and flux than formerly) it is quite possible that the amount of smoke from the flux will be considered excessive. However all rosin-based fluxes smoke when placed on a soldering iron tip; the amount of smoke produced when making a joint depends on the temperature of the iron and the amount of flux used. The smoke of rosin-based flux is less dangerous, though rather more irritating, than cigarette smoke. All that is required, after checking that the iron temperature is not excessive and that the right gauge of wire is used, is to insure good ventilation at the operator's workbench, together with a sensible attitude on the part of the operator, who will find that his throat gets rather dry if he inhales visible smoke.

The second point to remember is that many operators like to apply the flux-cored wire and iron to the job and then, as the solder starts to melt, push more solder wire into the joint. Flux expands more rapidly than does solder when heated; so if the wire is pushed rapidly into the joint under the hot iron, the pressure of the flux expansion builds up very quickly, and when the solder melts the flux will spatter. To avoid this, a suitable gauge of solder wire should be chosen so that there is no need to push extra solder wire into the joint.

When dip-soldering, the so-called 'liquid' fluxes are used. This is rather a misnomer because all fluxes are liquid at the soldering temperature; the fluxes used for dip-soldering are in fact solutions of solid flux in a suitable solvent. Most of the Multicore fluxes supplied solid in cored solder wire are also available in solution form. The ERSIN rosin-based fluxes are supplied as solutions in an alcohol, while ARAX flux can be supplied as a solution in water. In the case of rosin-based fluxes, the solutions are supplied at the concentration most suitable for general use. If they become more concentrated due to solvent evaporation they may be returned to their original strength by the addition of Multicore PC 70 thinners, the concentration being controlled by reading the density of the solution with a hydrometer.

2.5.5 CORROSIVITY OF FLUXES

In order to remove tarnish at a sufficiently high speed, flux must be acid. There is a certain risk that the flux will be so acid that its residues cause corrosion. In the case of inorganic salt fluxes, this risk is a near certainty and the residues must be removed by burning off or washing, as appropriate. It is possible however to formulate activated rosin fluxes whose residues are not corrosive. Test procedures are required to ensure that this condition has in fact been achieved. A number of tests have been developed and incorporated in public standards (see Table 3.3.2, p. 100 for list) and it is important to understand how these test operate.

Some tests depend on an assumed relationship between the acidity of the original flux and the corrosivity of the flux residue; BS 441 and DTD599a for instance limit the halide content of the flux, while QQ-S-571d and MIL-F-14256C limit the electrical conductivity of a water extract. No specification relies entirely on this relationship however; all include a direct corrosion test on the residues. In BS 441, DTD599a and DIN 8516 the test is done by melting flux and solder on sheet metal, with an additional sheet mounted ¼ inch above the molten flux to condense the flux vapours. After cooling, the metal sheets are exposed to a warm damp atmosphere, and examined after a specified period for visible corrosion products. Copper is the metal usually used, because the green copper corrosion product is clearly visible against the red metal background, and because copper is the metal most used in electronic work. In QQ-S-571d the direct corrosion test is done on copper wire of 0.0026 inch diameter, the criterion here being that the wire should not be corroded right through after a specified time of exposure to a warm damp atmosphere.

All flux enclosed in cored solder wire will, in ordinary use, be heated to soldering temperature and any corrosive volatiles removed from the residue. There is not the same guarantee with external fluxes, small quantities of which may escape heating. It appears then that the degree of acidity that can be tolerated in cored solder fluxes should be a little higher than in external fluxes, provided that the residues of both pass the direct corrosion test. This fact is recognized in DTD599a, which allows 0.7% halide in the fluxes of cored solders but only 0.5% in external fluxes. It is also recognised in the USA specifications; QQ-S-571d allows a water extract of flux from cored solder to have a resistivity of only 45,000 ohm-cm, while MIL-F-14256C requires the water extract from rosin flux solutions to have a resistivity of at least 100,000 ohm-cm.

Properly-formulated fluxes can only show their tarnish-removing power when either molten or dissolved, that is to say when they are liquid. When solid, they do not dissolve the tarnish at a perceptible rate. Flux solutions are liquid at room temperature and will dissolve tarnish at this temperature. A drop of flux solution placed on a sheet of copper will have dissolved an appreciable quantity of copper oxide before it dries, the amount dissolved depending on how much was present to start with and whether warmth was used to hasten the drying of the flux. The copper oxide dissolves by reacting with the flux resin acids to form copper salts, which are green. Both BS 441 and DIN 8516 state that this green colour formed within the rosin during drying or during soldering (when the same reaction takes place) shall not be taken as evidence of corrosion. In fact, it is only evidence that the flux can do the work for which it was intended – the dissolving of tarnish.

49

2.6 WORKPIECE MATERIALS

2.6.1 WETTING OF METALS BY SOLDER

Whether, and how easily, a particular metal or alloy can be soldered depends on two main factors. These are, first, whether solders will readily form an alloy with the metal; and second, whether a flux can be found which will remove such tarnishes as are likely to be present.

It has already been mentioned that most soft solders are based on tin. The reason for using tin is that this metal will alloy with a very wide range of other metals. With some metals, notably lead, zinc and cadmium, it alloys by forming a eutectic of lower melting point than either of the constituent metals (see tin-lead equilibrium diagram, Figure 38, p. 37). With most other metals (the commonest being gold, silver, copper, iron and nickel) tin reacts to form an intermetallic compound which is relatively hard and brittle. This compound is the 'cement' which holds the solder on to the workpieces. There are some elements, for example titanium, silicon and chromium, with which tin does not react at all. These elements cannot be soldered.

The tin attacks the workpiece metal first at the grain boundaries. If these boundaries are already filled with hardening additions, as is the case with some stainless steels, the workpiece will be very difficult to solder. Plain stainless steels, whose boundaries are not sealed in this way, can be soldered quite easily if a strong enough flux is used. On some high-tensile steels, the attack of the tin at the grain boundaries is rapid and deep. This intercrystalline penetration seriously weakens the workpiece. The soldering of high-tensile steels is therefore forbidden by some standards such as the inspection instructions on soldering issued by the Ministry of Technology and the Air Registration Board. The designer should check whether these restrictions apply to his work.

Some workpieces consist of alloys, the constituent metals of which have already fully reacted with each other. Tin reacts much more slowly with these compounds. A common example is the difficulty of wetting the tin-copper compound with tin. The compound is already fully reacted and will only redissolve very slowly in molten tin. Copper wires coated with a very thin layer of tin are frequently very difficult to solder, because during storage the tin coating has reacted completely with the copper. The remedy is to use wires with a much thicker coating of tin, or with a coating of tin-lead alloy; the lead dilutes the tin and retards the reaction, giving the wire a longer storage life. Stronger flux does not help the soldering of tin-copper compound because the question is not one of tarnish removal.

50

When soldering bare copper, the solder first forms a thin layer of tin-copper compound which is the bonding medium. This is the reaction commonly called 'wetting'. If through presence of too much tarnish it does not occur, the condition is described as 'non-wetting'. If wetting is achieved but solder is allowed to remain molten for too long a time on the copper, the compound layer may grow to such a thickness that the solder runs back, because it wets the compound less readily than it wets the bare copper. This phenomenon is one cause of 'de-wetting'.

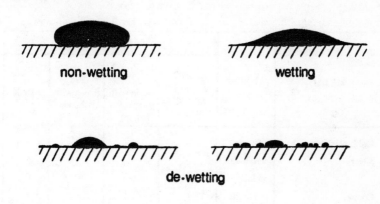

Fig. 43

Sometimes, metal parts for soldering or pre-tinning by dipping are cleaned with abrasive, particles of which remain embedded in the surface. These particles cannot be wetted by solder, but are small enough to be covered by solder during dipping. On withdrawal of the workpiece from the bath, the solder runs back off the workpiece. This is another type of de-wetting, which may be avoided by removing all abrasive powder before dipping. The powder can be wiped off hard metals such as steel with a cloth dampened with water or acetone, but it is much more difficult to remove from softer metals such as copper or brass. It is better not to use abrasive on these metals.

2.6.2 TARNISH REMOVAL

Fluxes are acids which clean the workpiece surface by dissolving the tarnish film. In nearly all fluxes, the acid which does the cleaning is hydrogen chloride. This acid is liberated in very minute quantities when the flux is heated, by decomposition of the activator. Unused hydrogen chloride is 'locked up' again (when the flux residue cools) by recombination with the activator base, leaving the residue neutral.

Whether a flux will work depends on whether the concentration of acid provided by the flux is enough to dissolve the particular tarnish present. The list below shows the type of tarnish likely to occur on common workpiece metals, together with the strength of flux needed to dissolve them.

METAL	TARNISH	REMOVED BY			
		R3, 380 (rosin with max.0.05% halide)	362P, 362 370 (rosin with max. 0.5% halide)	366 (rosin with 1% halide)	ARAX
Gold, platinum	none	+	+	+	+
Silver	sulphide	0	+	+	+
"	chloride	0	0	0	0
Copper	red oxide	+	+	+	+
"	black oxide	0	+	+	+
Brass	oxide	0	+	+	+
Zinc, cadmium	oxide	0	+	+	+
" "	passivated	0	0	0	+
Nickel, iron, steel	oxide	0	+	+	+
Stainless Steel	oxide	0	0	0	+
Aluminium, chromium	oxide	0	0	0	0

In this table, + indicates that the flux will remove the tarnish, 0 indicates that it will not. It is assumed that soldering is being done with an iron. Where flame soldering is used, a more active flux may be necessary to deal with the extra tarnish formed during heating by the flame. Note that when soldering gold, a flux is still needed even though the gold is free of tarnish. This is because whether or not the workpiece is tarnished, there ·are solder oxides to be removed before the solder will flow. Note also that silver chloride (which may be present on silver plate, derived from the plating bath) will not dissolve in any chloride flux and has to be scraped off.

2.6.3 PLATINGS

The problem of soldering on to plate is rather more complex than that of soldering on to plain metals. Possible complications include the porosity of the film; poor adhesion of the film to the underlying metal or 'substrate'; inadequate thickness of plate; and inclusion of impurities derived from the plating bath.

'Electroless' plating solutions, which deposit a thin film of metal on a substrate by chemical action, are available for depositing a variety of metals. A well-known example is acid copper sulphate, which will deposit a film of copper on iron or mild steel. Usually, the film deposited from such solutions is too thin and porous to make a sound basis for a soldered joint.

Common platings are now considered individually.

Tin: this may be deposited by electroplating or by dipping the workpiece in molten tin after coating it with a suitable flux. It is most commonly applied to copper wire and to steel sheet. It makes an excellent basis for subsequent soldering, provided an adequate thickness of tin has been put on. A thickness of 0.0003 inches (7.5 microns) is usually sufficient. Very thin coatings (0.00003 inches, 0.75 microns) on copper rapidly become completely converted to the tin-copper intermetallic compound and are then extremely difficult to solder.

Tin-nickel: this coating probably contains a large proportion of the intermetallic compound; in consequence, though bright and resistant to wear and corrosion, it is also rather difficult to solder.

Tin-lead: electroplated or hot-dipped, this coating is the best for copper wire, as the lead dilutes the tin and slows the rate of compound formation. It may also be applied by hot roller-coating, so long as an adequate thickness is applied. The thickness should be about 0.0002 inches (5 microns). 30/70 tin-lead is the composition most often used.

Zinc and cadmium: these coatings are very easy to solder with activated rosin fluxes such as ERSIN Multicore 362; but if passivated they become very difficult to solder with anything but ARAX.

Nickel: provided an activated flux such as ERSIN Multicore 362 is used, nickel is readily soldered. Occasional difficulties are encountered due to poor plating practice, which may give a porous deposit containing plating salts and allowing the substrate to develop a tarnish film.

Silver: in principle easily soldered, in practice this coating may be difficult to solder due to its tendency to develop a sulphide tarnish film. The presence of even small traces of chloride in the plating bath will make the film unsolderable. Some specifications prohibit the use of silver-plated metals for parts which are to be soldered, and the use of silver is now largely restricted to the manufacture of certain types of capacitor consisting of ceramic with a silver coating to which wires are attached. The wires are soldered to the silver coating. To prevent the solder dissolving the thin silver film, leaving the ceramic bare, it is usual to use Multicore LMP silver-loaded solder.

Gold: gold is much used to improve the wear- and corrosion-resistant properties of sliding electrical contacts, and to improve or maintain soldering properties where these are inadequate or may become so on storage. The ease of soldering on to gold, and the quality of the joint so made, has been the subject of much discussion in recent years and opinions are divided. However, reviewing the literature from 1962 to 1967, the position appears to be as follows:

1. The tin-lead-gold eutectic, of composition 64.5 tin, 32.5 lead, 3 gold, melts at 177°C.
2 At soldering temperature, 60/40 solder rapidly dissolves large quantities of gold.
3. The resulting alloy is harder, and has higher tensile, creep and shear strength than the pure solder, but is more brittle. Whether the brittleness is dangerous depends on the type of stresses the joint is likely to meet in service.
4. Soldered joints on gold should therefore be made as quickly as possible, at as low a temperature as possible, to avoid dissolving too much gold. This means using a low-melting solder alloy such as TLC, LMP, K or Sn 60 (see Table 3.2.1), as a cored solder wire of as fine a gauge as practicable.
5. Joints can easily be made on gold plate thicker than 0.0002 inch (5 microns) but may de-wet if heated too long or at too high a temperature.

6. On thinner gold plate, wetting may be difficult to achieve unless the substrate has been previously polished, or plated with a smooth undercoat of copper or nickel.

7. 'Hard gold', that is gold containing small hardening additions of cobalt, is unsuitable as a finish for surfaces which are to be soldered.

Owing to the existence of the low-melting tin-lead-gold eutectic, solders for use at higher temperatures might become hot-short (see Section 2.4.4 p. 40) if used on gold-plated surfaces. It is not practical to make a gold-loaded soft solder to supress solution of gold, as such an alloy, to be effective, would have to contain at least 25% of gold.

2.6.4 SOLDERABILITY

Solderability is the property of a workpiece surface which permits it to form a good bond with a specified soft solder alloy in the presence of a specified flux and at a specified temperature. When attempting to measure solderability, one must distinguish between the extent of wetting which can be achieved and the time required to achieve it.

The extent of wetting depends on the chemical nature of the workpiece metal, and reference should be made to Sections 2.4, 2.5, 2.6.1, and 2.6.2 to find suitable solder-flux combinations for soldering a given material. The extent of wetting may be measured in two ways. The first is to measure the area covered by a standard weight of solder when it is melted on a flat surface of the workpiece metal under specified conditions (temperature, time, type of flux). A variant of this method is to measure the final height of the solder, which is roughly inversely proportional to the area of spread. The second way of measuring the extent of wetting is to measure the contact angle, that is the angle enclosed between the solder surface and the workpiece surface (Figure 44). This angle can be measured by shadow projection after removal of flux residues. The cosine of the contact angle is a convenient measure, and may vary from -1 (contact angle $180°$, total non-wetting) to +1 (contact angle $0°$, perfect wetting), but is a constant for a given solder/workpiece combination.

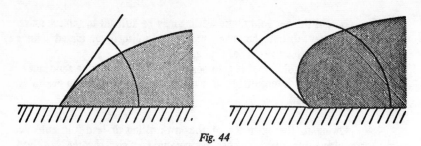

Fig. 44

The time needed to achieve the required extent of wetting, however, may vary between different batches of work, and in one batch may vary with storage conditions and time. Methods for measuring soldering time are therefore very important for the control of production of soldered joints, particularly if machine soldering of any type is used, as soldering machines, unlike the human operator, cannot be made to give extra attention to the occasional difficult joint.

Soldering time measurements are usually made using 60/40 tin-lead solder at a temperature of either 235°C or 370°C, depending on the production soldering method to be controlled by the test. Since soldering times with activated fluxes are often too short for accurate measurement, non-activated rosin flux is usually used for the test.

Suppose the automatic soldering machine, in production, has to make a soldered joint in 1.5 seconds, using an activated flux, this 1.5 seconds being the actual dwell time of the workpiece in contact with molten solder. Workpieces which prove satisfactory on production with activated flux may have a measured soldering time with non-activated flux of, let us say, 4 seconds. Then the production line will run satisfactorily if it is fed only with batches of workpieces having a soldering time, on test, not greater than 4 seconds. In this way one may set up solderability standards for the guidance of the department supplying the workpiece.

It is emphasized that the example given above is only an example, and the exact ratio of soldering time on test to soldering time on production will vary considerably with the production method used. If the production engineer wishes to use soldering time tests, he must first establish what this ratio is for each type of workpiece he uses.

Two types of soldering time test are in use, one for component termination wires and one for flat stock such as tags or printed circuit boards. The soldering time of component termination wires is measured by the globule test (BS 2011 Part 2T 1966) (J.A. ten Duis, Philips Technical Review 1958/9, 20, 158). The equipment required, together with the solder and flux, is available from Multicore Solders. The method is to immerse the wire horizontally in a globule of solder held

Multicore Solderability Test Machine   *(11743-A*
Mark 2
Fig. 45

on a heated block; both the solder and the wire are first coated with a flux solution. The wire, when immersed, splits the solder globule in two; the time taken for the halves of the globule to flow round the wire and unite above it is a measure of the soldering time. The size of solder globule used is chosen according to the diameter of the wire to be tested, to ensure that flow of the solder over the wire can only occur if the wire is truly wetted; not enough solder is used to sink the wire. Figure 46 a, b and c illustrate the procedure viewed from the end-on position.

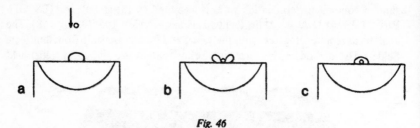

Fig. 46

The test is widely used by makers of wire and by makers of wire-ended components. In the equipment as marketed by Multicore Solders, the temperature of the globule is controlled in the range 200 – 250°C by a thermocouple which acts through a pyrometer and thyristor, regulating the heating current. The time is measured by a built-in digital stop-clock, started automatically and stopped by releasing a button held depressed during the test. This minimizes any error due to the response-time of the operator. It also allows the average response-time of the operator to be measured. The operator is asked to release the button as soon as he sees the clock start; the clock reading is then his response-time. In work where the highest accuracy is required, the average response-time for a particular operator may be substracted from his soldering time measurements.

In spite of the great care taken to standardize the solder, the flux and the temperature for this test, the results on a supposedly uniform batch of workpieces will still be found to vary. A typical set of results is shown in Figure 47, which gives the frequency distribution of results for 50 tests on solder-coated copper wire. This variation is due to slight variations in the surface condition of the wire along its length. This variability does not cause much trouble in practice but it does mean that a single soldering time test is of little value; the mean of at least ten should be taken.

The soldering time of flat stock may be determined by taking a number of samples and dipping them in a bath of molten solder, each sample being dipped for a slightly shorter time than the one preceding. The soldering time is the shortest time giving adequate wetting. Once again, non-activated flux and 60/40 solder at 235°C are used. The weakness of this test is the difficulty in defining unambiguously what is meant by adequate wetting; but the method is very simple. Mechanical dipping is needed to ensure that a precisely defined dipping time is obtained. (C.J. Thwaites, Electrical Manufacture 1964, 8 (5), 18).

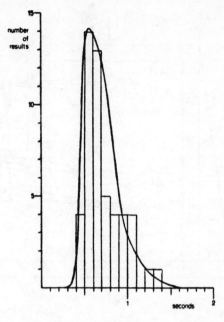

Fig. 47

Both the globule test and the dip test are methods which give a time measurement of practical importance, using procedures basically similar to practical soldering. They are not intended to give much information about the physics of the soldering process. To get such information one must use some other test, based on the fact that the soldering process consists of the wetting of a liquid by a solid, and which will indicate how the forces involved change during the process. For this purpose the ideal instrument would be a continuously-recording surface tension balance, capable of operating at soldering temperatures. Until recently the practical difficulties in constructing such an instrument have been too great, but they have now been resolved by ten Duis and van der Meulen (Philips Technical Review 1967, 28 (12), 362). The principle of this instrument, now called the Meniscograph, is shown in Figure 48. It consists of a lever L, very small movements of which can be detected by an inductive displacement gauge G. A specimen S is clipped to the end of the lever, its weight being counterbalanced by a weak spring which also supports the lever itself. The specimen is rapidly immersed to a predetermined depth in a solder bath B whose vertical movement is controlled by intermittent rotation of a cam C. This immersion produces forces of buoyancy and of rapidly-changing surface tension, which in turn produce very small displacements in the lever.

59

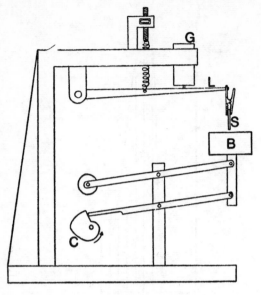

Fig. 48

For satisfactory operation the lever must be well protected from vibration and from heat radiated and convected from the bath.

The gauge is supplied by an oscillator, the output of which is modulated by small displacements of the gauge. After detection and amplification the signal is applied to a high-speed strip-chart recorder. Figure 49 (reproduced from the article mentioned above) shows the relative motion of speciment and bath surface, together with the resulting recording for solderable (a) and unsolderable (b) specimens. From such graphs the strength and speed of action of wetting forces under a variety of conditions can be derived.

It is sometimes found, when attempting to join two different surfaces, that though they are both solderable, their solderabilities differ considerably. This may be due to their shape, degree of roughness, degree of tarnish, or basic composition. In such cases the more easily soldered surface may draw solder away from the less easily soldered one, and the joint is difficult to make. Unless the solderability of the poorer surface can be improved, the only course is to pre-tin both surfaces heavily, and then sweat them together as quickly as possible, allowing a soldering time only long enough for the top surfaces of the tinning to melt and coalesce.

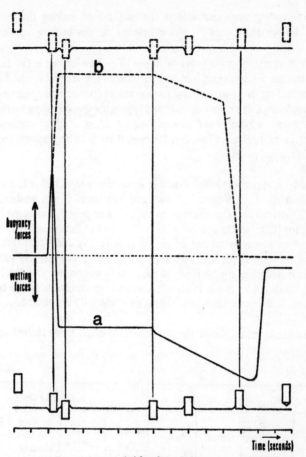

buoyancy
forces

wetting
forces

b

a

Time (seconds)

(with acknowledgements to Philips Technical Review
Fig. 49

2. 7 SOLDERING PROCEDURES

2.7.1 METHODS AVAILABLE

Very often a soldered joint could be made in several different ways with equally satisfactory results. So far, we have considered the solder, the flux, the workpiece shape and the workpiece material, and seen how the choice of any one of these limits the choice of the others. In this section, we shall see how the choice of heating appliance affects the method of making the joint, and in Section 2.8 we shall consider the efficiency of the heating appliance itself.

There are three main types of heater. The best-known is the pencil type, which includes the soldering iron and the torch. The second method of heating is the hot surface, the surface being molten solder (pot or bath soldering), hot oil (reflow soldering), or a hotplate. The third type is the space heating method, which includes oven, induction and radiant heating. Most of these methods require some degree of mechanization, and for each there is an appropriate solder form, such as bar, wire, pellet etc.

Solder is obtainable as flux-cored or solid wire or tape, either in a continuous length on a spool, or shaped and cut into 'preforms' (rings, washers, discs or pellets). Solder may also be obtained as bars, wire or pellets, protected by plastics packing, for filling and maintaining the solder level of baths and pots. Flux-cored wire, tape or preforms do not of course require any additional flux, but flux solutions are needed for use with solid wire, solid preforms, and solder baths. For reflow soldering, the workpieces are usually pre-tinned to a thickness such that additional solder is not required; but solder preforms may also be used for those parts of the assembly which cannot be adequately pre-tinned.

The table below shows the combinations of all these factors in common

HEATING		METHOD		SOLDER FORM			
Class	Example	Manual	Machine	Cored Wire	Cored Preform	Preform with flux solution	Bar solder with flux solution
Pencil	iron	+	+	+	+	–	–
	torch	+	+	+	+	–	–
Surface	pot	+	–	–	–	–	+
	bath	–	+	–	–	–	+
	reflow	–	+	–	+	–	–
Space	oven	–	+	–	+	+	–
	induction	–	+	–	+	+	–
	radiant	–	+	–	+	+	–

tip,

62

use. In this table a distinction is made between the solder pot and the solder bath. The solder pot is a small, usually circular, vessel of molten solder, in which workpieces are dipped by hand, often only one at a time. It is used for pre-tinning, and for soldering together the strands of a multi-strand wire to make a neat end which will not fray. The solder bath is rectangular and much larger. It is used for the continuous tinning of metal sheet, strip and wire, and for making large numbers of joints simultaneously, as for example on printed circuit boards. The dipping of the workpieces is done mechanically. This is known as 'mass soldering'.

Manual procedures have already been described in Part 1 and in Section 2.5.4. The next two sections are therefore devoted to some aspects of machine soldering and mass soldering.

2.7.2 MACHINE SOLDERING

Automatic soldering machines consist of a conveyor which brings up the work, a feed system for the cored solder wire, and a soldering head carrying either a soldering iron or a gas flame. A very convenient way of building such a machine is to incorporate the Multicore 3A Soldering Head (see Figure 50) into a conveyor. The 3A Head may be operated automatically or by a pedal, and incorporates its own solder feed together with a soldering iron.

Fig. 50

If the user wishes to build his own equipment, there are certain important points to consider. When designing the cored solder feed, it should be remembered that solder wire is soft and will not withstand long pushes or pulls up feed tubes. It is also unwise to pass the wire over many small pulleys, especially if these rotate in different planes, since excessive bending of the wire will result in frequent breakages. Re-threading in a complex solder feed system is time-consuming. The design should be as simple as possible, and should not require the solder wire to pass over more than one pulley; this should be of large diameter.

There may be certain restrictions on choice of solder when using an automatic machine equipped with an iron. The machine is likely to push the cored solder wire on to exactly the same part of the tip at each operation. If the bit is of plain copper, this may cause uneven erosion of the tip unless one of the Multicore SAVBIT alloys is used. It is advisable in any case to use a tip with a simple wedge or chamfered tip which is easily re-shaped; complex tip shapes made to fit a particular workpiece should not be used as they are difficult to maintain.

With pencil heating, whether the pencil is a soldering iron or a gas flame, it is usual to use flux-cored solder wire straight from the reel. For some work-pieces it may be more convenient to use a flux-cored solder preform. These are available in a large range of dimensions in most of the common solder/flux combinations.

Preforms are practically always needed when oven, induction or radiant heating is used. Where the joint design is such that the preform is held in place by the joint shape, a flux-cored preform is used. In some cases, however, it is possible that the preform could be shaken out of its intended position before it has melted. In these cases one should use a solid preform and a drop of flux solution or ERSIN Multicore Red Jelly flux, which will hold the preform in place while the work is moved into the heating zone. The oven should of course be well ventilated, so that flammable vapours can escape or burn off harmlessly before they reach a high concentration within the oven.

The use of induction heating is limited by the need to get the workpiece inside a coil of the right size and shape to give efficient generation of heat within the workpiece. The advice of suppliers of induction heating equipment should be sought on this point.

2.7.3 SOLDERING OF PRINTED CIRCUITS
2.7.3.1 Printed Circuit Assemblies

A printed circuit consists of a sheet of insulating material carrying a pattern in copper foil. The copper pattern provides electrical connection between the various circuit components (such as resistors, capacitors, transistors etc.) soldered to it. Manufacture of these soldered connections presents special problems, to which careful attention must be paid if reliable results are to be obtained.

Since the use of printed circuitry permits achievement of a high packing density (allows many components to be packed into a very small space), printed circuits are very often used in equipment to be carried in vehicles or missiles. The boards, and the soldered joints they carry, may therefore be exposed to very severe accelerations or vibrations, sometimes in extreme climates. Careful consideration must then be given to the mechanical as well as the electrical features of the joint, since in equipment intended for use in vehicles or missiles, reliability is of prime importance.

2.7.3.2. Materials

The designer of printed circuits will be well aware of the variety of materials and components available for the construction of printed board assemblies. Those who approach the problems of soldering from other angles may not be so familiar with this subject, and for their benefit short descriptions of the more commonly-used items are given here.

The simple printed circuit consists of a sheet or laminate of phenolic resin (such as Formica) reinforced with paper, and carrying on one side a sheet of copper foil. The desired circuit pattern is printed (usually by a silk-screen process) on the copper-coated face of the board, using a special ink termed the etch resist. The board is then immersed in an etching solution (usually an acid salt such as ferric chloride solution) which dissolves away all the copper not protected by the etch resist. When this process is complete, the etching solution is removed by thorough washing with water, and the etch resist removed by washing in an organic solvent. Holes are pierced in the board to accept the component terminations; the components are inserted; and the connections soldered.

Most printed circuits for the entertainments industry (record-players, tape recorders, radio and television receivers) are made in this way; but the more exacting requirements of the so-called 'professional' users (making instruments, control equipment, navigation aids, computers, communications and broadcasting equipment, missiles and space vehicles) has led to the development of many variations of the basic idea. For example it is now possible to obtain laminate clad on both sides with copper (double-sided board) or consisting of several layers of laminate interleaved with copper foil (multilayer boards). Connections between the foils on double-sided boards may be made by eyelets inserted into holes, but it is more usual now for the holes to have a layer of copper electroplated on to their walls (see Figure 51).

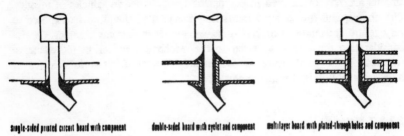

single-sided printed circuit board with component   double-sided board with eyelet and component   multilayer board with plated-through holes and component

Fig. 51

Plated-through holes are almost invariably used to interconnect layers on multilayer boards. Where component terminations are soldered into plated-through holes, the resulting joint has much greater strength than a joint on a plain hole.

Though the various types of laminate will generally withstand the chemical effects of the heat of soldering, they vary in the extent to which they are deformed by heat. This can be controlled by choice of board thickness, and of soldering time and temperature.

Any of the following may be met as the base material:

> paper/phenolic resin
> paper/plasticized phenolic resin
> linen/plasticized phenolic resin
> paper/epoxy resin

fibreglass felt or cloth/epoxy resin

fibreglass felt or cloth/polyester

fibreglass cloth/teflon

fibreglass cloth/melamine resin

fibreglass cloth/silicone resin

The conductor pattern may be made to serve other purposes than merely replacing the wiring of the older type of circuit assembly. Such purposes include:

edge connectors — a number of the conductor tracks are brought to the side of the board, thus forming a flat plug for insertion into a flat socket; connections can be made to the socket for power supplies, input and output signals, controls etc. The conductor tracks may be plated with gold at the edge which is to be inserted into the socket, to ensure good electrical contact. This gold film must be protected with a masking material during soldering, the mask being peeled off afterwards. Connections to the socket are made by hand soldering.

switch contacts — the printed circuit technique may be used for making the static contacts of rotary switches, using a foil or plating of platinum or rhodium alloy; this may be pressed into the laminate so that the top surfaces of laminate and contacts are flush. This technique may also be used for printed circuit motors. Connections will usually be made by hand soldering or by edge connectors.

printed components — careful design of the shape of conducting patterns can make parts of them act as components in the circuit; resistors or capacitors for example. Care must be taken that their values are not materially altered by the soldering process chosen. Printed resistors are usually made using films of manganin, constantan or nickel-chrome, often gold-plated on the areas to be soldered.

2.7.3.3 COMPONENTS

The components to be soldered to a board show a considerable variety of form. Some of them — small transformers, chokes, tube-bases etc. — are tag-ended, that is to say, the electrical terminations are made of sheet metal. This metal is usually tinned copper or tinned brass. As the tags are usually stamped out of the sheet after tinning, the cut edges are not protected from tarnish formation; this, combined with the presence of sharp edges on the cut metal and a long storage period before assembly, can cause difficulties in soldering. It may be necessary in these cases to use a rather strongly activated rosin flux such as ERSIN Multicore 366. This flux does not comply with the halide requirement of DTD.599a.

Components such as resistors and capacitors are usually cylindrical, rectangular or disc-shaped, with round wire terminations. The actual soldering of the wires should not present any difficulty, as it is now possible to obtain wire with a specified solderability (see BS 4393:1969, 'Tin or Tin-lead coated Copper Wire'); but the method of mounting the component on the board must be carefully considered. Figure 52 shows various mounting methods.

horizontal mounting of axially- and radially-terminated components

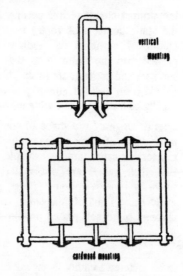

vertical mounting

cordwood mounting

Fig. 52

The vertical mounting method permits many more components to be mounted on the board, and also reduces the amount of heat absorbed by the components during soldering. The horizontal method gives better mechanical support to the component and less susceptibility to damage by vibration. The cordwood method allows a high packing density to be achieved and also gives excellent mechanical support, but it is important to insure that components and support rods expand more or less equally with heat, or some joints may be broken. If the assembly is to be filled (potted) with resin or rubber for added protection against vibration and damp, care must be taken to ensure that the potting resin does not put extra strain on the soldered joints. Some resins may shrink not only during but after curing or hardening, by about 2%. In the cordwood construction of Figure 52 for instance, if the adhesion of the potting resin to the two printed boards is good (as it must be to exclude moisture), the shrinkage of the resin will tend to pull the two boards together. Then the component must bend, or the soldered joints at the ends must give way, or the track will be peeled from the board. Extra mechanical support of the boards will merely cause the potting material to peel off them. The solution would be to use either:

1) a resin which does not shrink in the later stages of curing;

2) a soft rubber or foam which will stretch easily; or

3) stress-relieving loops in the component termination wires.

Transistors may be mounted direct on the board, or on small pads which give good mechanical support while maintaining a small extra clearance. This gives extra protection against the heat of soldering, which otherwise may crack the glass with which the transistors are sealed.

Transistors are usually sealed with glass to protect the transistor dice itself from corrosion. The terminations, which are brought out through the glass, must therefore be made of an alloy such as nickel-iron, which has the same thermal expansion characteristics as the glass. Unfortunately, the solderability of such wires is often poor, especially after the wires have been heated in the sealing process. Wires have often been given a coating of gold to improve the soldering characteristics, but such treatment is not successful if the bond of the gold to the underlying nickel-iron is poor. It is much improved if there is an undercoat of copper or nickel beneath the gold.

The most complex type of components are the microcircuits and integrated circuits, which may have as many as sixteen terminations. Some commonly used packages for these are shown in Figure 53, together with methods of mounting them. These circuits are expensive, and a single board may carry dozens of them; if one fails, it is out of the question to discard the whole board, but the large number of terminations on each component makes their removal by unsoldering rather difficult. From this point of view, lap-mounting is better than through–hole mounting. However it is much more difficult to hold the component in position during the initial soldering, and it is not easy to hold the leads parallel to the board. The solder is also being expected to provide all the mechanical strength of the joint. With lap mounting, soldering must be done by reflow or by hand; with through-hole mounting, soldering may be done with a solder bath.

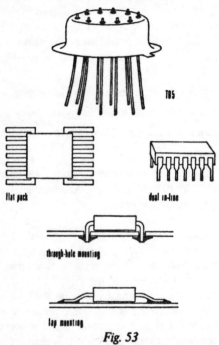

TO5

flat pack

dual in-line

through-hole mounting

lap mounting

Fig. 53

Though mention has been made above of some of the possibilities now available, many of these are still in a stage of rapid development, and opinions as to the best methods of assembly are varied. However it is probably true that the majority of printed circuit boards made at present are still of the

POSSIBLE METHODS FOR SOLDERING PRINTED CIRCUITS
(see Section 2.7.3 for description of individual processes)

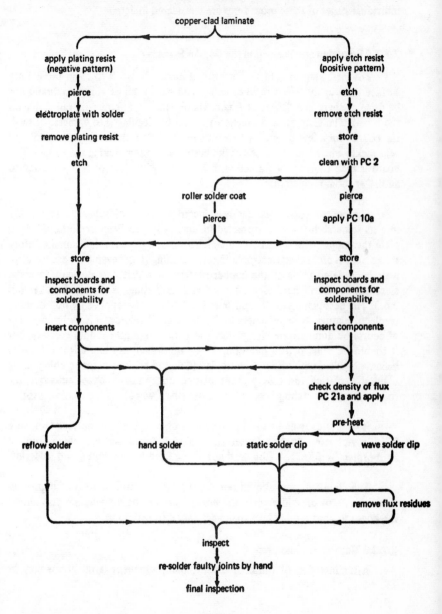

conventional single-sided type carrying discrete components. Possible procedures for soldering these are shown in the diagram on p.71; in what follows, the individual stages of these procedures are considered in detail.

2.7.3.4 Preparing and Preserving the Copper Surface

The first step in soldering a printed circuit board is to clean the copper surface thoroughly. Mechanical cleaning with wire wool or abrasives should not be done as there is a danger of fragments of wire wool or abrasive remaining on the board. The simplest and quickest method of cleaning is to immerse or swab the copper for a few seconds with Multicore PC 2 Tarnish Remover, an inhibited acid pickle which rapidly dissolves the tarnish without attacking the copper. The board is then thoroughly washed with water, rinsed with alcohol and allowed to air-dry at room temperature.

The copper pattern is readily soldered when clean, but will very quickly lose its solderability unless protected in some way. One way of doing this is to plate the copper with some other metal. This is best done on the laminate before the pattern is etched on; electroplating after etching is inconvenient because there may be isolated parts of the copper pattern to which it is difficult to make electrical contact. The solderability of various platings is discussed in Section 2.6.3. The best plating for this purpose is 60/40 tin-lead, applied by hot–dipping or electroplating, to a thickness of 0.0002 inch (5 microns). Hot–dipping may of course be done after etching, since electrical continuity is not necessary, but it should be done before mounting holes are drilled, as these might otherwise become blocked with solder. Electroplating should be done before etching, using a suitable plating resist to prevent plating on areas of copper subsequently to be removed by etching. The solder coating itself will act as the etching resist.

Boards already etched and pierced may be protected by applying Multicore PC 10a Activated Surface Preservative, a rosin-based lacquer which forms a hard protective film. This film need not be removed before fluxing and soldering.

The circuit pattern should not contain large unbroken areas of copper, as this is wasteful of solder when the board comes to be dipped, and also allows the board to absorb more heat than necessary during dipping.

2.7.3.5 Methods of Soldering

After insertion of the components, the component terminations may be

72

soldered to the conductor pattern individually by hand, with a soldering iron and cored solder wire. The soldering iron should have a narrow tip thermostatically controlled at 260°C. The solder should be 60/40, 19 to 22 swg (0.7 to 1.0 mm) containing five cores of ERSIN Multicore flux. Hand soldering is done on short production runs requiring very high reliability, or when the board is not more than 1/32 inch (0.8 mm) thick; such thin boards would be excessively warped by the heat of a solder bath. Hand soldering is also done to repair joints which have not formed properly when mass soldered, or which have failed in service. It is sometimes convenient, when hand soldering printed boards, to use ERSIN Multicore solder incorporating a red-dyed flux; it is then much easier to check that all joints have in fact been soldered, as the red flux residue is more easily seen.

It is however more usual for all the joints to be made simultaneously. This is known as mass soldering, and may be done in one of two ways – reflow soldering or bath soldering. In reflow soldering, components and boards which have been quite heavily pre-tinned before assembly must be used. The assembly is then held on the surface of a bath of oil heated to 230 – 250°C. (The oil used must of course have a flash-point higher than the operating temperature of the bath.) Alternatively, resistance, induction or hot-gas heating may be used. The tinning on components and boards then melts and runs together. If some component leads cannot be pre-tinned, they must be threaded through close-fitting cored solder rings or washers placed over the mounting holes. In such cases the mounting holes must be fitted with eyelets or internally plated, in order to make electrical contact with the circuit pattern on the underside of the board; or else the circuit pattern must be on the top of the board.

In bath soldering, the printed wiring pattern is on the underside of the board, with the components on top. The board may be applied to the bath in a number of ways, as illustrated in Figures 54 and 55. In these figures, the movement of the board is shown by broken lines. In the flow baths, the solder is continuously pumped in the directions shown by the solid arrows. With any of these methods, the speed of the board movement should be such that each part of the board is in contact with the solder for a time equal to at least 1.5 times the soldering time of the least-solderable component used.

STATIC BATHS

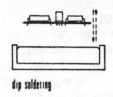

dip soldering

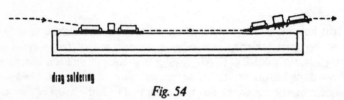

drag soldering

Fig. 54

The flow bath methods ensure uniformity of solder composition and a working surface always free from dross (oxide), but more solder is lost as dross than is the case with static baths. In static baths, lead is likely to sink, leaving the surface tin-rich; and the surface must be scraped free of oxide before every dipping. Commercial drag-soldering baths are available which have a very shallow bath to reduce alloy segregation, and a scraper to remove dross. The scraper is mounted at the front end of the board carrier.

2.7.3.6 Inspection before Soldering

Mass soldering depends for its success on rapid and complete wetting of every joint. If any joint is less than perfect it must be re-made by hand soldering. It is therefore essential to test the solderability of samples of components and boards at frequent intervals, using the methods described in Section 2.6.4, to ensure trouble-free operation. These tests should of course be done before the batches go to the production line.

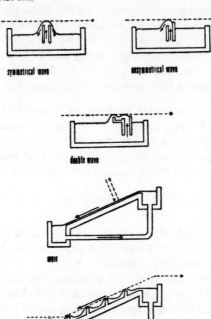

Fig. 55

2.7.3.7 Fluxing for Mass Soldering

Before soldering, the board must be coated with flux. The flux most generally applicable is Multicore Non-corrosive Liquid Flux PC 21a. This is a modified form of ERSIN Multicore flux which ensures rapid and complete wetting of the board by the flux; it also ensures that, on dipping the board, the flux flows readily away from the copper pattern ahead of the advancing solder, and does not become trapped within the joint. PC 21a may be applied to the board by dipping, brushing, spraying, wave, or roller coating. Special fluxes such as Multicore PC 25 Foam Rosin Flux are available from which a foam may be generated by bubbling air through a submerged porous stone. The board may then be passed over the foam to deposit a thin film of flux.

75

The flux solvent must be allowed to dry off before dipping. If solvent is still present when the board is dipped, bubbles of solvent vapour trapped beneath the board may prevent the solder from wetting the copper completely; the boiling of the solvent may cause local cooling of the solder, which apart from heating the board has then also to supply the latent heat of evaporation of the solvent; and voilent boiling may cause the solder to spatter out of the bath.

In most automatic soldering machines the film of flux solution is dried by passing the board over a heater placed between the fluxing and soldering positions. The heater should be adjusted so that, on reaching the soldering position, the flux film is slightly sticky or soft. Apart from removing the solvent, this procedure pre-heats the board, ensuring more rapid wetting by the solder.

2.7.3.8 Bath Filling

Tin contents outside the range 58 to 70 % should not be used as the working temperature required for sufficiently rapid wetting becomes too high. There is no point in using solders containing more than 63 % of tin as both the price and the working temperature rise with increasing tin content. For these reasons 60/40 or 63/37 are almost universally used as the bath filling. 65/35 may be used for adjusting the tin content of the bath should it fall more than 2 % below its nominal value in the course of use.

To ensure efficient operation and rapid wetting, the initial bath filling should be of high purity. İnevitably, some impurities will be picked up from the workpiece materials, but if the solder is initially of high purity it will be longer before the percentage of impurities rises too high. Solder for mass soldering of printed circuits needs to be exceptionally free–flowing if all the joints are to be successfully formed during the short immersion of the board. It should therefore contain no elements, either as major alloying additions or as impurities, which might form gritty, high–melting materials in the bath. This means excluding elements such as copper, silver, antimony, arsenic, iron, zinc and oxygen. Multicore EXTRUSOL solder bars, made to very high standards of purity, are most suitable for filling solder baths and maintaining the level. They are available packed in plastics film to prevent the formation of surface oxide during storage.

Many baths are so constructed that they must not .be switched on unless filled with .solder, otherwise the crucible or heating elements might overheat and be damaged. To avoid this danger when first filling a bath, Multicore EXTRUSOL pellets are recommended. The pellets melt rapidly because of their small size. They are also very useful, in small baths, for maintaining the level without cooling the bath too much.

The composition of the solder should be checked regularly, for example by chemical analysis using the methods of BS 3338 (see Section 3.3.3). Generally it is sufficient to check only the tin and copper content. Using a bath-filling of solder containing nominally 60 % of tin, the tin content should be kept between 58 and 62 %, and the copper content should not exceed 0.3%.

2.7.3.9 Soldering

When the board is to be dipped into static solder, the solder must be scraped free of dross immediately before dipping. When a solder wave is used, this is not necessary. The formation of dross can be largely prevented by the use of Multicore PC 41 Anti-oxidant Solder Cover.

The board must approach the solder surface at a slight angle so that any flux solvent vapour may escape. The solder temperature should be in the range 220 to 260°C, the usual temperature being 240°C. The average immersion time is between 2 and 4 seconds, very rarely longer than 5 seconds. The board should be removed slowly from the solder, allowing time for the excess solder to run off without freezing and so avoiding the formation of solder icicles, or of solder bridges between neighboring conductors.

2.7.3.10 Inspection after Soldering

Since the residues of Multicore PC 21a and PC 25 fluxes are completely non-corrosive, they may be left on the board; but it is sometimes easier to inspect the quality of the soldering if the flux residues are first removed. This is done by immersion cleaning, sometimes with ultrasonic agitation, in a suitable solvent such as Multicore PC 80 Solvent Cleaner (a solvent blend containing halogenated hydrocarbons). This blend is intended to combine maximum cleaning power with minimum risk of damage to component identification paints, but being a blend it is unsuitable for use in vapour degreasing plant. The advice of the manufacturer of the degreasing equipment should be sought in selecting solvents for use in it.

Whether or not flux residue removal is undertaken, the board must be thoroughly inspected for evidence of non-wetting or de-wetting (see Section 2.6.1); faulty joints must be re-soldered by hand, using cored solder and a soldering iron as described in Section 2.7.3.5.

2.8 HEATING

2.8.1 TEMPERATURE CHANGES AT THE JOINT

As a joining procedure, soft-soldering has many of the advantages of brazing or welding, with the added convenience that the operating temperature need not be so high. To gain full advantage of this requires that the supply of heat be well-controlled. It is therefore important to understand clearly the factors controlling the heating conditions.

Ideally, the flux, the solder and both workpieces should be heated instantly to a suitable temperature, and cooled instantly when the joint has been made, without heating anything outside the immediate neighbourhood of the joint. Figure 56 shows how the temperature would vary in this ideal case.

This of course is impossible to achieve in practice; the heating cannot be instantaneous, because heat flows quite slowly even in good conductors. At first the temperature rises quickly, but the higher it rises, the quicker the heat is conducted away to other parts of the workpiece. If flux solvent is present, its boiling will remove heat from the joint and an even longer time is required for the joint to reach soldering temperature.

The actual heating cycle at the joint is shown in Figure 57, in comparison with the ideal cycle shown in dotted line. The practical problem is, how to choose the soldering temperature T, and how to make the rise and fall in temperature

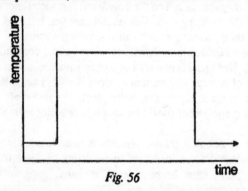

Fig. 56

as steep as possible. This clearly depends on the nature of both the joint and the heating appliance (iron, flame, bath, etc.). This will be discussed in terms of the soldering iron used with cored solder, but the principles are much the same for other heating methods.

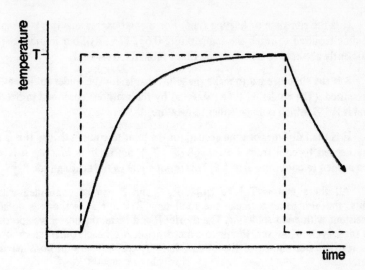

Fig. 57

The temperature changes occurring in the iron are shown in Figure 58. In this figure, T_0 is room temperature. T_{iron} is the temperature of the soldering iron tip; this temperature of course falls when the bit is placed on the workpiece. T is the temperature chosen for making the joint.

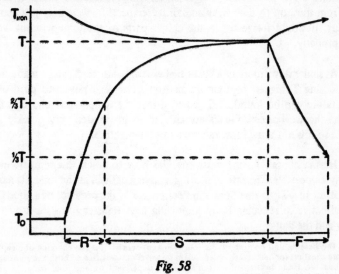

Fig. 58

79

R is the rise time or heating time. For theoretical reasons this is taken as the time required to reach the temperature $0.632 (T - T_0)$, but in practice it is sufficiently accurate to take R as the time required to reach $\frac{2}{3}T$.

S is the time needed to make the joint, that is, for the solder to flow as far as required. (The soldering time measured by the methods described in Section 2.6.4 is R + S, which is much easier to measure).

F is the fall time, or time needed for the joint to cool; in theory this is the time needed to cool from T to $0.368 (T - T_0)$, but again in practice it is the time needed to cool from T to $\frac{1}{3}T$. This is not equal to the heating time.*

All these factors T_0, T, T_{iron}, R, S and F can be controlled within limits, the aim being to make the total time R + S + F as short as possible consistent with good soldering. The shorter R and F are, the nearer we approach the ideal cycle. However, the factors are dependent on each other, so choosing one restricts our choice of the others. Each factor will now be considered in turn.

2.8.2 CONTROLLING THE TEMPERATURE AT THE JOINT

A temperature T must be chosen for making the joint. The choice of solder sets a minimum value for T, which must be at least high enough for the solder to melt. In practice, T should be at least $40°C$ above the liquidus of the solder used (see Table 3.2.1 for melting ranges of solders) because the solder is carrying heat from the iron to the workpieces; if its temperature were only just above its liquidus, it would freeze on to the colder parts of the joint without wetting them properly.

As solder flows more quickly at higher temperatures, S can be made shorter by choosing T higher, so long as an iron of enough power to produce this temperature can be found, and provided that the temperature chosen will not damage the workpieces. Fluxes are charred or inactivated very quickly above $400°C$, so it is not usual to work above this temperature.

Having chosen T, one must consider how to reach this temperature as quickly as possible. The rate of heating has been defined as the time, R, required to heat up to $\frac{2}{3}T$. As mentioned in Section 2.5.1, the presence of a good flux is very effective in reducing R by improving heat transfer from the iron to the solder and the work.

*Both the heating and cooling of the joint are exponential, like the charging of a capacitor. The time constant for heating, R, is dependent on the characteristics of both the joint and the iron, but the time constant for cooling, F, is dependant on the joint only. In general, therefore, F is not equal to R.

R can also be kept short by not using a thicker gauge of solder wire than is strictly necessary. Using a thick wire is wasteful, not only of solder but also of heat and therefore of time.

The final factor controlling R is the heating effectiveness of the iron, in relation to the size of the workpieces. This is considered in the next Section, 2.8.3.

S, the soldering time, is dependent on the soldering temperature T, and the solderability of the workpiece in relation to the particular flux and solder chosen. Choice of temperature has already been considered, and the solderability of various materials has been discussed in Section 2.6.

F, the cooling time, depends very much on the surroundings of the joint, and is considered in Section 2.8.4.

2.8.3 HEATING EQUIPMENT

It must be admitted that, because the measurements needed cannot be made accurately enough, it is not generally worth while to attempt to solve heating problems in soldering by calculation; but an understanding of how the heat is transferred is useful in deciding how to get better results from an existing system or how to choose a new one.

From the point of view of heating effectiveness, heating equipment is classified as follows:

TABLE IV

Class	Examples	Rate of heating dependent on:
I. Heat generated in the workpiece itself.	Resistance, induction and radiant heating.	Power.
II. Heat conducted from a hot gas.	Flame (torch), oven.	Power, and gas temperature.
III. Heat conducted from a hot liquid.	Solder bath, hot oil.	Temperature, heat capacity and thermal conductivity of the liquid.
IV. Heat conducted from a hot solid.	Soldering iron, hotplate.	Heater power; size, conductivity and temperature of bit, and its surface condition.

Obviously, in all classes the rate of heating depends also on the heat capacity and thermal conductivity of the workpieces, to which the heating equipment must be well-matched, neither too weak nor too powerful.

The surface condition of the tip is very important as good heat transfer will not be obtained if it is heavily pitted or not well tinned. Plain copper tips can be kept in good condition by always using Multicore SAVBIT solder. If for any reason SAVBIT cannot be used (for example, when special high- or low-melting solders are required) then an iron-plated copper tip should be used instead. Some reduction in the wear of a copper bit can also be made by wiping excess solder off it immediately after use.

To get rapid heating, the temperature of the tip (T_{iron}, Figure 58) should be as high as possible, but in practice, the life of the tip will be shortened, the flux may be charred, and the workpiece overheated if T_{iron} is too high. In most cases, the tip temperature need not be more than 60 to 70°C above the solder liquidus. The temperature may be controlled by controlling the supply voltage with a variable transformer (the temperature reached is roughly proportional to the voltage applied) or by using a thermostat whose temperature-sensing element is mounted in the tip itself. This is much more satisfactory because it enables one to use an iron of much higher power without danger of overheating. Use of an 'energy regulator', which switches on and off at short intervals, is not so good unless the tip has a high heat capacity. To some extent, a high heat capacity in the tip will make up for low temperature and low heater power; the tip discharges its heat into the workpiece during the relatively short soldering time, and is recharged from the heater afterwards. Before the invention of the electric soldering iron, the practice was to use a very large tip, heated in an oven or fire; little heat was lost when carrying the tip from the fire to the workpiece. However, the small tips needed for electronic work cool very quickly when withdrawn from the heat source. A small tip in good contact with a relatively powerful thermostatically-controlled heater is therefore the best tool for electronics.

Whether the tip is large or small, it must be made of a material with the highest possible conductivity. This limits the choice of material to pure silver or pure copper. The difference in conductivity between these metals is so small that the choice can be based on price – silver is of course far too expensive for general use, though it might be of value for specialised applications in micro-electronics. The disadvantage of both copper and silver is that they both dissolve rapidly in solder. The solution rate can be reduced by alloying the copper with certain other metals, but the thermal conductivity is seriously reduced. It is best therefore to use a pure copper tip in conjunction with SAVBIT solder, or to use an iron-plated copper tip.

Some assessment of the effective power (rated power x efficiency) of a soldering iron may be obtained by pushing cored solder wire on to the heated tip as fast as it can be melted, and noting the time required to melt a given weight of wire. Irons may be compared in this way. The thermal conductivity of different bits may be compared by the same method; for example, it will be found that a tinned copper tip will melt solder roughly twice as fast as an iron-plated copper tip of the same dimensions mounted in the same iron. In consequence, when using an iron-plated tip, a more powerful heater is required than when using a tinned copper bit.

2.8.4 CONTROLLING THE TEMPERATURE NEAR THE JOINT

While the joint is being made, heat may be radiated or convected from the heat source to neighbouring parts, or conducted to them direct through the workpiece metal. In electronic work particularly, this may damage the neighboring parts, and ways must be sought to minimize this heating.

In many cases, the work can be so laid out that heat radiated direct from the tip, or carried upwards in convection currents of hot air, does not damage nearby parts. In cases where the lay-out of the work cannot be designed with this in mind, it may be necessary to use screens of reflecting or non-conducting material. These must of course be clipped into place to leave the operator's hands free for the iron and solder wire.

Where space is very restricted, as in many electronic circuits, there may not be room to place a screen. The only possibility then is to insure that the soldering can be done in the shortest possible time. Close attention must therefore be given to choosing components of best solderability, and choosing a flux with best balance between activity and corrosion properties. It has already been mentioned that the soldering time can be shortened by using a higher soldering temperature. Though the high temperature at the joint transmits heat to the surroundings at a greater rate, it does so for a shorter time, so the total heating of the surroundings may be less when a higher soldering temperature is used.

Heating of nearby parts by direct conduction through metallic connections can be reduced by clipping 'heat sinks' or 'thermal shunts' to appropriate parts. Heat sinks or shunts are relatively massive metal clips, temporarily fixed to metallic connections IN BETWEEN the soldered joint and the part to be protected. Being massive and therefore slow to heat, they intercept and drain off the heat flow before it reaches the sensitive parts. However, they must not be used indiscriminately. If placed too close to the joint, they may seriously reduce the rate of heating in the joint itself. They must be removed soon after the joint has been completed, or they will act as a heat reservoir which will itself heat the part to be protected. It is most important that they are not inadvertently placed beyond the part to be protected, as they will then merely insure that ALL the heat from the joint drains through the heat-sensitive part.

Transistors are very often mounted on clips or plates which are intended to remove the heat generated within the transistor while it is operating. Such heat sinks do not necessarily give any protection against overheating the transistor while its electrical connections are being soldered, because in many cases the heat from the connection being soldered must pass through the heat-sensitive region before reaching the heat sink.

It must be accepted that despite all precautions, some heating of nearby parts is inevitable. The effects of this can be reduced if the nearby parts are cooled with a jet of high-pressure inert gas before, during or after soldering. Such gases are available in small aerosol dispensers. When the high-pressure gas escapes from the jet, it expands very rapidly, and in doing so quickly cools the immediate surroundings. Care must be taken that the sudden shrinkage induced in a part so quickly cooled, does not crack the part, or the joint itself.

2.8.5 FLOW OF HEAT

There is a fairly close analogy between flow of heat and electric current, which can help in thinking about heating problems in soldering. The analogy is based on the following comparisons:

$$
\begin{array}{rcl}
\text{temperature (}^{\circ}\text{C)} & : & \text{potential (volts)} \\
\text{quantity of heat (joules)} & : & \text{charge (coulombs)} \\
\text{heat flow (watts)} & : & \text{current (amperes)} \\
\text{thermal resistance (}^{\circ}\text{C/watt)} & : & \text{resistance (ohms)} \\
\text{thermal capacity (joules/}^{\circ}\text{C)} & : & \text{capacitance (farads)}
\end{array}
$$

The equation for the flow of heat in terms of thermal conductivity is identical with the equation for the flow of electric current in terms of electrical conductivity; and the law for the rate of charging of an electrical capacitor is formally equivalent to Newton's Law of Cooling.

The analogy, though exact, is limited, and there are important differences that must be borne in mind. Only the range of units listed above, and the two equations mentioned, should be used. There is no complete circuit; the heat should be thought of as flowing from a source (the heating element) to a sink (the surroundings at room temperature), through an array of 'components' consisting of thermal resistances and thermal capacities. Thermal insulators and conductors do not differ in conductivity nearly as much as their electrical counterparts, and the connections between components contribute considerably to the total resistance. In drawing a flow diagram to represent an actual situation, extra components must therefore be inserted to represent these effects.

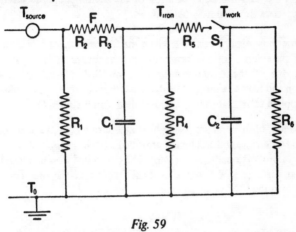

Fig. 59

The diagram of Figure 59 illustrates the flow of heat when making a joint with a soldering iron. The heat flow from the source is equal to the (electrical) wattage of the soldering iron heating element, at the temperature T_{source}. Some heat is lost through the handle (R_1), the outside of which is at room temperature T_0. The remainder flows into the tip through the small resistances R_2 and R_3. The tip has a thermal capacity C_1 and is constantly losing heat to the air from its exposed surface R_4. R_5 is the thermal resistance of the end of the tip, the part that is applied to the joint. This, before applying the iron to the joint, is at the unloaded temperature T_{iron}.

Application of the iron to the flux-cored solder wire and the work is represented by closing the switch S_1. When the flux melts and wets the solder, work, and iron tip, R_5 is considerably reduced. The heat capacity of both solder and work is represented by C_2; clearly, this is unnecessarily increased if too thick a solder wire is used.

85

R_5 is reduced still further when the solder melts; the temperature of the work T_{work} then rises rapidly to a value a little below T_{iron}. Meanwhile T_{iron} itself has fallen somewhat, to an extent dependent on R_6, the thermal resistance of the work.

T_{iron} and T_{work} could be measured by mounting thermocouples in holes drilled close to the surfaces of the iron tip and workpiece respectively; but it is not satisfactory to attempt to measure either of these temperatures by placing a thermocouple between the tip and the work. This is because R_5, though small, is not negligible, and the exact position of the thermocouple in relation to R_5 cannot in practice be accurately defined.

In a thermostatically–controlled iron the temperature at F is used to switch on and off the electric current supplying the heat source. It can be shown that if two irons, one of them thermostatically–controlled, are otherwise of similar construction and have the same unloaded tip temperature T_1, then when the two irons are applied to similar joints the controlled iron is cooled less.

Unloaded, both irons are losing heat at the rate KT_1, K depending on tip dimensions and surface finish. The uncontrolled iron A is supplying heat to its tip at a rate W_A, proportional to its wattage. The controlled iron B is supplying heat to its tip at the rate mW_B, where m is the fraction of the time for which the thermostat is in the 'ON' position.

$$KT_1 = W_A = mW_B$$

(It follows that the controlled iron, to maintain a temperature equal to that of the uncontrolled iron, must have a higher wattage, since $m < 1$). When a load is is applied, the uncontrolled iron temperature falls to T_{2A} and its tip loses heat at a rate $(K+k)T_{2A}$; but it still supplies heat at the old rate W_A. Then

$$T_{2A} = \frac{W_A}{K+k} = \frac{mW_B}{K+k}$$

The controlled iron when similarly loaded losses heat at a rate $(K+k)T_{2B}$. The thermostat responds by increasing its 'ON' time from m to $m + \delta m$. Then

$$T_{2B} = \frac{(m+\delta m)W_B}{K+k} > \frac{mW_B}{K+k}$$

PART 3
REFERENCE TABLES

3.1 JOINT FORMS

TABLE 3.1 TYPICAL JOINT FORMS

FILLING

1.  automobile bodies and general sheet metal work

2. food containers, to make them more easily washable

3.

BONDING

4. 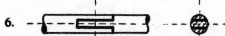 rod to rod

5.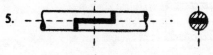

6.

7. 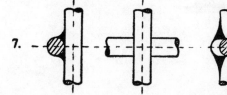 8.

TABLE 3.1 (continued) TYPICAL JOINT FORMS

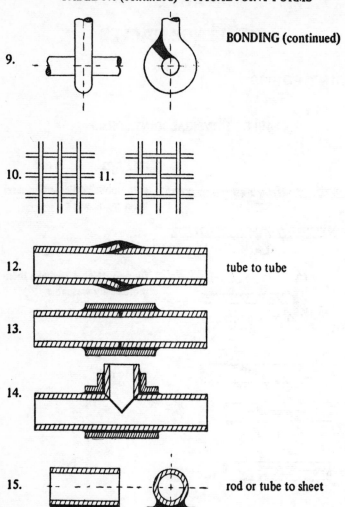

BONDING (continued)

9.

10.   11.

12.   tube to tube

13.

14.

15.   rod or tube to sheet

TABLE 3.1 (continued) TYPICAL JOINT FORMS

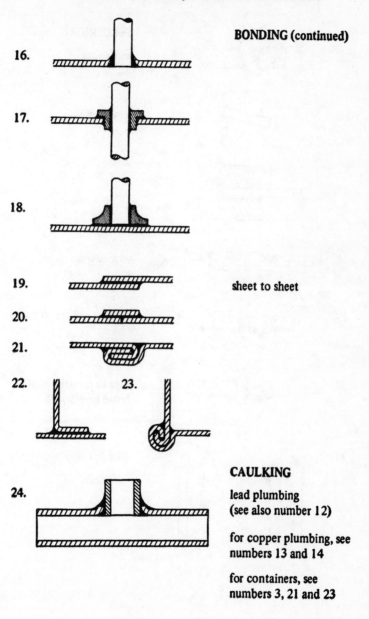

BONDING (continued)

16.

17.

18.

19.   sheet to sheet

20.

21.

22.   23.

CAULKING

24.   lead plumbing
(see also number 12)

for copper plumbing, see
numbers 13 and 14

for containers, see
numbers 3, 21 and 23

TABLE 3.1 (continued) TYPICAL JOINT FORMS

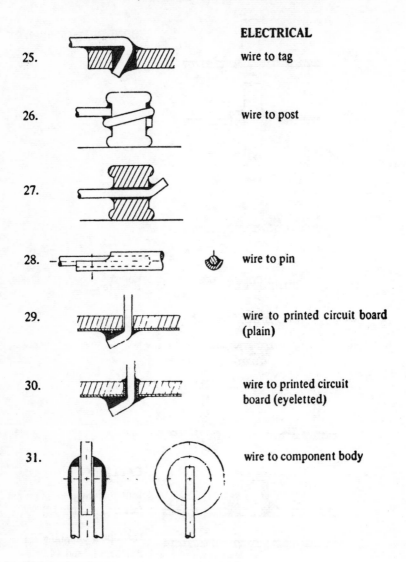

ELECTRICAL

25.   wire to tag

26.   wire to post

27.

28.   wire to pin

29.   wire to printed circuit **board** (plain)

30.   wire to printed circuit board (eyeletted)

31.   wire to component **body**

TABLE 3.1 (continued) TYPICAL JOINT FORMS

ELECTRICAL (continued)

32.

33.

34.   lead-through capacitor
to sheet

THERMAL

35.   refrigerator cooling
coils to sheet

Section A - A

36.   automobile radiators
lockseam tube

37.   fin-to-tube joint:
– in fin and tube matrix

TABLE 3.1 (continued) TYPICAL JOINT FORMS

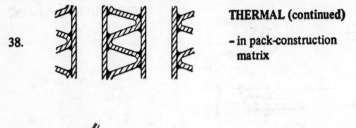

THERMAL (continued)

38.   – in pack-construction
      matrix

39.   header tank to tube-plate

reference is made to this table in Section 2.3.1.

TABLE 3.2.1 PROPERTIES OF SOLDERS

ALLOY	COMPOSITION CODE	NOMINAL COMPOSITION, %						STANDARD	MELTING RANGE °C		DENSITY g/cm³	U.T.S.	
		Tin	Lead	Antimony	Cadmium	Copper	Silver		Solidus	Liquidus		tonf/in²	N/mm²
PT	99.75/-	100	–	–	–	–	–	BS 3252	232	232	7.3	0.7	11
K	60/40	60	40	–	–	–	–	BS 219, BS 441	183	188	8.5	3.8	59
F	50/50	50	50	–	–	–	–	BS 219, BS 441	183	212	8.9	3.0	46
R	45/55	45	55	–	–	–	–	BS 219	183	224	9.1	2.8	43
G	40/60	40	60	–	–	–	–	BS 219, BS 441	183	234	9.3	2.7	42
H	35/65	35	65	–	–	–	–	BS 219	183	245	9.5	2.6	40
J	30/70	30	70	–	–	–	–	BS 219	183	255	9.7	2.5	39
V	20/80	20	80	–	–	–	–	BS 219, BS 441	183	275	10.0	2.4	37
Sn 63	63/36.7/0.3Sb	63	36.7	0.3	–	–	–	QQ-S-571	183	183	8.4	3.9	60
Sn 60	60/39.7/0.3Sb	60	39.7	0.3	–	–	–	QQ-S-571	183	188	8.5	3.8	59
Sn 50	50/49.7/0.3Sb	50	49.7	0.3	–	–	–	QQ-S-571	183	212	8.9	3.0	46
Sn 40	40/59.7/0.3Sb	40	59.7	0.3	–	–	–	QQ-S-571	183	234	9.3	2.7	42
28A	28/70.5/1.5Sb	28	70.5	1.5	–	–	–	BS AU 90	185	254			
95A	95/0/5Sb	95	0	5	–	–	–	BS 219	236	242	7.3	2.8	43
Savbit 1	50/48.5/1.5Cu	50	48.5	–	–	1.5	–	DTD.900/4535	183	215	8.9	3.5	54
TLC	50/33/17Cd	50	33	–	17	–	–	–	145	145	8.5	4.0	62
HMP	5/93.5/1.5Ag	5	93.5	–	–	–	1.5	BS 219	296	301	11.1	2.3	36
LMP	62/36/2Ag	62	36	–	–	–	2	–	179	179	8.5		
Sn 96	96/0/4Ag	96	–	–	–	–	4	QQ-S-571	221	221	7.5		

ALLOY : The names used by Multicore Solders Limited are listed here. In most cases, the names used are those given in the standards quoted in Column 9.

COMPOSITION CODE : A brief description of the composition, giving the weight percent of tin, lead and other metals present in that order. The code is the same as that used in Table 3.3.1, where alloys appearing also in the above list are marked with an asterisk (*). Except for tin and lead, the chemical symbols are used to denote which metals are present. Sb = Antimony, Cd = Cadmium, Cu = Copper, Ag = Silver.

NOMINAL COMPOSITION : An expanded version of the composition code, to clarify its use.

STANDARD : A specification number in this column indicates that the alloy as made by Multicore Solders Ltd. complies with that standard. For composition limits and maximum permissible impurities, reference should be made to the standards themselves.

MELTING RANGE : For explanation of the terms 'solidus' and 'liquidus' see Section 2.4.2. For conversion to °F, see Table 3.4.1. Data taken from the relevant standards.

U.T.S. : Ultimate tensile strength in tons force per square inch and in newtons per square millimeter.

reference is made to this table in Sections 2.4.1 and 2.8.2

93

TABLE 3.2.2 TYPICAL APPLICATIONS OF SOLDERS

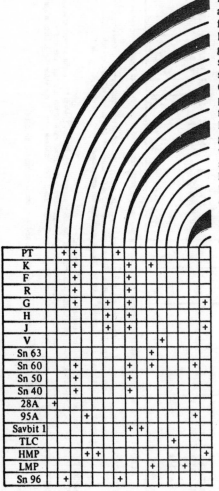

FILLING:
automobile bodies
food containers
BONDING:
general
service at high temperatures
services at low temperatures
CAULKING:
plumbing
food vessels
ELECTRICAL:
general
with copper soldering-iron bits
solder baths
lamp-capping
heat-sensitive components
on silvered surfaces
THERMAL:
refrigerators
automobile radiators

Solders in order of increasing			
solidus (°C)		liquidus (°C)	
TLC	145	TLC	145
LMP	179	LMP	179
Sn 63	183	Sn 63	183
K	183	K	188
Sn 60	183	Sn 60	188
F	183	F	212
Sn 50	183	Sn 50	212
Savbit 1	183	Savbit 1	215
R	183	Sn 96	221
G	183	R	224
Sn 40	183	PT	232
H	183	G	234
J	183	Sn 40	234
V	183	95A	242
28A	185	H	245
Sn 96	221	28A	254
PT	232	J	255
95A	236	V	276
HMP	296	HMP	301

3.8 CONVERSION CHARTS

3.3.1 Fahrenheit · Celsius (Centigrade)

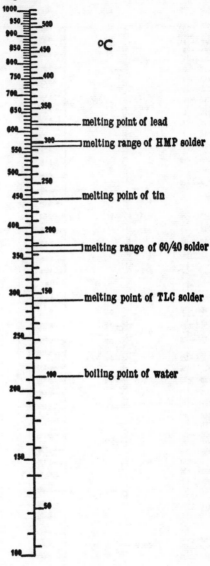

°F

°C

melting point of lead

melting range of HMP solder

melting point of tin

melting range of 60/40 solder

melting point of TLC solder

boiling point of water

3.3.2 S.W.G. - Inches - Millimetres

3.3.3 Pounds, ounces - Kilograms, grams

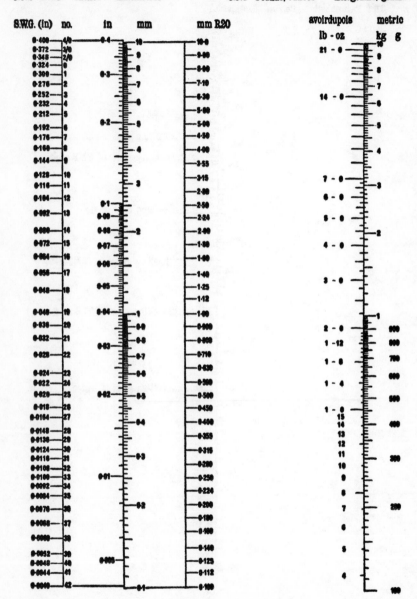

96

3.3.4   Tons, hundredweight, quarters, pounds · Kilograms

3.3.5 Pints, fluid ounces - cubic centimetres

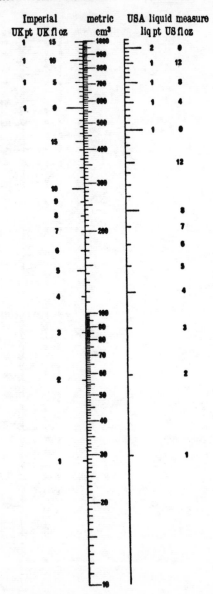

3.3.6 Gallons - Litres

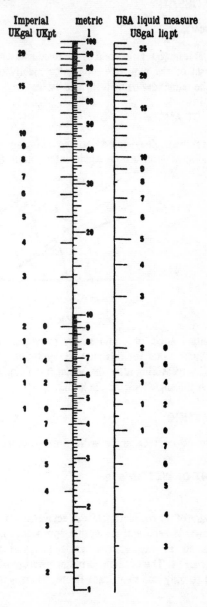

3.5 GLOSSARY

COLOPHONY

A natural resin (q.v.) obtained as the residue after removal of turpentine from the oleo-resin of the pine tree, consisting mainly of abietic acid and related resin acids, the remainder being resin acid esters.

CONTACT ANGLE

In general the angle enclosed between half-planes, tangent to a liquid surface and a solid-liquid interface at their intersection (see Figure 60). In particular,

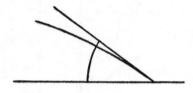

Fig. 60

the contact angle of liquid solder in contact with a solid metal surface. An approximate value for this may be determined, by shadow projection or other means, by measuring after the solder has solidified. Note that the contact angle is always the angle INSIDE the liquid.

DE-WETTING

Increase of contact angle with time (decrease of cosine of contact angle).

EXTENT OF WETTING

The cosine of the contact angle. Perfect wetting is approached as the contact angle falls towards zero and its cosine approaches unity. Complete non-wetting is approached as the contact angle increases towards 180° and its cosine approaches -1. The cosine is a better measure of extent of wetting as it can be quoted to only one significant figure, whereas the contact angle in degrees will often contain two significant figures (implying an accuracy which would often be spurious). In Figure 61, if a distance of 1 mm be scribed with dividers as shown, a travelling microscope used to measure the distance L would give an approximate value for the cosine directly, when the angle is appreciably less than 90°. Otherwise a similar measurement can be made using shadow projection.

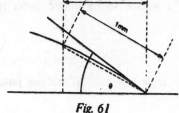

Fig. 61

FLUX ACTIVITY

The property of a flux which allows the smallest contact angle between molten solder and a solid surface to be achieved.

NON-WETTING

Formation of a contact angle greater than 90° (cosine of contact angle negative).

ROSIN

A synonym for colophony (q.v.), which term is preferred for use in the writing of standards because of the common confusion between the specific term 'rosin' and the generic term 'resin'. The term 'rosin' arose in 17th Century English as a mis-spelling of 'resin', and is still current in ordinary English and standard American. The terms 'colophony' and 'Colophonian resin', on the other hand, were used by Pliny to describe resin from Colophon (a town in Lydia, Asia Minor). In many languages, dictionaries record the use of the generic term 'resin' in the specific sense 'colophony', though a specific term equivalent to 'rosin' usually exists as well; the correct translation will be found to be the name of the type of resin used in the treatment of violin bows.

RESIN

Any vitreous (i.e. glassy, non–crystalline) organic solid, natural or synthetic, insoluble in water; usually flammable, electrically non–conducting and yellow or brown in colour.

SOLDERABILITY

The property of a surface which allows it to be wetted by molten solder.

SOLDERING TIME

The time required for a surface to be wetted under specified conditions.

WETTING

Formation of a contact angle less than 90° (cosine positive).

WETTING POWER

The property of a molten solder which allows it to wet a solid surface.

INDEX